EVENTS
THAT CHANGED THE
WORLD

EVENTS
THAT CHANGED THE
WORLD

igloo

igloo

First published in 2010
by Igloo Books Ltd
Cottage Farm
Sywell
NN6 0BJ

www.igloo-books.com

ISBN 9-78085-734-417-5

2 4 6 8 10 9 7 5 3 1
B044 0810

Author: Michael Heatley and Martin J Howard

Printed and manufactured in China

CONTENTS

INTRODUCTION

"Everything flows and nothing stays," said the Greek Heraclitus in around 500 BCE. For him, change was the fundamental truth underlying everything that is caught up in the flow of time.

History is a testament to that philosopher's insight. Every day societies and individual lives across the globe are shaped and reshaped in small and large ways. Fashions come and go, famine gives way to plenty, monarchs and governments are swept away, science provides us with technologies that our ancestors would have seen as magic, discoveries are made, wars are won and lost. As Tennyson later put it, 'The old order changeth, yielding place to the new.'

The world is in a constant state of flux – but every so often events occur that have a vastly more profound effect than the everyday shifting tides of politics and progress. Since we invented the wheel there have been certain moments on which history itself has turned. Some of them – like the moon landing of 1969 – were immediately recognised as great stepping stones in the history of humankind, witnessed by millions of people. At other times – for example the day that a bunch of geeks launched a new computer program – it is only when we look back that we can see the moment as pivotal. However, whether it was Christopher Columbus sighting the New World, setting in motion events that would lead to the rise of a great superpower, or a young man called Elvis Presley making a disc that would redefine popular culture forever, such moments have reverberated down the centuries. In a great domino chain of cause and effect, they have changed the world in ways that the people involved could never have imagined.

In these pages are descriptions of 100 events that have shaped the world we live in. Some have flowed from the act of putting pen to paper with an idea, such as Charles Darwin's Origin of Species. Other moments have taken place behind the closed doors of little-known laboratories. Still more have taken place before humanity's fascinated gaze on television, or, like the World War II D-Day landings, have involved the lives and deaths of thousands. Not all represent change for the better: the Wall Street Crash caused untold misery in the United States and around the globe, and the terrible events of September 11, 2001, have cost countless more lives than those of the people trapped in the World Trade Center that day. And the sinking of the Titanic and the explosion of the Challenger space shuttle are tragic reminders of human fallibility.

But the events in these pages also show our ability to achieve great feats, such as conquering the world's highest peak and reaching out into space, and our ingenuity in making leaps of scientific progress. Moments such as Live Aid in the summer of 1985 demonstrate the depth of human generosity and our willingness to be moved to great acts of compassion. And the last entry, on the election of the United States' first black president only 53 years after Rosa Parks was arrested for refusing to vacate her seat on a bus for a white man, serves to remind us how rapidly progress can happen: how quickly events can change the world.

Left: Nelson Mandela stands and raises his fist to the South African crowd after his release from Robben Island.

Above: Baronial coats of arms and royal seals surround the Magna Carta on this facsimile of the document.

Right: A painting showing King John signing the Magna Carta at Runnymede in 1215.

AT A GLANCE

The Magna Carta was a charter drawn up by barons and agreed to by the English King John in 1215. One of its aims was to limit the king's power to levy taxes on the barons. But, more significantly, it also secured the liberty of all free men. Therefore it can be regarded as the original guarantee of human rights, inspiring the English, the Canadian and the US Bill of Rights.

SIGNING OF THE MAGNA CARTA

RUNNYMEDE, ENGLAND
1215

The Magna Carta (Great Charter) is the most famous document ever produced, and was one of the most important in medieval Europe. It was drawn up to safeguard the rights of the nobility against the greedy King John, who kept raising taxes to fund his largely unsuccessful wars against France. However, more significantly, the charter also enshrined the rights of all free men of the realm: it promised them fair laws and access to legal courts without payment, and included the 'habeas corpus' clause, which meant no imprisonment without trial. In short it was the first ever bill of rights.

King John signed the charter, most reluctantly, at Runnymede, near Windsor Castle. He had been brought there by the barons who had united to take London and capture the king; they had considerable support from the people in carrying out this coup (and this favor would be repaid). Whilst the barons respected the king's right to govern, they were outraged not only by the massive feudal dues and taxes they had to pay, but also at the way he levied taxes – those who were out of favor could be saddled with a crippling tax debt whilst his favorites were excused. The wars in France were seen as just an opportunity for the monarchy to settle old scores and it was soon after another humiliating English defeat at Bouvines, France, that the nobles decided to come together.

There was mutual distrust at Runnymede, so there were clauses in the Magna Carta enabling the barons to enforce it through a council of 25. The barons knew that as soon as they disbanded their armies the king would assert his authority and destroy them, so they would not disarm. Their fears were probably justified. As soon as John got back to London he petitioned the Pope for permission to cancel his oath, which Rome soon granted.

King John's inability to act in good faith forced the barons to take the measures they did. Also, he badly overreached himself in his dealings with the nobility, and with the war in France. When it became obvious that the king was not going to abide by the charter, the barons had to choose whether to obey him or depose him. There was a split in their ranks. So there was general relief when, in October 1216, the king died. Ironically, subsequent rulers were more powerful than John, but the Magna Carta survived and was reissued in different forms. Even today some parts of it are legally valid, though the protection given by habeas corpus is now seen by many as being denied in the UK by the Prevention of Terrorism Act 2005.

cōmīnuacionē amittebāt: ut q̄ dee-
rant tormētis replerē punitū: et ipso
quidem tuus mirabilit tranſiret: illi
aūt nouā morte inuenirēt. Diē enī
creatura ab ſuū gen9 ab inicio refigu-
rabaz deſeruiēs tuis preptis: ut pue-
ri tui cuſtodirentur illeſi. Nā nubes ca-
ſtra toz obūbrabat: z ex aqua q̄ ante
erat terra arida apparuit: z ex mari ru-
bro via ſine īpedimēto: z camp9 ger-
mīnans de profūdo nimio: per quē
omnes natio tranſmit-q̄ tegebāt tua
manu uidētes tua mirabilia et mon-
ſtra. Tanquā equi enim depauerunt
eſcam: et tanquā agni exultauerunt
magnificātes te domine qui liberaſti
illos. Memores enī erāt adhuc eoz
que in incolatu illoz facta fuerāt: que-
admodū p natione animaliū eduxe-
it terra muſcas: et p piſcibs eructauit
flumine multitudinē ranaz. Nouiſſi-
me aūt viderūt noua creaturā auiū:
cum abducti cōcupiſcentia poſtulaue-
runt eſcas epulationis. In allocutio-
ne enī deſiderij aſcendit illis de mari
ortigometra: et vexationes peccatori-
bus ſupuenerūt non ſine illis q̄ ante
facta erāt argumētis p vim fluminū.
Iuſte enim patiebātur ſecūm ſuas ne-
quicias. Quōs vero deteſtabilē hoſpitali-
tatē inſtituerūt. Alij quidem ignotos
non recipiebāt aduenas. Alij autem
bonos hoſpites in ſeruitutem redige-
bant. Et non ſolum hoc: ſed z alius
quidem reſpect9 illoz erat: quū inuiti
recipiebāt extraneos. Qui autem cum
leticia receperūt hos qui eiſde uſi erāt
inſtitutis: ſeuiſſimis afflixerunt dolo-
ribs. Percuſſi ſunt autem cecitate-ſicut
illi in foribus iuſti: cū ſubitaneis coo-
periti eſſet tenebris. Vnuſqꝫq̄ː trāſitū
hoſtij ſui querebat. In ſe enī elementa

dū cōuertūtur ſicut ī organo qualitatis
ſonus immutatur: et omia ſuū ſonum
cuſtodiūt. Unde eſtimari ex ipſo viſu
certo poteſt. Agreſtia enī in aquatica
cōuertebant: et q̄cunq̄: erāt natātia ī
terra tranſiebāt. Ignis ī aqua valebat
ſupra ſuā virtutē: z aqua extinguentis
nature obliuiſcebaz. Flamme econtrario
corruptibiliū animaliū nō vexaret
carnes coabulātiū: nec diſſoluebant
illā que facile diſſolubaz ſicut glaci-
es bona eſcam. In omnibus enim ma-
gnificaſti ppłm tuū domine- z honora-
ſti: et nō deſpexiſti ī omni tpe et ī omni
loco aſſiſtēs eis. Explicit lib ſapie. In-
cipit płog9 ſup lib̄ ſŷrach ī ecleſiaſticū

Ultos nobis z magnos
p legem z ꝓphetas alioſq̄
qui ſecuti ſunt illos ſapi-
entia demōſtrata ē ī quibs
oportet laudare iſrah̄el de doctrina z ſapientie cauſa: quia nō ſolum ipſos lo-
quentes neceſſe eſt eſſe peritos: ſed etiā
extraneos poſſe et diſcentes et ſcriben-
tes doctiſſimos fieri. Auus me9 ibeſus
poſtq̄ ſe amplius dedit ad diligentiā
lectionis legis z ꝓphetarū z alioz li-
broz qui nobis a parentibs noſtris
traditi ſunt voluit z ipſe ſcriber aliqd
hoz q̄ ad doctrinā z ſapientiā pertinēt:
ut deſiderātes diſcere et illoz periti fiāt
magis magiſq̄: attendant animo: et
cōfirmētur ad legitimā vitā. Hortor
itaq̄: venire vos cum beniuolentia et
attentiori ſtudio lectionē facere: z veni-
am habere in illis in quibus videmur
ſequentes imaginem ſapientie: z defi-
cere in verboz compoſitione. Nā defici-
unt verba hebraica: quādo fuerint trāſ-
lata ad aliā linguā. Nō aūt ſolum
hec: ſed z ipſa lex et ꝓphet ceteraq̄: alio-
rum libros nō parua habēt differētiā

GUTENBERG INVENTS THE PRINTING PRESS

STRASBOURG, A FREE REPUBLIC, NOW IN FRANCE
C. 1440

Above: An undated illustration showing Johannes Gutenberg checking proofs in his workshop.

Left: A Gutenberg Bible, opened at Ecclesiastes. The first major work to be manufactured on a printing press, the bible's printed copies were considerably cheaper to buy than hand-scribed bibles. Now priceless, only 48 copies of the Gutenberg Bible still exist, and of these only 21 are complete.

AT A GLANCE

One of the most important events in human history, the invention of the printing press made it possible for texts to be printed quickly and cheaply, ensuring the spread of privileged knowledge to levels of society who would not until then have been able to afford books. The effect was immense, and it is no exaggeration to say that human progress was immeasurably speeded by Johannes Gutenberg's invention.

The invention of moveable type and the printing press is, without doubt, one of the most significant events in human history. Before it, all texts were laboriously copied out by hand, a process that could take weeks, months or even years, and books were available only to the very rich. Gutenberg's invention, however, sparked an age in which much previously arcane knowledge became widely disseminated. Today, many observers and historians regard the advent of the printing press as the beginning of the modern world.

The inspiration that led German goldsmith, Johannes Gutenberg to invent a complete process of printing is lost in the mists of time, though legend reports that the idea came to him 'like a ray of light' in 1439. But in the year 1440 he was experimenting in Strasbourg with a mixture of older technologies, such as the screw press, and ideas that he himself had pioneered. An invention of his own – a mould for each character – allowed him to produce large numbers of type letters, to be fixed within a frame for a job, then reused. Faster by far than hand-copying, producing Gutenberg's printed works was still time-consuming, demanding the production of the type characters, and hand-setting them to be inked and printed onto vellum or parchment sheets. The pages were usually decorated by hand in the time-honored manner of illuminated texts.

Gutenberg did not include his name or the date on his work, making it difficult to know which texts were printed on his press. It is thought that one of his earliest works was a German poem and that he produced a Latin grammar book for schools. In 1452, he began his most famous project, a printed bible. Published in 1455 in a run of about 180 copies, the Gutenberg Bible (also known as the 42-line Bible as each page contains 42 lines, without punctuation or indented paragraphs) bankrupted Gutenberg. Although he was later awarded a pension and honors by Archbishop Adolph von Nassau, the invention of the, by now, elderly Gutenberg did not bring him financial success. But his process had caught on, and new printing presses were being set up across Europe.

The impact was immense. The unstoppable dissemination of printed writings led directly to the Renaissance, the Protestant revolution, the dawn of modern science, the Enlightenment, and mass education. Without the printing press, human progress would have been unimaginably slower. As American writer Mark Twain wrote, four centuries after Gutenberg's death, 'What the world is today, good and bad, it owes to Gutenberg. Everything can be traced to this source, but we are bound to bring him homage ... for the bad that his colossal invention has brought about is overshadowed a thousand times by the good with which mankind has been favored'.

COLUMBUS MAKES LANDFALL

THE BAHAMAS
OCTOBER 12, 1492

Above: An artist's impression of Christopher Columbus making landfall in the New World.

Left: Replicas of the Pinta, *the* Santa Maria *and* Niña *set sail from Spain 500 years after Columbus.*

Overleaf: An illustration showing Christopher Columbus kneeling before Queen Isabella and King Ferdinand of Spain after his return from the New World.

It was the Italian-born adventurer Cristoforo Colombo (known to the English-speaking world as Christopher Columbus) whose arrival in the New World kick-started the Spanish colonization of that continent. And while Columbus did not actually discover the Americas – that had already been done by the ancestors of the American natives, and by Vikings, Irish, Phoenicians and probably others from the eastern side of the Atlantic – it was his explorations that would be continued by other European countries, changing the continent forever. In the USA, the second Monday in October is still celebrated as Columbus Day.

Columbus was searching for a new trade route to the Indies, and was receiving financial support for his voyages from King Ferdinand and Queen Isabella of Spain. In the knowledge that the world was round, he suggested that a westward route from Europe to the Indies could be shorter and more direct than the perilous overland and coastal trade routes through what is now known as the Middle East. If true, this would give Spain control of the lucrative spice trade commanded until then by the Arabs and Italians.

In 1492 he set sail from Spain, taking his three ships, *Santa Maria*, *Pinta* and *Santa Clara* (later renamed *Niña*), to the Canary Islands to stock up on provisions. He made landfall in the Bahamas on October 12. Having underestimated the circumference of the Earth, he believed he had reached the Indies – hence the islands became known as the West Indies. His actual landing point remains the subject of discussion; the three most popular choices are Watling Island (San Salvador today), Cat Island, and Grand Turk.

He was motivated both by personal gain, having been promised his share of the riches – gold, pearls and spices – and by spreading Christianity, but his crew treated the local people, particularly the womenfolk, poorly. Furthermore, he lost the *Santa Maria*, the largest of the three ships entrusted to him, when it ran aground on Christmas Day and had to be abandoned.

Columbus returned to Europe without the promised treasure, but even so Ferdinand and Isabella gave him the title of Admiral of the Ocean Sea. He made three more voyages, the last in 1502, but never did manage to reach India and the Far East, his original goals. In fact, he never even reached the mainland of the American continent. He did, however, make it to Cuba (which he thought was China) and many other Caribbean islands. And when he died in 1506, two years after returning from his fourth voyage, he was still convinced that his journeys had been along the east coast of Asia.

Above: A portrait of Ferdinand Magellan looking to the stars for navigational assistance.

MAGELLAN SETS SAIL FOR SOUTH AMERICA

SEVILLE, SPAIN
AUGUST 10, 1519

Portuguese-born sea captain Ferdinand Magellan set sail in August 1519 on the *Trinidad*, accompanied by four more ships. His intention, like that of Christopher Columbus before him, was to voyage to the Indies by sailing westward via the Americas rather than eastward as suggested by the prevailing land and coastal trade routes. Magellan, who had obtained Spanish nationality in order to serve Spain, also believed that the Pacific Ocean was much smaller than the Atlantic; according to the maps of the day, Japan was only a few hundred miles west of Mexico.

Magellan made initial landfall in Brazil, then sailed south in search of a river that he believed would take him through the continent to the ocean on its far side. But trial and error failed to locate any river. Eventually, in 1520, he discovered the narrow sea-passage now known as the Strait of Magellan, separating the southernmost tip of the South American continent from Tierra del Fuego. He was the first known European to reach that island.

He passed through the strait into the ocean which, due to its placid nature, he named the Pacific *(Tepre Pacificum,* 'peaceful sea'), and he sailed on for three months. But his crew suffered desperately, having to eat rats and drink polluted water to stay alive.

No land was sighted until in March 1521 Magellan reached the Philippines– but then on April 27, while attempting to convert the natives to Christianity, he was killed in the Battle of Mactan. It took 18 months for the expedition to sail on around Africa and return to Spain. By that time only 18 sailors were left alive of the original 250, and just one ship, the *Victoria*, out of the original five. But in September 1522, the surviving crew members had become the first known men to sail around the world, a journey that had taken three years.

Magellan's expedition had proved that Europeans could reach Asia by sailing west. But he failed in his quest to find a faster route to Asia from Spain, his route being much longer than the one around Africa. However, his voyage changed people's understanding of the Earth. The full size of the globe came to be understood, since the voyage was logged at 14,460 Spanish leagues – 60,440 km or 37,560 miles. The crew also found that despite having kept close watch on time, they turned out on their return to be a day behind, and so it was realized that what came to be known as the International Date Line would need to be established.

AT A GLANCE

Ferdinand Magellan's expedition from 1519 to 1522 was the first known to circumnavigate the world, even though he himself did not survive to return to Spain. He navigated the strait at the tip of South America, connecting the Atlantic and the Pacific Oceans, and he named it for himself.

Right: A 17th-century map of the Strait of Magellan, the route from the Atlantic to the Pacific.

TIER

AME

MAR

DEL

NORT

RI

P

R

Exquisita & magno
aliquot mensium pe
riculo lustrata et
iam retecta Freti
Magellanici Facies.
Eigentlicke afbeeldinghe der Magella-
nischer Strate die nu met veel gevaers
eltelijeke Maenden doorsien, Van
nieus ondeckt is.

Dese Eijlanden die in gheene Pascaerten aengeteeckent bevon-
den en worden, Liggen van d'incomste der Strate Magellani
O.N.O verscheijden 50 mijlen op de hoochde van 51 graden.

Het Derde Nau

Capo d'Hollande
Capo Forward
Elisabeths Baij
Cordes Baij
Magdel Baij
de quade Baij

20
20
15
13
12

Pinguyns
Eijlanden

Het tweede
Nau

8 7 6
13
7
13
25
't Heerste Nau
18 13 25 20

35
8 9
10 10
15 15
14
44
6 6 10 15

Above: A portrait of the astronomer and mathematician Nicolas Copernicus, dating to the 16th century.

Right: An engraving of the Copernican model of the solar system made by Andreas Cellarius in 1661. By then, although De Revolutionibus *had been withdrawn from circulation by the Catholic church, Copernicus' ideas had become widespread.*

AT A GLANCE

The publication of Copernicus' De Revolutionibus *dismissed the belief that the heavenly bodies revolved around the Earth and that, therefore, humanity was at the center of the universe. The book became one of the most influential ever published, inspiring a revolution in astronomy and in science itself.*

COPERNICUS PUBLISHES *DE REVOLUTIONIBUS*

FROMBOK, POLAND
1543

Commonly known as *De Revolutionibus*, the full title of Nicolas Copernicus' scientific masterpiece was De Revolutionibus Orbium Coelestion, or *On the Revolutions of the Heavenly Spheres*. Within it, the author set out his theory – supported by mathematics and observation – that the planets of the solar system orbit the sun, shattering the Western belief that God had placed the Earth at the center of the universe and set the heavenly bodies in motion around it.

Copernicus, like many scientists of his day, was active in many fields. From a tower in the walls of Frombok he made perforce naked-eye observations of the heavens (telescopes were not invented until the early 17th century); he also studied mathematics, medicine, Greek and Latin, and painted. He was a Catholic cleric, a physician, a diplomat and a magistrate.

But it is for his work in astronomy that Copernicus is remembered. Beginning around 1505, when he was 32 years old, he began formulating the theory that the solar system was heliocentric, revolving round the Sun. Denial of the geocentric model (in which the universe revolves around the Earth) – originally proposed by the great Roman astronomer and mathematician, Ptolemy, and sanctioned by the Roman Catholic church – was close to heresy, but Copernicus spent more than 20 years quietly perfecting his alternative theory, sending only a few summaries of his ideas to close friends. By the early 1530s, his writings on the subject, which would become De Revolutionibus, were all but complete, though Copernicus was reluctant to publish. In 1539, however, he took on a student, Georg Joachim Rheticus, who urged Copernicus to allow his work to be printed. He finally relented and De Revolutionibus was published in a run of 400 copies in 1543. Soon after, Copernicus died.

Although he had written it in a dense style that would be understood only by other mathematicians and astronomers, and care was taken to present it as a mathematical novelty not to be taken as reality, the book soon came under attack. De Revolutionibus was withdrawn from circulation by order of the Catholic church's Sacred Congregation in 1616, and remained on its index of forbidden books until 1758. But the cat was out of the bag, and the copies already in print had a dramatic impact. Circulating among the greatest thinkers of the day, they inspired new generations to look at the world in fresh ways. Copernicus' ideas were enthusiastically taken up by later astronomers such as Kepler, Galileo and Bruno, who expanded upon them, to the fury of the church, who resented the removal of humankind from its position at the center of the universe. Copernicus' work, then, represents not only a monumental leap in human understanding of astronomy, but the start of a revolution in scientific thinking.

DEFEAT OF THE SPANISH ARMADA

ENGLISH CHANNEL/LA MANCHE
1588

Above: Sir Francis Drake completes his game of bowls on Plymouth Hoe before setting sail.

Left: The Spanish Armada advances up the English Channel to meet its fate.

AT A GLANCE

The Armada was sent by Philip II of Spain in the summer of 1588 to invade England. The Armada's defeat signaled the decline of Spain as a great European power, as well as the end of the Spanish trade monopoly in North America and Asia. English sea dog Sir Francis Drake became a folk hero, reputed to have finished his game of bowls before routing the foe.

The Armada, a 130-vessel naval force sent by Spain to invade England in July 1588, was repulsed by the British fleet, with the flamboyant Sir Francis Drake under the command of Lord Howard of Effingham. The Spanish plan had been that their ships would pick up soldiers in the Netherlands, then controlled by Spain, and ferry them across to England – but it was doomed to failure.

Three reasons lay behind Spain's action. First, its monopoly on trade in the Americas was being threatened by English privateers, and secondly its Catholic King Philip II wanted to reverse the Protestant ascendancy in England since Elizabeth had become queen; he saw this as a 'great evil'. Thirdly, England was helping the Dutch to resist Spanish rule, Protestantism being on the rise in the Netherlands, too.

The Armada, including 22 fighting galleons, sailed in a crescent shape to offer the cumbersome galleons maximum protection at the centre. As the Armada approached the coast of Cornwall on July 29, beacons were lit from hilltop to hilltop through the English countryside to warn the queen in London of its approach.

Sir Francis Drake is sometimes portrayed as showing admirable calm by finishing his game of bowls before setting sail, but the tide and wind were against him and he knew there was no point setting off till later; and when the British fleet did meet the Armada, its guns were ineffective against the massive timbers of the galleons. But when the Spanish dropped anchor off Calais to await overnight for the arrival of their troops from the Netherlands, Drake set light to a number of fireships, which drifted into the Spaniards' midst.

The Armada scattered in panic, and so the Spanish galleons were more vulnerable to British gunfire. Worse, bad weather made it impossible for them to follow their favored style of naval battle, firing broadsides at the enemy ships before boarding them. Three of their galleons were sunk, with 600 men killed and 800 wounded; the rest found their escape route back down the Channel blocked by headwinds and the English, and were forced to sail up the east coast of England and round Scotland to return home.

Just over 60 ships out of the original force of 130 returned to Spain – half the fleet had been sunk or wrecked. Over 20,000 Spanish sailors and soldiers were killed, whereas the English, throughout the whole campaign, lost no ships and only 100 men in battle. However, over 7,000 English sailors died from disease, mostly dysentery and typhus, while the Armada remained in English waters. Defeated King Philip II of Spain blamed the Armada's failure on the weather, saying, "I sent you out to war with men, not with the wind and waves." Whatever the truth, Sir Francis Drake's reputation was immeasurably enhanced, while Spain's reputation as a world power was significantly damaged.

PILGRIMS ARRIVE AT PLYMOUTH

MASSACHUSETTS, USA
DECEMBER 17, 1620

Above: Plimoth Plantation is a recreation of the original Plymouth settlement in Massachusetts. The Plantation is famous for its authenticity; costumed interpreters speak an approximation of the Pilgrims' English and the details of life in the village are as close as possible to what they would actually have been in the 1620s.

Left: Titled The Mayflower on her Arrival in Plymouth Harbor, *this 1882 painting by William Halsall captures passengers coming ashore in the New World on a cold December day.*

Overleaf: The First Thanksgiving *by Jean Leon Gerome Ferris depicts the celebration of the pilgrims' plentiful harvest after months of hardship.*

AT A GLANCE

The arrival of the Puritan pilgrims at Plymouth Harbor on December 17, 1620, marked the start of the American ideals of offering liberty and sanctuary to the oppressed, and has become an important part of the country's mythology.

The landing of the Puritan pilgrims at what was then known as Plymouth Colony has resounded down the years of American history. They were not the first Europeans to establish a colony in North America – Jamestown in Virginia had been founded 13 years earlier – but the notion of a band of weary and persecuted folk finding sanctuary and liberty in the new world is a powerful one and has helped shape American culture.

In 1620, an exodus of 102 people sailed from Plymouth in England, to cross the Atlantic in the desperately cramped *Mayflower*. But their journey had really begun 34 years earlier with the formation of a congregation by Puritan Richard Clyfton in Babworth, Nottinghamshire. Refusing to recognize the authority of the Church of England, the congregation was constantly threatened with legal action, and in 1606 and 1607 they relocated to the Netherlands. Although they were able to conduct their services in peace there, problems soon arose. The group was slowly being assimilated into mainstream Dutch life, and there were fears of Spanish invasion and persecution by a rigidly Catholic regime. In 1619, a request was sent to England for a land grant in the New World, which was given under the condition that the congregation's beliefs remained officially unrecognized. The area, to be called New England, was north of Jamestown, at the mouth of the Hudson River.

On September 6, 1620, the Mayflower sailed alone from Plymouth, Devon, after the *Speedwell*, a ship that had been expected to accompany it, was found to be leaking. Of the original 121 passengers, only 102 could be accommodated aboard the single ship and the cargo of supplies for that number of people made space aboard the small vessel extremely cramped. Over the following weeks, they faced storms, sickness and the death of a member of their company (as well as the birth of a child, named Oceanus), but on November 10, the *Mayflower* sighted land at what is now Provincetown Harbor, on the tip of Cape Cod. After the area had been explored, the ship sailed westward again, weighing anchor at Plymouth Harbor on December 17.

Over that first winter, more than half of the settlers died of diseases they were already suffering from when they had arrived in the New World. Nevertheless, they succeeded in building the colony's first houses and, with the help of the local Native American tribe and a plentiful first harvest the following fall, slowly began to thrive. Over the centuries, since the passengers of the *Mayflower* set foot on the shore of their new home, their story has become symbolic of American ideals of freedom, endurance and hope. The pilgrims' arrival and their early struggles have reached an almost mythical status and are celebrated in art, literature and film, and remembered in the USA each year on Thanksgiving.

23

Above: A portrait of Sir Isaac Newton painted by Sir Godfrey Kneller at the beginning of the 18th century.

Right: The title page of Philosophiæ Naturalis Principia Mathematica. *Written in Latin, original copies are rare and valuable, though Trinity College still owns Newton's own copy, which bears his notes for revisions to the second edition.*

AT A GLANCE

Isaac Newton's Philosophiæ Naturalis Principia Mathematica *was a work of staggering vision and clarity of thought. Containing groundbreaking observations on the effects of gravity on celestial bodies as well as laws of motion that provided the basis of classical mechanics, its publication sparked a revolution in science. Among the most important works ever produced, Newton's* Principia *remains a pillar of science more than three centuries after it first appeared.*

NEWTON PUBLISHES THE *PRINCIPIA*

CAMBRIDGE, UK
JULY 5, 1687

Famously inspired to think about gravity by watching an apple fall from a tree on his mother's farm, Isaac Newton dreamed up groundbreaking ideas on the subject which were fully articulated in one of the greatest works of science ever written, *Philosophiæ Naturalis Principia Mathematica* or *Mathematical Principles of Natural Philosophy*.

Now considered by many to be the most important scientist in history, Isaac Newton showed an early interest in developments in astronomy, philosophy and mathematics on entering Trinity College, Cambridge, at the age of 18 in 1661. He failed to shine as an undergraduate, but his private work was marked by brilliance and during the two years after he had gained his degree, he made impressive strides in a number of scientific fields; as a result he was invited back to Trinity College in 1667 as a Fellow. He expanded on his work in optics, showing that light was made up of the spectrum of colors, building the first refracting telescope and setting out his findings in a book called *Opticks*, which rivals the subsequent *Principia* in its scientific significance. He also developed calculus and spent much of his time dabbling in alchemy. A somewhat eccentric man, Newton was prone to becoming so lost in his own thoughts that he would be overcome by them before even getting out of bed, he was often found sitting and staring into space in his nightshirt for hours on end.

Work on this next book began in 1679, following a correspondence with Robert Hooke, himself a giant in the field of natural philosophy. The appearance of Halley's Comet during the winter of 1680–1681 also excited his interest in the orbits of celestial bodies. Published in 1687, the three-volume *Philosophiæ Naturalis Principia Mathematica*, breathtaking in its scope, was immediately recognized as a scientific masterpiece. Within its pages Newton expressed laws and observations that remain current almost three centuries after his death, setting out his three laws of motion and his law of universal gravitation, applying them to the movement of celestial bodies with startling accuracy and explaining for the first time, the movement of the tides. The *Principia* also considered the size of all known bodies in the solar system including the Sun itself, demonstrated that the Earth was not a perfect sphere, recognized that the Sun was not at the center of the galaxy and described the orbits of comets.

The sheer scope of the Principia set it apart from all scientific work that had preceded it and set the stage for a revolution in the fields of mathematics and physics. Beyond this, Newton's clarity of expression and his methodology, which favored experimental proof, became a model for scientists who came after him. It also brought Newton a great deal of acclaim. In 1689, he became a Member of Parliament and in 1703 he was made President of the Royal Mint. In 1705, well established as the foremost figure in European science, he was knighted, becoming Sir Isaac Newton.

PHILOSOPHIÆ

NATURALIS

PRINCIPIA

MATHEMATICA.

Autore *JS. NEWTON*, *Trin. Coll. Cantab. Soc.* Matheseos
Professore *Lucasiano*, & Societatis Regalis Sodali.

IMPRIMATUR·
S. PEPYS, *Reg. Soc.* PRÆSES.

Julii 5. 1686.

LONDINI,

Jussu *Societatis Regiæ* ac Typis *Josephi Streater*. Prostat apud
plures Bibliopolas. Anno MDCLXXXVII.

INVENTION OF THE SPINNING JENNY

LEIGH, LANCASHIRE, ENGLAND
1764

Above: An illustration depicting James Hargreaves' Spinning Jenny.

Left: A woman working in an automated cotton mill in the early 20th century.

AT A GLANCE

The invention of the Spinning Jenny was representative of the industrial revolution, by which mechanization replaced hand-driven skills and enabled greater profits to be made by manufacturers and mill owners. Resistance from the working classes was inevitable, but ultimately futile.

The invention of the Spinning Jenny was the single most important event of the early industrial revolution. It introduced mass production to the spinning of cotton, a vital stage in the process of making cloth. This mechanization began the transformation of cloth production from a cottage industry to factory production in the 'dark satanic mills' of industrial England.

As with so many important innovations, several men laid claim to it, and other men's innovations certainly paved the way for it. In 1733 John Kay patented a flying shuttle, which allowed a weaver to make cloth wider than the reach of his outstretched arm. In 1760, his son Robert devised the drop box, a way of making patterns by using three colors of weft (the woven, horizontal thread) on a single loom. Wider cloth and multiple yarns meant that weavers needed more thread; the first Spinning Jenny allowed one spinner to run six spindles at a time, instead of the previous single spindle.

Its invention is generally credited to Thomas Highs of Leigh in 1764, although the idea was more fully developed three years later by James Hargreaves in Blackburn. Hargreaves' new machines were destroyed by rioting spinners who feared that they would be put out of work. They were right of course; ten years later, there were 20,000 Spinning Jennies operating in Britain.

Hargreaves fled to Nottingham, arriving there at about the same time as Richard Arkwright, an entrepreneur who further developed the Spinning Jenny by using water power. Arkwright opened his first water-powered mill at Cromford in Derbyshire, and eventually had a chain of Arkwright mills from Lancashire to Lanarkshire in Scotland. He too faced resistance to his innovations when protesters burnt down his mill at Birkacre in Lancashire in 1779.

That year, Samuel Crompton combined the ideas of Arkwright, Hargreaves and Highs in the Spinning Mule, a machine capable of producing finer thread than its predecessors. Further innovations followed, leap-frogging one another in the race to increase output and improve quality. In 1785 a steam engine by James Watt was used to power a cotton mill for the first time, and the Rev Edmund Cartwright patented a power loom.

Cartwright looms were the target for arsonists in Manchester in 1792. But the rioters and arsonists couldn't stop progress; the technology was applied to other industries. In due course mechanization transformed not only manufacturing processes but the structure and politics of British society. It changed the very landscape of Britain, too, which became dotted and crossed by mills and factories, canals and railways, and new towns and cities.

COOK SETS SAIL FOR THE PACIFIC

PLYMOUTH, ENGLAND
1768

Explorer and cartographer Lieutenant James Cook set sail from Plymouth in his converted coal-carrier, the *Endeavour*, in 1768, bound for the Pacific. He had been ordered by the Royal Society to observe Venus passing in front of the sun, an event that could be used to help measure the distance from the sun to the Earth.

Cook reached New Zealand, which had previously been discovered by the Dutchman Abel Tasman, in 1770; Cook circumnavigated and charted both north and south islands before continuing westwards. When he reached the east coast of New Holland (later to be known as Australia), he named his anchorage Botany Bay, and the land itself New South Wales; on 26 August, he claimed it for Britain and King George III. Then he sailed northwards, on a four-month voyage along the eastern coast of the continent.

In 1788 the British Captain Arthur Phillip followed Cook, to find a perfect natural harbour which he named after Britain's then Home Secretary, Lord Sydney, and the British started settling the continent, mainly through the transportation of British convicts.

Cook was the first person to accurately chart a large part of the Australian coastline, his 12 years sailing around the Pacific Ocean contributing much to European knowledge of the area. On his second voyage, on *Resolution*, he managed to determine longitude with higher accuracy than anyone had achieved before, using the newfangled chronometer and a Gregory Azimuth Compass. He also understood how important it was to eat vegetables to reduce scurvy, the sometimes fatal illness that resulted from dietary deficiency on long voyages. He succeeded in completing his first voyage without losing a single man to the disease.

Cook is ranked with Vasco de Gama and Columbus among explorers, and is considered a major figure in Australia's modern history. Many places, both on the east Australian coast and in New Zealand, have been named after him or the *Endeavour*, and many of the names he gave to places in 1770, such as Botany Bay and the Whitsundays in the Great Barrier Reef, are still used today. He died on an expedition to Hawaii in 1779, his third voyage of discovery, and is commemorated by a statue in Greenwich, London, UK.

AT A GLANCE

In 1770, Lieutenant (later Captain) James Cook was the man who discovered Australia. He was an innovator in the process of long-distance sea travel and navigation, reaching six of the seven continents during his lifetime, and is rightly remembered as one of the foremost explorers of his era.

Left: Landfall at Botany Bay.

Inset: Captain Cook's orders to discover Australia, on display in the Public Records Office, London.

IN CONGRESS, JULY 4, 1776.

The unanimous Declaration of the thirteen united States of America.

When in the Course of human events, it becomes necessary for one people to dissolve the political bands which have connected them with another, and to assume among the powers of the earth, the separate and equal station to which the Laws of Nature and of Nature's God entitle them, a decent respect to the opinions of mankind requires that they should declare the causes which impel them to the separation.

We hold these truths to be self-evident, that all men are created equal, that they are endowed by their Creator with certain unalienable Rights, that among these are Life, Liberty and the pursuit of Happiness.— That to secure these rights, Governments are instituted among Men, deriving their just powers from the consent of the governed,— That whenever any Form of Government becomes destructive of these ends, it is the Right of the People to alter or to abolish it, and to institute new Government, laying its foundation on such principles and organizing its powers in such form, as to them shall seem most likely to effect their Safety and Happiness. Prudence, indeed, will dictate that Governments long established should not be changed for light and transient causes; and accordingly all experience hath shewn, that mankind are more disposed to suffer, while evils are sufferable, than to right themselves by abolishing the forms to which they are accustomed. But when a long train of abuses and usurpations, pursuing invariably the same Object evinces a design to reduce them under absolute Despotism, it is their right, it is their duty, to throw off such Government, and to provide new Guards for their future security.— Such has been the patient sufferance of these Colonies; and such is now the necessity which constrains them to alter their former Systems of Government. The history of the present King of Great Britain is a history of repeated injuries and usurpations, all having in direct object the establishment of an absolute Tyranny over these States. To prove this, let Facts be submitted to a candid world.

He has refused his Assent to Laws, the most wholesome and necessary for the public good.

He has forbidden his Governors to pass Laws of immediate and pressing importance, unless suspended in their operation till his Assent should be obtained; and when so suspended, he has utterly neglected to attend to them.

He has refused to pass other Laws for the accommodation of large districts of people, unless those people would relinquish the right of Representation in the Legislature, a right inestimable to them and formidable to tyrants only.

He has called together legislative bodies at places unusual, uncomfortable, and distant from the depository of their Public Records, for the sole purpose of fatiguing them into compliance with his measures.

He has dissolved Representative Houses repeatedly, for opposing with manly firmness his invasions on the rights of the people.

He has refused for a long time, after such dissolutions, to cause others to be elected; whereby the Legislative powers, incapable of Annihilation, have returned to the People at large for their exercise; the State remaining in the mean time exposed to all the dangers of invasion from without, and convulsions within.

He has endeavoured to prevent the population of these States; for that purpose obstructing the Laws for Naturalization of Foreigners; refusing to pass others to encourage their migrations hither, and raising the conditions of new Appropriations of Lands.

He has obstructed the Administration of Justice, by refusing his Assent to Laws for establishing Judiciary powers.

He has made Judges dependent on his Will alone, for the tenure of their offices, and the amount and payment of their salaries.

He has erected a multitude of New Offices, and sent hither swarms of Officers to harrass our people, and eat out their substance.

He has kept among us, in times of peace, Standing Armies without the Consent of our legislatures.

He has affected to render the Military independent of and superior to the Civil power.

He has combined with others to subject us to a jurisdiction foreign to our constitution, and unacknowledged by our laws; giving his Assent to their Acts of pretended Legislation:

For Quartering large bodies of armed troops among us:

For protecting them, by a mock Trial, from punishment for any Murders which they should commit on the Inhabitants of these States:

For cutting off our Trade with all parts of the world:

For imposing Taxes on us without our Consent:

For depriving us in many cases, of the benefits of Trial by Jury:

For transporting us beyond Seas to be tried for pretended offences

For abolishing the free System of English Laws in a neighbouring Province, establishing therein an Arbitrary government, and enlarging its Boundaries so as to render it at once an example and fit instrument for introducing the same absolute rule into these Colonies:

For taking away our Charters, abolishing our most valuable Laws, and altering fundamentally the Forms of our Governments:

For suspending our own Legislatures, and declaring themselves invested with power to legislate for us in all cases whatsoever.

He has abdicated Government here, by declaring us out of his Protection and waging War against us.

He has plundered our seas, ravaged our Coasts, burnt our towns, and destroyed the lives of our people.

He is at this time transporting large Armies of foreign Mercenaries to compleat the works of death, desolation and tyranny, already begun with circumstances of Cruelty & perfidy scarcely paralleled in the most barbarous ages, and totally unworthy the Head of a civilized nation.

He has constrained our fellow Citizens taken Captive on the high Seas to bear Arms against their Country, to become the executioners of their friends and Brethren, or to fall themselves by their Hands.

He has excited domestic insurrections amongst us, and has endeavoured to bring on the inhabitants of our frontiers, the merciless Indian Savages, whose known rule of warfare, is an undistinguished destruction of all ages, sexes and conditions.

In every stage of these Oppressions We have Petitioned for Redress in the most humble terms: Our repeated Petitions have been answered only by repeated injury. A Prince, whose character is thus marked by every act which may define a Tyrant, is unfit to be the ruler of a free people.

Nor have We been wanting in attentions to our Brittish brethren. We have warned them from time to time of attempts by their legislature to extend an unwarrantable jurisdiction over us. We have reminded them of the circumstances of our emigration and settlement here. We have appealed to their native justice and magnanimity, and we have conjured them by the ties of our common kindred to disavow these usurpations, which, would inevitably interrupt our connections and correspondence. They too have been deaf to the voice of justice and of consanguinity. We must, therefore, acquiesce in the necessity, which denounces our Separation, and hold them, as we hold the rest of mankind, Enemies in War, in Peace Friends.

We, therefore, the Representatives of the united States of America, in General Congress, Assembled, appealing to the Supreme Judge of the world for the rectitude of our intentions, do, in the Name, and by Authority of the good People of these Colonies, solemnly publish and declare, That these United Colonies are, and of Right ought to be Free and Independent States; that they are Absolved from all Allegiance to the British Crown, and that all political connection between them and the State of Great Britain, is and ought to be totally dissolved; and that as Free and Independent States, they have full Power to levy War, conclude Peace, contract Alliances, establish Commerce, and to do all other Acts and Things which Independent States may of right do.— And for the support of this Declaration, with a firm reliance on the protection of divine Providence, we mutually pledge to each other our Lives, our Fortunes and our sacred Honor.

John Hancock

Button Gwinnett
Lyman Hall
Geo Walton.

Wm Hooper
Joseph Hewes,
John Penn

Edward Rutledge.

Thos Heyward Junr.
Thomas Lynch Junr.
Arthur Middleton

Samuel Chase
Wm Paca
Thos Stone
Charles Carroll of Carrollton

George Wythe
Richard Henry Lee
Th Jefferson
Benja Harrison

Robt Morris
Benjamin Rush
Benja Franklin
John Morton
Geo Clymer
Jas Smith.
Geo Taylor
James Wilson
Geo Ross
Caesar Rodney
Geo Read
Tho M:Kean

Wm Floyd
Phil Livingston
Frans Lewis
Lewis Morris

Richd Stockton
Jno Witherspoon
Fras Hopkinson
John Hart
Abra Clark

Josiah Bartlett
Wm Whipple
Saml Adams
John Adams
Robt Treat Paine
Elbridge Gerry
Step Hopkins
William Ellery
Roger Sherman
Saml Huntington
Wm Williams
Oliver Wolcott

Above: The Assembly Room in Philadelphia where the Declaration was signed.

Left: The historic Declaration of Independence.

Overleaf: John Trumbull's Declaration of Independence depicting the presentation of the draft of the Declaration of Independence to Congress.

AT A GLANCE

In 1776, 13 colonies in North America united to sign Thomas Jefferson's Declaration of Independence, breaking free of the British Empire and becoming the United States of America. The new nation, founded principally because the colonists rejected the idea of being taxed without parliamentary representation, is now considered by many as the leader of the free world.

US DECLARATION OF INDEPENDENCE

PHILADELPHIA, USA
JULY 4, 1776

The birth of the United States of America in 1776 was the result of a struggle against British rule by her American colonies. The British government had run up debts in wars against France and India, and so had decided to increase taxation. But the British living in America resented this, especially because they had no say in the decisions made by the British parliament; their slogan 'No taxation without representation' summed up what they felt.

In September 1774, representatives of twelve of the self-governing provinces convened in Philadelphia, forming the First Continental Congress, in an attempt to coordinate a response to Britain's demands. But when their negotiations – and even their petition to King George III to intervene – proved fruitless, they decided to boycott British goods and services.

The citizens of Boston tipped British tea into their harbor as a protest against the taxation on tea and sugar, and many colonists refused to pay the stamp duty levied on documents. In 1775, colonist Patrick Henry expressed the feelings of many who until this time had considered themselves British subjects: he called for his fellows to place their loyalties to one side and put their lives on the line in the pursuit of liberty.

In 1776 the British Parliament passed the Prohibitory Act, creating a blockade of American ports and declaring American ships to be enemy vessels. This strengthened public support in the colonies, and John Adams, a keen supporter of independence, said that by doing this, Parliament had declared American independence before Congress had been able to do it.

On July 4, 1776, 55 men, representing the 13 colonies, each put their signature to the Declaration of Independence, drafted principally by Thomas Jefferson; it claimed sovereignty for the territories and rejected their allegiance to Britain. About 200 copies were printed and circulated throughout the colonies for public reading. The original document signed by Congress is now preserved in the National Archives, though several early copies also exist.

The War of Independence had actually already begun a year earlier, with skirmishes at Lexington and Concord in which about 55 men had died. The war continued, with France helping the colonists, until it was officially ended by the 1783 Treaty of Paris. This recognized the sovereignty of the USA over land reaching from Canada to the north to Florida to the south and to the Mississippi to the west. The Constitution of the United States followed five years later.

The signing of the Declaration is celebrated in the USA every July 4, Independence Day.

FALL OF THE BASTILLE

PARIS, FRANCE
JULY 14, 1789

Above: King Louis XVI, whose execution followed four years later, in 1793.

Right: A contemporary illustration of the Fall of the Bastille by artist Jean-Pierre Houel.

By 1787, it had become impossible to govern France effectively. Inflation was rampant, the state was impoverished by long wars, and outdated farming practices and ancient feudal systems combined to keep the peasants poor and hungry. Ministers of the king, Louis XVI, tried to carry out political reforms that year, but the aristocracy, who saw the proposed reforms as a threat to their status, thwarted them at every turn.

In May 1789, under pressure from both his government and the population as a whole, the king reluctantly gave the French people a role in government for the first time in history. The new National Constituent Assembly met for the first time on July 9 – but just two days later, the nobles persuaded the king to sack his finance minister, who had supported the reforms.

News of his dismissal spread rapidly through Paris. The people, believing that this was the start of a counter-attack by the old regime, protested by raiding tax offices and food depots. Skirmishes broke out as weapons and wheat were 'liberated'. On the morning of July 14, the angry demonstrators seized a hoard of 30,000 firearms, and began a hunt for gunpowder and shot.

The Bastille was an old fortress, so badly designed that it had been captured at every one of the six sieges in its 400-year history. As a prison it had already been slated for closure before the riots broke out; on the day it was stormed, it held only seven inmates. But the space left unoccupied by prisoners housed a huge arsenal of explosives, and it was for this that the rabble raided the building.

The frenzied crowd quickly overcame the inadequate defense force. Bloodthirsty after three days of rioting, the mob brutally murdered the prison governor and began an orgy of drunken celebration in the Paris streets – contemporary reports say that many of them dropped dead from sheer exhaustion. But the victorious revolutionaries somehow found the energy to demolish the building almost immediately, stone by stone. All that remain today are a few foundations, visible in the Bastille metro station, and some masonry re-used in the bridge over the Seine at the Place de la Concorde.

The importance of the Bastille as a prison and a garrison may have been exaggerated in the centuries since its overthrow, but its strength as a symbol of the violent destruction of the old order is undeniable. The French Revolution launched 60 years of political upheaval that would transform the social structure of Europe. *Quatorze juillet* 1789 was the beginning of the end of feudalism in France – it was the day that for the first time its ordinary people took control of their destiny.

AT A GLANCE

The demolition of the Bastille prison in Paris in July 1789 signaled the beginning of the French Revolution, as the downtrodden people rose up against King Louis XVI and the aristocracy that had kept them subjugated. Today, France, now a republic, still celebrates 'le quatorze juillet' every year.

BATTLE OF TRAFALGAR

OFF CAPE TRAFALGAR, SPAIN
OCTOBER 21, 1805

Above: An engraved portrait of Horatio Nelson, who died during the Battle of Trafalgar but remains one of Great Britain's most admired national heroes.

Right: Admiral Nelson's **Victory** *fires her guns on the* **Redoubtable** *during the Battle of Trafalgar.*

By early 1805, the French leader Napoleon Bonaparte was the master of large swathes of Europe, and had amassed 150,000 soldiers and a vast flotilla of troop-carrier ships to invade England. The only protection Britain had was the British Navy, under the command of the great admiral, Sir Horatio Nelson, who had pinned down a large part of the French fleet, commanded by Pierre-Charles Villeneuve, at Toulon on the Mediterranean coast of southern France. Unable to protect his troop carriers, Bonaparte could not risk launching the invasion.

Napoleon ordered his commander-in-chief, Villeneuve, to sail his combined French/Spanish fleet to the West Indian island of Martinique, to be joined by more French ships. Bonaparte expected the British Navy to hasten after them, to protect British holdings in the West Indies. But Villeneuve was then to sail rapidly back to the English Channel (la Manche), to sweep it clear of the few British ships left there, allowing the troop carriers to do their work.

Villeneuve sailed to Martinique. But the rest of the fleet failed to join him, so with his ships in bad condition, and afraid that the British were poised to attack them, Villeneuve then went to Cadiz rather than the Channel. Bonaparte, his invasion plan frustrated, diverted his troops eastwards, into Germany.

Then on September 2, word that the French-Spanish fleet was at Cadiz reached Nelson, back in England, and on the 15th he set sail aboard his flagship, *Victory*, with the British fleet.

On October 20, Villeneuve's fleet set sail. Nelson ordered his fleet of 22 massive ships of the line, 6 frigates, and some smaller vessels to intercept Villeneuve's 33 ships of the line, 7 frigates, and smaller craft. The British ships were soon spotted by Villeneuve's fleet, which formed into line of battle during the night.

At 11.45 the next morning, about 21 miles (34 km) off Cape Trafalgar, Nelson ordered the message 'England expects that every man will do his duty' to be signaled to all British vessels. The British ships sailed into the French-Spanish line at a right angle. At 12.45 pm, Nelson's *Victory* fired a raking broadside at the *Bucentaure,* then locked masts with the *Redoubtable*. Fierce deck-to-deck fighting followed, during which Nelson was fatally wounded by a musket shot. While he lay dying, the French-Spanish fleet was slowly overwhelmed. A few ships escaped, but the British eventually captured 22 vessels and lost none. At 4.30 pm, on hearing of the victory, Nelson whispered "Thank God I have done my duty," and expired.

When news of the great victory reached Britain, the celebrations were tempered by the loss of their charismatic hero. Nevertheless, by vanquishing the greater part of the French fleet, Nelson had emphatically removed the threat of a French invasion of Britain, and set the scene for British dominance over the world's oceans – and hence most of the world – for the next century.

AT A GLANCE

The Battle of Trafalgar was the greatest sea battle of the Napoleonic age, during which a combined French and Spanish fleet was vanquished by the British Navy under Admiral Sir Horatio Nelson. While the battle had little impact on the Napoleonic wars in continental Europe, the victory meant that Napoleon Bonaparte was never able to threaten an invasion of Britain, and this helped ensure British naval dominance during the 19th century.

AT A GLANCE

Napoleon was defeated at Waterloo in 1815 by allied armies under Wellington from Britain and Blücher from Prussia. The defeat not only broke the French emperor's will and health but also his country's stranglehold over Europe, changing the face of the continent. He was sent into exile and he died six years later.

BATTLE OF WATERLOO

BELGIUM
JUNE 18, 1815

For 18 years Napoleon Bonaparte, in expanding his empire, had brought war to much of Europe, and this had turned many of its countries into enemies of France. These countries formed a coalition, and in 1814 Paris fell to their invading forces. Bonaparte was captured by them and sent into exile on the island of Elba, but he was held for less than a year; in February 1815 he escaped and rode up through France to Paris. There, he was hailed as emperor once again by the French people, and large parts of the French Army decided to serve under him.

Britain, Russia, Prussia and Austria formed an alliance to crush Napoleon once and for all. They each pledged 150,000 men for an invasion of France, which was planned for July 1. Napoleon, however – brilliant general as he was – seized the initiative, deciding to attack the individual enemy armies before they had a chance to combine forces against him.

He boldly invaded Belgium, and on June 16 his French army fought on two fronts, defeating Field Marshal Blücher's Prussian army at Ligny, and managing to stall the British army under the Duke of Wellington at Quatre Bras. Wellington's troops withdrew to the village of Waterloo, while the Prussians regrouped further east.

At Waterloo on the morning of June 18, battle recommenced. The French infantry advanced first, but were repulsed by British firepower and cavalry. Next, a French cavalry counterattack wreaked heavy losses on the British cavalry. But then the British infantry redcoats formed tight squares and advanced, and the French cavalry, despite repeated charges, were unable to penetrate them; the fearsome rapid fire of the British musketeers decimated the French.

The French managed, however, to capture La Haye farmhouse, a strategic position which their artillery used to launch a devastating bombardment onto the British squares. Napoleon sent in his crack troops, the Imperial Guard, to cut a path through the British forces and take on the Prussian army, now arriving on the field.

But for the first time in their history the Imperial Guard were defeated; it was the British guardsmen and light infantry who together achieved this. As the news of the Guard's disgrace spread, French morale collapsed – and Wellington chose this moment to signal a general advance. The French army fled, pursued and brutally cut down by the Prussian cavalry, vengeful from their defeat the day before.

Bonaparte was broken. His support in Paris melted away, and he fled the city, hoping to sail to America. But the Royal Navy had blockaded the ports, and less than two weeks later, Napoleon surrendered to a British sea captain. He was imprisoned this time on the remote island of St Helena, where he died in exile in 1821. France's power in Europe was broken, and Britain did not fight another major war for 100 years.

Above: Napoleon's defeat at Waterloo preceded his exile to the island of Elba.

Left: An illustration from the painting by H Chartier depicting the Battle of Waterloo.

Overleaf: A contemporary painting of the Battle of Waterloo, which broke Napoleon Bonaparte's grip on Europe and changed the course of the continent's history.

41

Above: Trains pass each other on the Liverpool and Manchester Railway, in an illustration by Clavell.

Right: The Northumbrian, *the first locomotive on the Liverpool and Manchester Railway, pictured during centennial celebrations in 1930.*

OPENING OF THE LIVERPOOL–MANCHESTER RAILWAY

UK
SEPTEMBER 15, 1830

The Liverpool and Manchester Railway Company (L&MR) was formed in 1823, and three years later the British parliament allowed it to construct the first public passenger railway line in the world. The route was a challenge for its engineer, George Stephenson, as in its 32 miles the line had to cross wide valleys, cut through stone hillsides and even in one section be floated across an apparently bottomless peat bog.

When the line was nearly completed, a competition of speed, strength and endurance was held on a test track at Rainhill, to find the best engine to run between the two cities. The winner was Stephenson's locomotive *Rocket*. But between the trial and the opening of the line Stephenson improved his design, and as a result it was another of his locomotives, the *Northumbrian*, which hauled the coaches full of eminent guests on the inaugural run on September 15, 1830.

The line was a double track, and the plan was for the *Northumbrian's* train to pause at a certain point to allow the dignitaries on board to view a procession of locomotives travelling on the other track. Some of the guests took advantage of the stop to get out and stretch their legs – and joy turned to horror at the first death on a passenger railway, when a member of parliament fell while attempting to get out of the way of the oncoming cavalcade. His legs were crushed under the *Rocket's* wheels, and he died soon afterwards.

Despite that discouraging event, the opening of the Liverpool and Manchester Railway made a phenomenal impact. Its immediate success – and the profits it made – prompted the railway mania of the 1830s and 1840s; by the end of those two decades, there were over 5,000 miles of railway in Britain, transforming the landscape.

The speed, convenience and comfort of rail travel hastened the end of long-distance coaches and horses. In fact, passenger traffic on the nation's roads never really grew until the car was invented. The rail freight service outshone the canal system, which could not compete with the speed at which the railway could carry perishable goods and urgent mail. This meant that the trains took over the transport of raw materials and products to and from the industrial heartlands.

Those heartlands went on to supply railways to the world, using the track gauge and other innovations introduced by Stephenson for the L&MR. The 19th century became known as the Railway Age, and Stephenson as the Father of the Railways.

AT A GLANCE

The opening of a 32-mile track between the northern British industrial centres of Liverpool and Manchester confirmed the railway as the coming mode of transport for both passengers and freight, ending the era of horse and coach. Rail would rule until the rise of motor transport in the next century.

PARLIAMENT PASSES THE EMANCIPATION ACT

LONDON, UK
JULY 26, 1833

The Emancipation Act in 1833 put the finishing touch to a gradual shift in social attitudes that had begun nearly 50 years earlier. Back in 1787, the Society for the Abolition of Slavery had been founded by Quakers, and that same year the British Prime Minister, William Pitt the Younger, had asked a young MP, William Wilberforce, to lead the abolition movement in parliament.

Wilberforce was an evangelical Christian, and it was these Non-Conformists and Dissenters who so strongly supported humanitarian progress. But the Church of England, the state religion, was at best indifferent, some of its clergymen even owning slaves themselves.

As the years went by, the British people became more and more opposed to the cruel injustices of the slave trade, but political and vested interests blocked every attempt to pass laws to restrict it. Although Wilberforce presented an abolition bill in Parliament almost every year from 1789 onwards, he had to wait for nearly 20 years, when in 1807 a new government was in power, for his bill to be passed.

It was an important first step, because it outlawed the trade in slaves carried out by British ships. But trade by other countries, particularly Portugal, continued – and in any case it was still legal to own slaves, as against transporting them. So Wilberforce was adamant that slavery itself must be ended, and he continued to campaign.

In 1823 a new Anti-Slavery Society was formed, and Wilberforce published a pamphlet that made his points with his usual verve and vigor. But the years of fighting and frustration had worn him down, and he began to take a less active role. He retired from Parliament in 1825, and in 1830 he chaired the Anti-Slavery Society for the last time. But by then the tide had turned, and the political will which Wilberforce had worked for so long to influence was at last reflecting the people's support for the cause.

At last, on July 26, 1833, the Abolition of Slavery Act had its final reading in the House of Commons, to become law on August 1 the following year. There were still compromises – slaves were to be reclassified as 'tied apprentices' for up to six years, and the government had to pay out over £20 million in compensation to the planters who had bought them. But it was the beginning of the end for a great inhumanity, and a sinking William Wilberforce was able to say, "Thank God that I have lived to witness a day in which England is willing to give twenty millions sterling for the abolition of slavery." He died just three days later, on July 29, 1833.

Above: A monument to William Wilberforce was erected in Westminster Abbey.

Left: A contemporary illustration of an anti-slavery public meeting held in Exeter Hall, London.

AT A GLANCE

The long, hard battle against slavery cost politician William Wilberforce his health and ultimately his life. But the Emancipation Act passed in 1833 gave thousands upon thousands of people their lives back, as the other politicians finally gave in to half a century of public opinion, and the vested interests of the ruling classes were overcome.

Above: An early telegraph receiver. Electric current flowing along a telegraph line energized twin electromagnets in the receiver. These attracted an iron bar which caused tape, pulled by a roller, to be pushed against an inking wheel. A short burst of current inked a short line – a dot – and a long pulse created a dash.

Left: A studio photograph of Samuel F. B. Morse, the inventor of Morse code.

INVENTION OF MORSE CODE

NEW YORK, USA
1835

Most famous today for its use as the international SOS distress signal, ··· — ···, Morse code has been in use since the development of Samuel F. B. Morse's electric telegraph system in the late 1830s. His code was adapted by his assistant, Alfred Vail, and it was his system that most resembles that used today, being refined in 1848 into Modern International Morse Code by Friedrich Clemens Gerke.

The development of the code is entwined with that of the telegraph system. In 1832, Morse, at that time an artist, became fascinated by electromagnetism and the possibilities it held for communication over a long distance. Over the following years, he developed a scheme for a single-wire telegraph system through which electrical pulses sent from a transmitting device controlled an electromagnet in a receiver. These pulses could, he suggested, be converted to marks on a piece of paper that moved along at a constant speed. However, in order to produce a meaningful message, Morse realized that the pulses would need to adhere to a simple code that could be easily converted into language. While working at New York University in 1835, he successfully demonstrated that pulse signals could be sent along a wire, and devised a simple code for translating them into text: Morse code was born.

Morse's original code involved sending pulses that corresponded to numerals that were then converted into letters of the alphabet. This, however, was later refined by Vail into a system where the shorter 'dots' and longer 'dashes' were combined, enabling them to correspond directly with letters and numbers.

Simple to understand and to operate, the code was used by Morse to send the famous, official opening message along the first telegraph line between Baltimore and the Capitol Building in Washington, D.C.: "What hath God wrought." As the telegraph system spread, its operators soon found that they could, without referring to the tape, understand the clicks coming down the telegraph line at rates exceeding 40 words per minute. The fact that it could be understood as a language in its own right allowed Morse code to make the transition to radio in the 20th century, using sound (rather than indentations or ink on paper) to express the dots and dashes, and the code could also be used silently with short and long flashes of light. There have been cases, too, of disabled people using it to communicate; for example, a radio operator who suffered a stroke was able to 'speak' to doctors by blinking his eyes in Morse code.

Morse code's adaptability and simplicity saw its use spread worldwide, and though the telegraph has long since been superseded by more sophisticated forms of communication, it remains in use internationally to this day.

AT A GLANCE

Devised by Samuel Morse and later refined by Alfred Vail, Morse code provided a simple, easy-to-understand code that was first used on primitive telegraph systems but was later adopted internationally for radio and other communications media.

Above: A portrait of Louis Daguerre, captured using his own invention in 1846.

Left: The daguerreotype process was used as far away as Japan by the mid-1840s, but was particularly popular in the USA, where photographers eagerly captured everything from family portraits to great national buildings, such as the Capitol in Washington, D.C.

AT A GLANCE

With exposure times of just 10 to 20 minutes and an unprecedented level of clarity and detail in the resulting images, the daguerreotype process pioneered by Louis Daguerre and Nicéphore Niépce heralded the beginning of practical photography.

INVENTION OF THE DAGUERREOTYPE

FRANCE
1839

Although many inventors had previously attempted to fix images using photo-sensitive materials, the daguerreotype was the first reliable photographic process to achieve a high level of detail, and the first to be widely used commercially.

The process was pioneered by a French artist, Louis J.M. Daguerre, and Nicéphore Niépce, a chemist who had been experimenting with the use of chemicals to capture images since 1793. In 1825, Daguerre was the successful owner of a theater called the Diorama, which featured huge images that Daguerre had created by using a camera obscura to project scenes. These were traced and colored before being cleverly lit to provide the illusion of time passing, and movement. Even with the scene faithfully projected, the process of making the 71 x 45 ft (22 x 14 meter) paintings was time-consuming, and Daguerre was keen to find a way in which images might be captured quickly and easily. In 1829, he entered into a partnership with Niépce, who had already had some success in this area with a process he called 'heliography'.

With Daguerre concentrating on refining a camera mechanism and Niépce on the chemical composition of the plates, the pair made some progress by coating copper sheets with iodized silver before Niépce's death in 1833. Undaunted, Daguerre used what he had learned from his collaborator to continue experimenting, and in 1835, after accidentally breaking a thermometer, he discovered that images could be developed using mercury vapor. Four years later, on January 7, 1839, his perfected invention was announced by the French Academy of Sciences. In the daguerreotype process, copper plates were prepared by exposing them to iodine, forming a light-sensitive silver iodide coating. After an exposure of 10 to 20 minutes, the plate was developed by placing it over heated mercury, then fixed in a bath of salt water and rinsed in hot water. While the images produced by this method were extremely fragile – and the chemicals dangerously toxic – the results were stunning. Daguerreotype pictures were perfect black and white mirror images that captured an astonishing level of detail.

The invention quickly proved a sensation. In August, 1839, the French government proclaimed Daguerre's process a gift 'Free to the World' and awarded him a pension. Over the next decade, the method spread around the world. Now, portraits – formerly the preserve of expensive artists – could be created quickly and cheaply, and early photographers were quick to capitalize on the opportunities the daguerreotype offered, traveling from town to town to practice the new art.

While the daguerreotype process itself was swiftly overtaken in later decades by more refined photographic methods, such as calotype and tintype, Daguerre's invention, marks the dawn of the age of photography.

Above: The south transept of the Crystal Palace, built for the Great Exhibition of 1851, being reconstructed in Sydenham.

Right: A contemporary engraving of the Great Exhibition, Main Avenue, looking east.

Overleaf: A contemporary engraving of the South Transept of the Crystal Palace.

AT A GLANCE

Britain's Great Exhibition of 1851 was the brainchild of Queen Victoria's husband, Prince Albert, and it was intended to publicize Britain's achievements. It more than met its aims, inspiring designers from many countries worldwide, while its profits funded three major museums that still inform and enlighten to this day.

THE GREAT EXHIBITION OPENS

LONDON, UK
MAY 1, 1851

By the mid-19th century Britain was at peace with itself and the world. It had not fought a war since defeating the French at Waterloo. It had survived political upheavals at home and abroad, including the chaotic year of 1848 when so many European nations had suffered armed revolt. And now, thanks to its own industrial revolution, Britain was experiencing an explosion of wealth.

It was Prince Albert, Queen Victoria's German husband, who had come up with the idea of a Great Exhibition. He had overcome early unpopularity by throwing himself into British life; he reinvented the Royal Family as role model for the nation's nuclear families, and he took a great interest in national politics.

Albert was a modern man, an admirer of innovation and the application of science. He was made President of the Royal Society for the Encouragement of Arts, Manufacture and Commerce in 1843 and, seeing the Society's annual exhibitions and the French Industrial Exposition of 1844, was inspired by the idea of staging an international festival of industrial design in Britain.

Although the Exhibition was to include almost as many overseas exhibits as British ones, the main idea was to show off the achievements of Britain and its Empire by comparison with the rest of the world. The very building in which it was housed, the Crystal Palace, was a marvel of engineering and modular mass production. It was longer than the French royal palace at Versailles and taller than Westminster Abbey, and its one million square feet of glass easily enclosed a number of full-size trees that were growing on the site in Hyde Park, in the heart of London.

In this way, Britain demonstrated to the world its belief in its mastery over nature and science. The Exhibition gave the British a sense of superiority, security and confidence which helped keep their morale high for the next hundred years. But the Exhibition also acted as a forum for the international exchange of ideas; some of the exhibits from overseas producers, including Britain's industrial successors, the USA and Germany, inspired a new wave of simpler design and more efficient mass production.

The Crystal Palace was dismantled after the exhibition and rebuilt in south London, where in 1911, as the home of the Festival of Empire, it briefly relived its former glory. It burned down in 1936.

The Great Exhibition was visited by six million people between May and October 1851, and was a fabulous money-spinner. The profits – £186,000, or over £16 million ($24 million) in today's money – were used to found the Science Museum, the Natural History Museum, and the Victoria and Albert Museum in neighboring Kensington.

PERRY BOMBARDS TOKYO – JAPAN OPENS UP TO THE MODERN WORLD

TOKYO, JAPAN
JULY 8, 1853

Above: Commodore Matthew Perry meets the Japanese royal commissioner at Yokohama.

Left: US naval forces sail into Tokyo harbour.

AT A GLANCE

A blunt display of naval might by the United States in 1853 helped break down the barriers that the proudly insular Japanese rulers had put up against the Western world. The agreement that resulted from this demonstration helped change the form of government in Japan, made trade easier, and opened up lines of communication between Japan and the Western world that would last for nearly a century.

In the mid-19th century, Japanese ports were closed to foreigners, apart from a handful of Dutch and Chinese traders at Nagasaki. Japan's rulers, the feudal Tokugawa shogunate, resisted contact with outsiders, both commercial and diplomatic. The USA and other nations had tried to open channels of communication, but had been consistently rebuffed. Then in 1849, after Captain James Glynn had secured the release of some American sailors imprisoned in Nagasaki, he recommended to the US Congress that the United States should send in a diplomatic mission – backed up, if they felt it necessary, by force.

For the US government it was vital to gain access to Japanese ports, in order to restock its commercial whaling fleet with coal and other supplies, and the prospect of trading with Japan was a bonus. So in 1852, US President Millard Fillmore ordered Commodore Matthew C. Perry to sail the US Navy's East India Squadron to Japan, to establish diplomatic relations.

Perry had had a distinguished naval career. In 1822, he had taken the Caribbean island of Key West for the USA. During the Mexican–American War, he had been appointed Commander of the Navy's Home Squadron, and he had personally led the attack on Tabasco, in central Mexico, in 1847. Having modernized the US fleet, he was known as the 'Father of the Steam Navy'.

Four black vessels arrived in Tokyo Harbor on July 8, 1853, causing amazement amongst the native population, who had not seen steamships before. The Japanese told Perry to carry on to Nagasaki, but he refused and ordered his ships, with their powerful Paixhans shell guns, to bombard Tokyo harbor. The Japanese, realizing that they could not defend themselves against such might, allowed Perry to deliver a formal request from the US President for a treaty.

In February 1854, Perry returned to Japan, and was given a document which agreed to most of the United States' demands. This became the Convention of Kanagawa, or the America–Japan Treaty of Amity and Friendship. It led to commercial trade between the United States and Japan, and also contributed to opening up of Japan to other Western nations, with the resulting blending of cultures.

This hastened the downfall of the Tokugawa shogunate and the modernization of the Japanese state. Commodore Perry, meanwhile, received a grant of $20,000 from the US Congress as a reward for his work in opening up trade relations between Japan and the rest of the world.

ON

THE ORIGIN OF SPECIES

BY MEANS OF NATURAL SELECTION,

OR THE

PRESERVATION OF FAVOURED RACES IN THE STRUGGLE
FOR LIFE.

By CHARLES DARWIN, M.A.,

FELLOW OF THE ROYAL, GEOLOGICAL, LINNÆAN, ETC., SOCIETIES;
AUTHOR OF 'JOURNAL OF RESEARCHES DURING H. M. S. BEAGLE'S VOYAGE
ROUND THE WORLD.'

LONDON:
JOHN MURRAY, ALBEMARLE STREET.
1859.
P. ʒ̄̄̄.

The right of Translation is reserved.

*Above: The title page of Charles Darwin's
revolutionary book,* On the Origin of Species,
published in 1859.

*Right: An 1875 photograph of naturalist
Charles Darwin.*

AT A GLANCE

*Medical student Charles Darwin's
enquiring mind encouraged
him to look beyond the Biblical
explanation of Earth's creation and
to suggest an alternative means
of evolution. His* On the Origin of
Species *became a standard text
in spite of vehement religious
opposition.*

DARWIN'S *ORIGIN OF SPECIES* PUBLISHED

LONDON, UK
NOVEMBER 24, 1859

The young Charles Darwin had taken a keen interest in natural history, or 'natural theology' as it was known. According to prevailing wisdom, God had created a fixed order of natural life, and any variations in it were according to God's laws. But Darwin was aware of new theories of evolution which were beginning to challenge that entrenched Christian view.

As a medical student in Edinburgh, he had spent more time studying marine invertebrates than attending surgery demonstrations, which he found upsetting. It was, however, as a geologist that he joined the survey ship HMS *Beagle* in 1831 on its second voyage around the world. During that five-year journey he studied fossil records as well as plant and animal life.

His observations, including those of the differing species of finches found on the islands of the Galapagos group, suggested to him the notion of natural selection. He reasoned that a sequence of variations in a given species could over time lead to the evolution of a new species, if those variations were favorable for the survival in a particular habitat.

It was survival of the fittest This realization implied that the natural order was not fixed by God; it could change – indeed had changed – in response to circumstances. It was a theory which directly contradicted the accepted ideas of natural theology, and Darwin proceeded with caution, aware of the hostility his views might arouse.

While he conducted more research and built his reputation as a biologist, other scientists were independently converging on his ideas. In 1844, an anonymous publication, *Vestiges of the Natural History of Creation*, contained a crude version of evolutionary theory and provoked the fury of the clergy, but spurred Darwin and others to greater fieldwork and study.

A paper delivered in 1855 by one of those other scientists, Alfred Russel Wallace, convinced Darwin of the need to get into print with his ideas, and so *On the Origin of Species by Means of Natural Selection, or the Preservation of Favoured Races in the Struggle for Life* finally appeared, more than 20 years after the voyage of the *Beagle*. To avoid controversy, his text actually made no reference at all to the evolution of human beings – nevertheless he still faced the angry condemnation of those opposed to the idea of mankind being 'descended from the apes'.

The concept of evolution was quickly adopted by the scientific community, but only in the 1930s was Darwin's theory of natural selection fully accepted. It is now the cornerstone of the life sciences, although the recent resurgence of fundamentalist Christianity has created new opposition to it.

Above: Richard Gatling received patents for drills, toilets and tractors, but is best remembered for the Gatling gun.

Right: The patent diagram for the Gatling gun, the world's first practical multiple-barrel machine gun.

Below: US soldiers use a Gatling gun during the Philippine Insurrection in 1899.

AT A GLANCE

Invented during the American Civil War of 1861, the multi-barreled Gatling gun was one of the first machine guns. Weapons using its rotating-barrel concept were still being used a century later in Vietnam, proof of its inventor's forward thinking.

INVENTION OF THE GATLING GUN

USA
1861

The Gatling gun won its place in military history for being the world's first rapid-fire weapon that by means of mechanical rotation of barrels could shoot more quickly than any hand-cocked weapon. The sustained bursts it delivered could amount to 200 rounds per minute – an amazing rate of fire for its time. It was effectively one of the first machine guns.

When Dr Richard Gatling invented the gun in 1861 during the American Civil War, he expressed the rather naïve belief that the gun's potential to kill and maim would make future soldiers think twice before engaging in battle. Failing that, it would reduce the numbers of soldiers needed to risk their lives on the battlefield.

It was first used by the Union in the Civil War in its victory over the Confederates, but was so radical in design that Gatling was unable to persuade the government to buy it. But Major General Benjamin F. Butler privately purchased 12 guns for $1,000 each, to be used on the Petersburg front in 1864.

The original Gatling had revolving barrels needing manual cranking, and so it ceded the honor of being the first true fully automatic weapon to the Maxim gun, invented by the American-born British inventor Sir Hiram Maxim in 1884, which made use of the fired projectile's recoil force to reload. This made it more efficient and less labor-intensive than the Gatling. The first Gatling, which used percussion caps, was supplanted in 1867 by a model using metallic cartridges, which was less prone to jam. This was bought in numbers by the US Army and had a firing rate of 600 rounds per minute.

Gatling, the son of planter and inventor Jordan Gatling, not only invented the gun that bore his name, but also patented a seed-sowing rice planter in 1839 that was later adapted into a successful wheat drill. In 1870, Richard Gatling and his family moved to Hartford, Connecticut, near the Colt Armory where the Gatling gun was manufactured.

By 1876 the Gatling gun had a theoretical rate of fire of 1,200 rounds per minute. Some time later, Gatling-type weapons were invented that diverted a fraction of the gas pressure from the chamber to turn the barrels. Later still, electric motors supplied external power.

New, improved models continued to be produced until the early 20th century when with the advent of the automatic machine gun the US Army declared the Gatling obsolete. The Gatling concept made a comeback, however, in the late 1940s/early 1950s for aircraft; developed versions were also extensively used for air-to-ground operations in the Vietnam War.

No. 47.631.

R.J. Gatling
Battery Gun.
1½ Inch to 1.Ft.

Patented May. 9. 1865.

47 631

Fig: 1.

47,631.—Battery Gun.—Richard J. Gatling, Indianapo-
lis, Ind.:

First, I claim making the series of barrels with their aggregate
locks and cartridge cavities to revolve on an axis, while the requisite
stations to perform the loading directly into the rear end of the barrel, exploding, and the cartridge case returning operation, are retained by the impingement of points on the revolving mechanism,
upon fixed detents, cams or incline planes; these several operations
being performed consecutively without stopping the rotation of the
barrels, when the gun is in operation.

Second, I claim the locks, figures 12 and 13, which revolve with the
barrels and breech and are operated by the cam races and springs
during their revolution.

Third, I claim the cam ring, figure t, which is rigidly attached to
the discharge of the stationary casing, and which by means of its
cam faces controls the longitudinal reciprocating movement, the
locks by means of the lugs and the impingement of the bolt ends of
the lock upon it, substantially as described.

Fourth, I claim the caps to be placed over the cavity in the carrier
in such or the best substantially as described.

Fig. 2.

Richard J. Gatling

Witnessed
Edward H. Knight
Alex. S. C. Haught

Above: A photographic portrait of Louis Pasteur, the founder of modern microbiology.

Left: Pasteur at work in his laboratory. The pioneer of the pasteurization process, Pasteur did work that has been used in helping prevent disease.

AT A GLANCE

Louis Pasteur's discovery of the pasteurization process, which kills microbes in liquids, was not only a significant development in its own right, but led Pasteur to develop the germ theory of disease in ways which would lead directly to the production of new vaccines. In proving that disease is spread by micro-organisms, he also sparked a revolution in medical treatment and the development of antiseptics.

PASTEUR TESTS PASTEURIZATION FOR THE FIRST TIME

FACULTY OF SCIENCES, LILLE, FRANCE
APRIL 20, 1862

The work of Louis Pasteur in proving that disease is spread by micro-organisms, and his development of immunology, marks a significant landmark in the history of medicine and has contributed to the saving of many millions of lives around the world. His first breakthrough, which led to further groundbreaking work, was pioneering the sterilizing technique that now bears his name.

The son of a poor French tanner, by the age of 27, in 1849, Louis Pasteur had earned degrees in Letters and Mathematical Sciences, and was appointed Professor of Chemistry at the University of Strasbourg, where he met his wife. The couple married in May 1849, and over the years had five children, though three of his daughters died of typhoid, spurring Pasteur's efforts to combat disease.

By 1854, he had been made Dean of the Faculty of Sciences at Lille University. Already interested in the controversial germ theory that other scientists – notably Agostino Bassi – had developed, which suggested that micro-organisms were responsible for spreading sicknesses, Pasteur soon had a chance to investigate it. At the request of a local brewer whose products were regularly spoiled by going sour, Pasteur showed that the brewer's beer, as well as wine, milk and other liquids, were spoiled by micro-organisms that came from the environment; until then, it had been accepted that liquids putrefied spontaneously. Next, he set about devising a process that would kill micro-organisms while leaving liquids drinkable, and with his colleague Claude Bernard he developed the technique of rapid heating and cooling. First tested on April 20, 1862, his simple but effective method was later widely adopted. It slows the rate of growth of microbes, giving pasteurized products a longer shelf life. Still used globally today, the method has prevented much suffering.

Over the following years, Pasteur adapted his theories and, by showing that micro-organisms attacking silkworm eggs were causing an epidemic, he saved the silk industry; he also proposed that the vaccination technique developed by Edward Jenner against smallpox could be used to fight other diseases. He discovered that artificially weakened forms of a disease could act as a vaccine, sparking a radical new approach to immunology and the production of many new vaccines, including a rabies vaccine. His work also inspired Joseph Lister to pioneer the use of antiseptics in surgery.

Although Pasteur's ideas were often ridiculed during his own lifetime, he was eventually hailed as a national hero in France, and a new medical institute in Paris was named in his honor. Dying in 1895, he was given a state funeral and laid to rest within the institute.

Above: The surrender by Lee to Grant at Appomattox Court House ended the American Civil War.

Right: General Lee poses on his horse, Traveler, after the end of the war.

AT A GLANCE

The controversial issue of slavery sparked the American Civil War in 1861, seven Southern (pro-slavery) states having declared their independence from the Union, and another four joining them. Their defeat after a bloody four-year conflict cost over a million military and civilian lives, and the scars on the relatively new nation took a long time to heal.

LEE'S SURRENDER MARKS THE END OF THE AMERICAN CIVIL WAR

APPOMATTOX, VIRGINIA, USA
APRIL 9, 1865

The surrender of Confederate General Robert E. Lee to his Union counterpart, General Ulysses S. Grant, ended the American Civil War to all intents and purposes. They agreed terms during the morning of April 9, 1865, and Lee formally surrendered to Grant shortly after midday. The historic encounter took place at Appomattox Court House, site of the final battle of the Appomattox Campaign, the decisive series of skirmishes which had begun a couple of weeks earlier.

The origins of the war had lain in the election of Republican Abraham Lincoln, a fervent anti-slavery campaigner, as President of the United States in 1860. Although slavery was being gradually abolished in the North, it remained legal in the Southern states, where it was seen as an important part of the economy. By the time Lincoln took up office in March 1861, seven of those states had already declared their independence from the Union: South Carolina had been the first to secede, in December 1860, followed by Mississippi, Florida, Alabama, Georgia, Louisiana and Texas.

The North responded by calling for a volunteer army from each state of the Union. This led to the border states of Virginia, Arkansas, Tennessee and North Carolina also seceding from the Union, to join the seven Southern states in their newly formed Confederate States of America. Lincoln's government declared that secession was illegal, and refused to recognize the Confederacy as a sovereign state. Hostilities began on April 12, 1861, when Confederate forces captured Fort Sumner, a Union stronghold in Charleston, South Carolina.

The Union quickly seized control of the border states, while Lee made some gains in the east. But in 1863, Union victories at Vicksburg and Gettysburg split the Confederate forces. At that point, the Confederate army had clearly lost the war, but they staggered grimly on for nearly two more years. Their last hope was to reunite Lee's Army of North Virginia with General Joseph E. Johnston's troops in South Carolina, but Lee's defeat at Appomattox in April 1865 prevented this. The remaining Confederate troops surrendered within a month, and the war was declared over by President Andrew Johnson on August 20, 1865.

The civil war was the bloodiest conflict in American history, with 620,000 soldiers killed and an estimated half million civilian lives lost. It was one of the world's first industrialised conflicts, and its use of mass-produced weapons and trench warfare foreshadowed World War I. Victory for the Union meant that in 1865 slavery was abolished throughout the United States by the Thirteenth Amendment to the United States Constitution.

War Department, Washington, April 20, 1865.

$100,000 REWARD!
THE MURDERER
Of our late beloved President, ABRAHAM LINCOLN,
IS STILL AT LARGE.
$50,000 REWARD!
will be paid by this Department for his apprehension, in addition to any reward offered
by Municipal Authorities or State Executives.
$25,000 REWARD!
will be paid for the apprehension of JOHN H. SURRATT, one of Booth's accomplices.
$25,000 REWARD!
will be paid for the apprehension of DANIEL C. HARROLD, another of Booth's accomplices.

LIBERAL REWARDS will be paid for any information that shall conduce to the arrest of either of the above-named criminals, or their accomplices.

All persons harboring or secreting the said persons, or either of them, or aiding or assisting their concealment or escape, will be treated as accomplices in the murder of the President and the attempted assassination of the Secretary of State, and shall be subject to trial before a Military Commission and the punishment of DEATH.

Let the stain of innocent blood be removed from the land by the arrest and punishment of the murderers.

All good citizens are exhorted to aid public justice on this occasion. Every man should consider his own conscience charged with this solemn duty, and rest neither night nor day until it be accomplished.

EDWIN M. STANTON, Secretary of War.

DESCRIPTIONS.—BOOTH is 5 feet 7 or 8 inches high, slender build, high forehead, black hair, black eyes, and wears a heavy black moustache.
JOHN H. SURRATT is about 5 feet 9 inches. Hair rather thin and dark; eyes rather light; no beard. Would weigh 145 or 150 pounds. Complexion rather pale and clear, with color in his cheeks. Wore light clothes of fine quality. Shoulders square; cheek bones rather prominent; chin narrow; ears projecting at the top; forehead rather low and square, but broad. Parts his hair on the right side; neck rather long. His lips are firmly set. A slim man.
DANIEL C. HARROLD is 22 years of age, 5 feet 6 or 7 inches high, rather broad shouldered, otherwise light built; dark hair, little if any) moustache; dark eyes; weighs about 140 pounds.

GEO. F. NESBITT & CO., Printers and Stationers, cor. Pearl and Pine Streets, N. Y.

Above: A poster offers a reward for the apprehension of Lincoln's assassin.

Left: A contemporary illustration of Abraham Lincoln's assassination by John Wilkes Booth.

AT A GLANCE

Abraham Lincoln, the first US President to be assassinated in office, was killed in 1865 in an act of revenge for his key role in the American Civil War against the pro-slavery South. He paid the ultimate price for his convictions, but his death could not derail emancipation, nor – as hoped by the assassin – reverse the result of the war.

DEATH OF ABRAHAM LINCOLN

WASHINGTON, DC, USA
APRIL 14, 1865

On Good Friday, April 14, 1865, Abraham Lincoln became the first US President to be assassinated whilst in office. He was shot whilst watching a play in a private box at Ford's Theater, Washington, DC, with his wife and two guests.

Lincoln's assassin was John Wilkes Booth, an actor, Confederate sympathizer and outspoken supporter of slavery. He was outraged by Lincoln's proposal to abolish slavery. With General Lee's defeat at Appomattox, the South had clearly lost the American Civil War, but Booth believed that they could still win it, because, despite the surrender document signed by Lee on April 9, their General Johnston was fighting on. So Booth and his co-conspirators decided to strike a blow for the Confederacy by kidnapping the President and three other high-ranking members of his administration. But then, after he heard Lincoln declare his intention to give former slaves the vote, Booth, enraged, changed his plan to assassination.

Although attempts by others had failed, Booth succeeded. In the theater, he waited for a particular line in the play to raise a loud laugh and muffle the sound of the shot. Lincoln's bodyguard was absent, and Booth was able to creep up close behind the president and shoot him in the back of the head. Lincoln collapsed, to die early the next morning.

After the shooting, Booth jumped down onto the stage shouting, "*Sic semper tyrannis!*" Latin for 'Thus always to tyrants', the state motto of Virginia. Then, despite breaking his ankle, he managed to escape from the theater in the confusion. He fled to Virginia where, on April 26, 1865, he was killed trying to escape from Union soldiers.

Abraham Lincoln was the first Republican president of the USA. Before that he had been a lawyer and a state legislator in Illinois, and he had served as a member of the House of Representatives. He was a vehement opponent of slavery, and his election as president in 1860 sparked the secession of the Southern States and the start of the American Civil War. In 1862, he issued the first Emancipation Proclamation, which freed all slaves in the Confederacy. He was re-elected in a landslide victory in 1864, his main campaign promise being to enact the Thirteenth Amendment, abolishing slavery; this became law in December 1865.

Lincoln's leadership style was strong yet moderate. But his successor Andrew Johnson and the radical Republicans in the Senate imposed tougher terms on the South than Lincoln had planned. So the murder of Lincoln effectively delayed America's healing process, prolonging the bitterness between North and South; reconstruction of the USA as a whole was a long-drawn-out process, taking from 1865 to 1877.

GREGOR MENDEL PUBLISHES EXPERIMENTS ON PLANT HYBRIDIZATION

BRNO, AUSTRIA-HUNGARY
1866

Above: An Augustinian monk whose work was ignored during his own lifetime, Gregor Mendel is now recognized as the 'father of genetics'. This photographic portrait dates to about 1880.

Right: Gregor's research was based on the breeding and crossbreeding of different strains of the common garden pea plant, of which he grew about 29,000 over a period of eight years.

AT A GLANCE

Overlooked at the time it was written, Gregor Mendel's Experiments on Plant Hybridization *was based on observations he made over eight years of painstaking research; it described hereditary principles for the first time. Rediscovered in the early 20th century, his work is now viewed as the foundation of modern genetics.*

The momentous work of the monk, Gregor Mendel in the field of genetics and heredity was ignored and forgotten. But during the 20th century it was rediscovered and recognized as being of enormous importance.

Baptized Johann Mendel two days after his birth on July 20, 1822, he took the name Gregor on entering the Augustinian Abbey of St. Thomas in Brno in 1843. After studying physics at the University of Vienna, he returned to the abbey and became a monk and a teacher. In 1856, he began to experiment with the breeding of pea plants, growing about 29,000 over the next eight years, crossing differing strains and observing the inherited characteristics of the plants. This led him to propose two new genetic principles, the Law of Segregation (the 'First' Law) and the Law of Independent Assortment (the 'Second' Law), which he explained in a paper called *Versuche über Pflanzen-Hybriden (Experiments on Plant Hybridization)*.

His paper set out an almost complete theory of heredity. It demonstrated that the offspring of white- and purple-flowered pea plants produced only purple flowers, though further descendants produced white flowers in a 3:1 ratio when crossed with the offspring of true-breeding white and purple varieties. The same was true of the length of the plant's stem and the shape of its seeds and pods. This led him to conclude that the plants contained 'factors', i.e. genes, that were either dominant or recessive. Theorizing that each new plant inherited factors from both of its parent plants, he described the process of heredity, in which the offspring contained genetic information from both parents with recessive information hidden, to reappear in later generations when the dominant factor is absent. Characteristics could skip generations.

His methodical approach proved principles that laid the foundations of genetic science, though, at the time, few noticed. In 1865, he addressed the Natural History Society of Brünn, and in 1866 published *Experiments on Plant Hybridization*. He then devoted his life to religion and died in 1884 thinking that his work had been forgotten. In 1900, however, other scientists began duplicating it, unaware of his success. Mendel's paper was brought to light and found to have already covered the ground that new scientists were retreading. During the 1930s, his discoveries were combined with the evolutionary theories of Charles Darwin to produce 'modern evolutionary synthesis'. The union of ideas offered a more complete model of evolutionary biology than Darwin had been able to give and, largely unchanged, remains the standard for today's biologists.

INVENTION OF DYNAMITE

GERMANY
1866

Above: Alfred Nobel, the Swedish chemist and engineer who invented dynamite and bequeathed his fortune to institute the Nobel Prizes.

Left: Miners insert dynamite into a rock wall to extract iron ore.

AT A GLANCE

Dynamite has been used all over the world to help create railways, roads, tunnels and canals, as well as to demolish and rebuild. Alfred Nobel was the man who invented it, by combining volatile nitroglycerin with silica. It was one of 355 patents he amassed during his eventful lifetime.

Alfred Nobel, the Swede whose millions endowed the prizes that bear his name, accumulated much of his wealth by his invention of dynamite. He had enjoyed an eventful childhood, his engineer/inventor father going bankrupt in 1833, the year of Alfred's birth, then taking the family to live in St Petersburg, Russia. In 1850, Nobel's father sent him abroad to study chemical engineering.

Nobel's father's mechanical workshop flourished during the Crimean War but went bust as the war ended. As Alfred, who returned to Sweden in 1863 with his father, searched desperately for new products, Nikolai N Zinin, his chemistry teacher, reminded him of nitroglycerin. This had been invented by Italian chemist Ascanio Sobrero in 1846 but was liquid and thus difficult to handle.

Alfred's younger brother Emil was killed in one of his nitroglycerine experiments in 1864, but Alfred persevered and formed the company Nitroglycerin AB in Stockholm, Sweden. Around this time Nobel also developed a detonator (blasting cap) using a percussive shock rather than heat for ignition.

He set up the Alfred Nobel & Co Factory in Krümmel near Hamburg, Germany, and in 1866 established the United States Blasting Oil Company in the USA. But when the Krümmel plant was destroyed by an explosion, Nobel decided to make nitroglycerin safer for the user.

Experimenting on a raft anchored on the River Elbe, Nobel discovered that by mixing it with *kieselguhr* (a siliceous deposit also known as diatomaceous earth), a paste-like substance was formed that could be inserted into the holes drilled for mining and then ignited.

He called this mixture 'dynamite' and in 1867 received US patent number 78317 for his invention. Dynamite made Nobel's name and was soon used for blasting tunnels, cutting canals and building railways and roads across the globe.

Although he lived in Paris, Nobel travelled widely, and during the 1870s and 1880s built up a network of factories across Europe to manufacture explosives. In 1894, he bought an ironworks at Bofors in Sweden that became the nucleus of the Bofors arms factory.

When he died in 1896 in Italy, Alfred Nobel held 355 patents, in the fields of electrochemistry, optics, biology, and physiology. He left a will dedicating his fortune to create five prizes that would promote peace and honor scientific and cultural achievements; there were to be prizes in the fields of physics, chemistry, medicine, peace and literature. A new prize, the Sveriges Riksbank Prize in Economic Sciences in Memory of Alfred Nobel, was first awarded in 1969.

DAS KAPITAL PUBLISHED

LONDON, UK
1867

Above: A portrait of political thinker and author Karl Marx.

Right: The reading room at the British Museum in London where Marx wrote Das Kapital, *photographed in 1900.*

AT A GLANCE

Karl Marx's Das Kapital *is the first detailed examination of capitalism, the way it works and its effects on society. In it, he examines the economic laws that govern its operation, with special emphasis given to the dehumanization of exploited workers. The power of this work is such that its arguments have inspired and inflamed sociologists, economists, historians and revolutionaries to the present day.*

Karl Marx is often thought of as the father of modern socialism, and in his most important work, *Das Kapital* (*'Capital'*), he developed his radical theories about class struggle and the economic laws of a capitalist society. Exiled in London, he saw for himself the harsh working conditions and relentless exploitation of the labor force. He was also influenced by the radical political theories of his friend Engels, whose views he largely shared. Researched in the library of the British Museum, the first volume of *Das Kapital* was published in 1867; the rest was uncompleted at his death in 1883.

Marx traced the roots of capitalism back to the time when workers had become separated from the raw materials and land. They were therefore forced to work for owners who had enough money to pay for both materials and land and still make a profit. Products could be highly desirable and costly, but the workers would still only receive the 'exchange value' which was payment related to the labor they put in, not to what the product was worth.

In a capitalist society all the profits go to the owner, whereas the workers' pay is unrelated to the profits and they may have only just enough to live on. Although Marx's sympathies were clearly with the working classes, it was rare for Marx to make moral judgments. It is clear, though, that he believed capitalism was harmful, reducing the workers to wage slaves, many doing a single repetitive task.

The object of the capitalist is to produce a large amount of 'surplus value' – i.e. profit. Much of this profit is then ploughed back into the production of more commodities or services, absorbing more wage earners. In this way capitalism is a self-perpetuating system. Clearly, a return to pre-industrial ways could not happen because the worker was now dependent on the owner for factories and other means of production. Ironically, the workers were actually commodities themselves, selling their labor-power for a daily wage; and there was always going to be a plentiful supply of labor to support capitalism's growth, with a reserve army of the unemployed.

For Marx, modern capitalism was all to do with the pursuit of money as an end in itself. However, he did believe that the system was ultimately unsustainable, leading to a diminishing number of monopoly capitalists who would be overthrown by the working classes (as outlined in the earlier work *The Communist Manifesto*). In fact, he even expected an international socialist revolution in his own lifetime, but he was to be disappointed.

AT A GLANCE

It took just six years to lay the 1,700 miles of track needed to complete the railroads span across the American continent from east to west. Its opening in 1869 consigned horse-drawn coaches and wagon trains to history, allowing people and goods to move freely, and encouraging trade right across the continent, from one coast to the other. Suddenly, the mighty USA somehow seemed smaller.

COMPLETION OF THE TRANSCONTINENTAL RAILROAD

PROMONTORY SUMMIT, UTAH, USA
MAY 10, 1869

The opening of the world's first true transcontinental railroad linked the eastern and western seaboards of the United States by rail for the first time. Originally known as the Pacific Railroad, the line was hailed as one of the greatest engineering feats in American history. There had been talk of a transcontinental railroad since 1830, when the steam railway had been developed in Britain and exported to America. Much of the debate concerned which route the railroad should follow through some unforgiving terrain, and even then the 1,700-mile route finally selected, crossing rugged mountains and seemingly endless plains, was desperately hazardous in places.

During Abraham Lincoln's presidency, Congress had passed the Pacific Railroad Acts of 1862 and 1864, authorizing the construction and operation of the line. Congress sold US Government Bonds to raise money for the project, and supported it by donating government-owned land along the way. This made good business and political sense, as the railroad would be vital for trade, commerce and travel between the eastern and western halves of the country, helping bind them closer together, and making them easier to govern.

In 1863, construction of two separate sections began, to meet each other in Utah. The Central Pacific Company built the 600-mile western section, which began in Sacramento, California, and passed over the mountains of the Sierra Nevada, through Nevada State and into Utah. The eastern section, laid by Union Pacific, started its 1,100-mile journey from its junction with the existing US rail network at Council Bluffs, Iowa, and ran to Utah through Nebraska, Colorado and Wyoming. The railroad bypassed the Great American Desert, but branch lines were built to serve Denver, Colorado, and Salt Lake City, Utah.

On May 10, 1869, the Transcontinental Railroad was opened to traffic. To join the two sections at Promontory Summit, the Last Spike was driven – embarrassingly, at his second attempt – by Leland Stanford, former Governor of California and President of Union Pacific. His golden spike was removed immediately afterwards, to be replaced by a standard iron one. A railway bridge over the Missouri River from Council Bluffs to Omaha, Nebraska, was completed in 1873.

The passenger service, which became known as the Overland Route, put an end to the slow and hazardous journeys out west by stagecoach and wagon train, because railroad transportation of passengers and goods was far cheaper, quicker and safer. This allowed the west to be opened up to settlement to a far greater extent than before, and this expansion of the region made it richer faster.

Left: Railroad workers celebrate at the driving of the Golden Spike in Utah.

Below: Another view of the completion of the US transcontinental railroad.

Above: An aerial view of the Suez Canal. To the left is the Nile Delta, to the right is the Sinai Peninsula.

Right: US navy ships traveling through the Suez Canal.

Overleaf: The official opening of the Suez Canal, depicted by Edouard Riou.

Below: Canal creator Ferdinand de Lesseps with some of his engineers.

OPENING OF THE SUEZ CANAL

EGYPT
NOVEMBER 17, 1869

The opening of the Suez Canal in November 1869 marked the completion of a ten-year construction project aimed at connecting the Mediterranean Sea to the Red Sea. Ships could now travel between Asia and Europe without having to sail the hazardous thousands of miles around Africa, dramatically improving worldwide trade. The canal, together with the Transcontinental Railway across the United States that had been opened six months earlier, allowed circumnavigation of the globe with previously unknown speed. It also encouraged more European colonization of Africa.

In 1798, Napoleon Bonaparte had discovered evidence of an Ancient Egyptian waterway in the area and considered the construction of a new canal, but he ultimately abandoned the project; it was another Frenchman, Ferdinand de Lesseps, a former diplomat in Egypt, who was to play a major role in developing the canal. In 1854, Egyptian ruler Said Pasha granted de Lesseps a concession to build the waterway. The Suez Canal Company was established for the purpose but, apart from the French, most people in European did not believe the scheme would be feasible, so financial support for it was low.

Work began in April 1859. An estimated 1.5 million people labored on the construction of the canal, with up to 30,000 working at any one time. The use of forced Egyptian labor was a controversial aspect of the project, but even so, when the canal opened to shipping in November 1869, the project had cost more than double its original estimate. Running from Port Said in the north to the city of Suez at its southernmost tip, the canal is 119 miles long. Shipping may move in only one direction at a time, and there are two crossover points: at Ballah By-Pass and the Great Bitter Lake. There are no locks.

Britain purchased Egypt's shares in the Canal Company in 1875. Seven years later, during a civil war in Egypt, British troops moved in to protect British interests in the canal. In 1888, the Convention of Constantinople declared the canal a neutral zone under British protection. In 1936, a treaty with Egypt allowed Britain to continue to retain control, however, Egypt broke this agreement in 1951, and this led to the withdrawal of all British troops in 1956.

That same year, nationalization of the canal by Egypt's President Nasser and the freezing of its assets provoked the Suez Crisis. War was averted by the creation of the first ever United Nations peacekeeping force, to ensure continued international access to the canal. However, during the 1967 Arab–Israeli conflict, the Six Day War, UN troops were withdrawn, and the canal was closed to shipping – with the side-effect of speeding the building of supertankers – until 1975, when it reopened.

AT A GLANCE

Former French diplomat Ferdinand de Lesseps pushed through the development of a canal which, when opened in 1869, meant that ships plying between Asia and Europe no longer had to take the far longer and more hazardous route around Africa. Despite several military conflicts over access through the years, the Suez Canal remains in use today.

ALEXANDER GRAHAM BELL DEVELOPS THE TELEPHONE

BOSTON, MASS., USA
MARCH 10, 1876

Above: Model of Alexander Graham Bell's first electric speaking telephone.

Left: An old-fashioned rotary phone, surrounded by more modern cellphones.

Edinburgh-born Aleck (Alexander) Bell's father, uncle and grandfather had all worked in the field of elocution, and as a boy Aleck experimented with resonance and the mechanics of speech. At the age of 16, he and his brother built an automaton with adjustable lips and bellows which said the word 'mama'.

Bell's own interest in the science of sound was spurred on by his mother's deafness, and after the family moved to the USA he taught the Visible Speech System; this had been devised by his father for writing down sounds by showing the actions of tongue, lips and throat, used to help the deaf to speak. In 1873 he was appointed Professor of Vocal Physiology and Elocution at Boston University.

Boston was at the time a melting pot of creative scientific innovation, and Bell was so stimulated by the environment that he took himself to the brink of exhaustion, teaching by day and experimenting through the night. He became obsessed with the idea of transmitting sound by electricity. With no formal training in electronics, he was convinced, after he had misunderstood a German scientific text, that it had already been achieved, and that 'my failure was due only to my ignorance of electricity'. It was not – but without that misreading he might never have pursued the idea.

On February 14, 1876, he filed a patent application for a 'method and apparatus' called the acoustic telegraph, which he had originally devised as a means of sending multiple Morse code telegraph messages down a single wire. He found that the same method could carry the multiple harmonic overtones of speech. On March 10, three days after the patent was granted, he famously used his invention for the first time, to say to his electrical mechanic Thomas Watson, waiting in a neighboring room: 'Mr Watson, come here. I want to see you.'

The Bell Telephone Company was formed in 1877, when Western Union turned down the chance to buy the patent for $100,000 on the basis that the phone was nothing more than a plaything. Within ten years, 150,000 Americans owned a telephone. It made millionaires of Bell and of its investors, and indeed of many others in future years in the massive telecommunications industry which it spawned.

Over the next 18 years Bell Telephone faced over 600 lawsuits from rival claimants to the invention. The company lost none of the cases.

AT A GLANCE

The invention of the telephone by Alexander Graham Bell revolutionized communication as the 19th-century world knew it. Prior to this, Morse code had been the cutting edge of technology. Bell's invention came from techniques for teaching speech to the deaf, and laid the foundations for the mobile communications revolution of a century later.

Above: A photograph shwing the inner workings of a Tesla coil.

Right: Nikola Tesla, the man whose experiments led to use of alternating currents in electrical machinery, in his laboratory, 1910.

AT A GLANCE

Nikola Tesla developed the alternating current system of electricity that is still used today, over a century later. Though derided by many as a 'crazy inventor', his mind can in retrospect be seen as one of the greatest in science. And while his inventions failed to make him rich, his name is celebrated in the Tesla Effect, the term used to describe wireless energy transfer.

NIKOLA TESLA LIGHTS THE CHICAGO WORLD'S FAIR

CHICAGO, USA
1893

Inventor and engineer Nikola Tesla was born in 1856 in the village of Smiljan, then part of the Austro-Hungarian Empire and now in Croatia. Having worked as an electrical engineer in Germany, Hungary and France, he migrated to the USA in 1884 and made many discoveries in the field of electromagnetism in the years that followed.

Tesla worked briefly with fellow inventor Thomas Edison in New Jersey, but they fell out and became bitter rivals. Tesla's system of generating alternating current (AC) electricity had advantages over Edison's direct current system, and this became apparent when George Westinghouse, founder of the Westinghouse Electric Company, bought patent rights to Tesla's system and used it to light the World's Columbian Exposition at Chicago in 1893. Edison's company, General Electric, had also bid for the exposition's lighting contract, but his proposal cost roughly twice as much and would have produced less light and a lot more heat.

The success of Tesla's AC generator was confirmed when Westinghouse gained a contract to build the massive turbines at Niagara Falls. The same principle is still used to provide light and electricity today. The Tesla Coil is used in radios, television sets and a wide range of other electronic equipment; invented in 1891, it has never been improved on. This is the basis for modern AC systems; no electrical system in the world today would work in the same way without Tesla's innovations.

When Tesla became a US citizen in 1891, he was at the peak of his creative powers. His projects included the new types of generators and transformers, a system of AC power transmission, fluorescent light and a new type of steam turbine. He became intrigued by the concept of wireless transmission of power. The Tesla Effect refers to an application of this type of electrical conduction, the movement of energy through space and matter rather than the production of voltage across a conductor.

In 1943, the year of his death, the US Supreme Court upheld Tesla's patent number 645576 in a ruling that served as the basis for patented radio technology in the USA. He had predated Marconi's breakthrough, which he claimed used his patents, but he never saw a penny in compensation. Sadly, despite having sold the rights to his AC system, Tesla died in debt.

FIRST WOMEN TO GET THE VOTE

NEW ZEALAND
1893

In the UK, women's suffrage had been an ongoing issue since the mid-19th century, and it wasn't until 1918 that some women received the right to vote, with full electoral privileges not granted until a decade later, in 1928. But across the other side of the world in New Zealand, females had been voting since 1893.

Above: Prime Minister Jenny Shipley addresses a news conference in 1999. Shipley was the first woman to be elected Prime Minister of New Zealand.

Left: A group of English suffragettes demonstrating in 1924 for the same right to vote that had already been granted to women in New Zealand over 30 years previously.

Under British rule, the country had held its first parliamentary elections in 1853, after the British had passed the New Zealand Constitution Act a year earlier. However, as in its ruling nation, voting in New Zealand at that time was far from an equal opportunity, or even a human right; only certain members of society were allowed their say, depending on their age, race, sex and social status.

But in the second half of the 19th century the voting criteria in New Zealand began to expand rapidly; first to gold miners of any ethnic origin, followed by the Maori people – and parliamentary seats being created for Maoris – in 1867. By 1879 the government had implemented universal male suffrage, allowing all men in the country, including European settlers, the right to vote.

Vastly improved opportunities for New Zealand women in the 19th century, not least in education, created a challenge to the engrained social view that women should be confined to domestic matters. One of the movement's most notable members was British-born Katherine Sheppard, who helped form and lead the New Zealand wing of the Women's Christian Temperance Union.

In the 1870s and 1880s, support for the suffrage movement grew amongst members of parliament, but the Liberal government was at odds with the issue, their cabinet member Richard Seddon being strongly opposed to it. When in April 1893 he succeeded John Ballance as premier of New Zealand, the future looked bleak for the country's females.

But the huge amount of support from both men and women on petitions that had narrowly failed in past years could not be ignored. After a bill was passed in lower parliament, it rested on the Legislative Council. After Seddon pushed some councilors too far, they changed their votes, to pass the bill 20 votes to 18.

So New Zealand became the first nation to award all females the vote. It was a monumental step in women's rights, though the first woman wasn't voted into parliament for another 40 years when Elizabeth McCombs was elected. And in 1997, Jenny Shipley became the country's first female prime minister, completing a journey for women that had taken over a century.

AT A GLANCE

Votes for women was a controversial issue throughout the world. But when in 1928 Britain's women finally secured their right to vote on the same terms as men, New Zealand women had already been voting for a quarter of a century.

FIRST MODERN OLYMPIC GAMES ARE HELD

ATHENS, GREECE
1896

Above: An American athlete at the Olympic Games of 1896. The USA topped the medal table in the games' inaugural year, winning (according to the IOC's reviewed scheme) 11 gold medals, as well as seven silver and two bronze.

Left: A hand-colored postcard of the Panathenaic Stadium in Athens during the Olympic Games of 1896.

AT A GLANCE

The first modern Olympic Games was organized by the IOC, who invited amateur athletes from around the world to compete. Since that first event, in 1896, the games have been organized every four years (apart from wartime) and have grown to become the world's foremost sporting competition.

While attempts to revive the ancient tradition of the Olympic Games in Greece had previously been made, 1896 saw the first to be organized by the International Olympic Committee (IOC). Since then, the games have become the world's greatest sporting competition with athletes entering from almost every country on Earth and victors winning international glory.

Now held every four years, following the tradition of the ancient Olympic Games, the Olympics were revived as an international competition by Baron Pierre de Coubertin, a French academic with an interest in health and athletics. The idea came to him in 1889 and over the following five years he arranged a grand conference, inviting athletes, sports organizers and enthusiasts. In 1894, at the Sorbonne in Paris, he developed his ideas, calling for a competition that would uphold the ideals of the ancient games and incorporate many of its features. For de Coubertin it was important that the competitors were amateurs from all levels of society, and he also stressed another feature of the Greek games – that for the duration of the competition, warring city-states would lay down their arms and declare a truce. Not only should the games be a great arena of athletic competition, he argued, but they should have a role to play in promoting peace and friendly competition between nations. The IOC proposed the first two games, the first of which was to be held in Athens in 1896 and the second in Paris, four years later.

Hosted by Athens' specially refurbished Panathenaic Stadium, the first games, which offered 43 events, was attended by 241 athletes from 14 countries. Winners were awarded a silver medal and an olive branch, and runners-up a bronze medal with laurel, though the IOC has since retroactively designated first, second and third places as gold, silver and bronze. In 1896, the USA topped the winners table with what would have been 11 gold medals, Greece were close behind with 10, and Germany, six. Several events were contested by teams made up of athletes from different nations, a feature that would continue throughout the early games.

The 1896 Olympics were hailed as a resounding success and the Paris games of 1900 saw over 1,000 athletes in attendance and an enlarged program of events. Since then the games have become firmly established as the most prestigious international sporting competition. With changed rules that allow sponsorship and the entry of professional athletes, they have expanded to include the Winter Olympics, which are also held every four years, as well as the Paralympic Games for disabled competitors and the Youth Olympic Games for younger athletes.

Above: A modern X-ray machine, made possible by the discoveries of Marie Curie.

Right: An illustration of Marie Curie and Pierre Curie in their Paris laboratory.

AT A GLANCE

Marie Curie's work opened the doors to many new opportunities in medical research, with X-rays helping to diagnose ailments early, and using radium to help sufferers of many different strains of cancer. Her legacy gave many some people the chance to survive a disease previously untreatable by orthodox medicine.

MARIE CURIE DISCOVERS RADIUM

PARIS, FRANCE
1898

Marie Curie, born in Poland, was a dedicated woman whose work with her husband Pierre would help millions through aiding the development of X-ray technology, and help battle the most feared disease of the late 20th century, cancer.

Marie was born into a highly academic family; her parents were teachers, and it was no surprise when she moved to Paris aged 24 to study at its world-famous university, the Sorbonne. It was here she met and married Pierre Curie and began the research that would change their lives and make their names.

They were continuing the work of physicists Wilhelm Conrad Röntgen and Henri Becquerel; the former had discovered X-rays and the latter radioactivity. Marie and Pierre were researching radioactivity – though the pair had yet to coin the term – in the mineral uraninite.

In exploring the uraninite ore, they removed the radioactive elements uranium and thorium, and while doing so detected a much higher level of radioactivity than before. In June 1898 a new element, hundreds of times more active than uranium, was identified and named polonium, after Marie's native country.

By the end of the year, the Curies had discovered yet another element, this one a million times more radioactive than uranium. They named it radium, and it would be key to their future work. It would later be used as a source of radiation in radiotherapy to prevent cancer cells from dividing, but also had other applications.

After separating it and determining its atomic weight, Curie compiled her research and results into a doctoral thesis. She presented it to her examination committee, two of whose members went on to receive the Nobel Prize in later years; they described it as 'the greatest scientific contribution ever made in a doctoral thesis'.

The Curies were awarded the Nobel Prize for physics in 1903 for their research into radiation begun by Becquerel. After Pierre's sudden death in 1906, Marie carried on her work, becoming the first woman to be made a professor at the Sorbonne and the first person to win two Nobel Prizes, the second being awarded to her in 1911 for her discoveries of polonium and radium.

Curie used her knowledge to aid the war effort in 1914, bringing X-ray machines to the battlefield in vehicles and using radioactive gas to treat diseased tissue. She died in July 1934 from leukemia – a tragic consequence of her many years of close contact with the element she had brought to the world's attention.

Marie's two Nobel Prizes put her in an elite bracket of four multiple winners – a fitting honor for a woman who had dedicated her life to science and left a legacy of hope for sufferers of cancer.

Above: A portrait of Guglielmo Marconi dating from around 1920.

Right: Marconi pictured with transmitting and receiving apparatus circa 1901, the year that the first transatlantic transmission was made.

Overleaf: In this 1922 photograph, Marconi listens for radio signals from space.

AT A GLANCE

Marconi's transmission and reception of the first transatlantic radio signal propelled him to international fame and set the stage for the development of commercial radio and, later, television. Marconi's company, which played a major role in the founding of the BBC, would be active in both fields.

MARCONI RECEIVES FIRST TRANSATLANTIC RADIO SIGNAL

ST. JOHN'S, NEWFOUNDLAND, CANADA
DECEMBER 12, 1901

At 12.30 pm on December 12, 1901, at Cabot Tower on Signal Hill, St. John's, on the eastern coast of Canada, Guglielmo Marconi picked up three dots on his wireless telegraph equipment. Morse code for the letter S, the signal had traveled 2,200 miles (3,500 km) across the Atlantic Ocean from Poldhu in Cornwall, England. The reception was faint and Marconi's equipment crude, which has led to the suggestion that all Marconi really picked up was atmospheric interference – but this event is generally accepted as the moment that radio came of age.

While Marconi is rightly considered a great figure in the history of broadcasting, his genius lay not so much in invention itself as in improving on existing technology. His earliest experiments drew on the work of Heinrich Hertz who had shown that radio waves could be created and detected. In 1895, Marconi began building his own apparatus using components pioneered by others, and he transmitted signals over a distance of nearly a mile outside his home in Pontecchio, Italy. The following year, aged 21, he took his apparatus to Great Britain, where he found support for his work. By March 1897, he had succeeded in transmitting a Morse code signal over a distance of 3.7 miles (6 km) on Salisbury Plain. Two years later, Marconi's radio messages had crossed the English Channel.

His ambition was to send a message across the Atlantic, and in 1900 he began preparing a powerful transmitting station at Poldhu. In 1901, he crossed the Atlantic and set up a receiver on Signal Hill; the three dots he received there on December 12 traveled 2,120 miles (3,400 km) further than any signal previously sent, bringing him fame and international acclaim. On January 18, 1903, his stations on either side of the Atlantic successfully transmitted and received a Morse code greeting from President Theodore Roosevelt to British King Edward VII, and in January 1909, Marconi became a hero after the sinking ocean liner *Republic* transmitted a distress signal using his equipment; the rapid response of other radio-linked ships in the area ensured the survival of crew and passengers. After *Titanic* alerted nearby ships before she sank in 1912, it became a legal requirement for all ocean-going vessels to carry the radio equipment Marconi had helped pioneer.

Many other scientists and inventors contributed to the development of radio, but Marconi's groundbreaking work, and that of his Wireless Telegraph and Signal Company, was a major force in perfecting the technology as well as extending its commercial use. After that first weak transatlantic signal, radio rapidly became a ubiquitous technology that connected the world.

FOUNDING OF THE WOMEN'S SOCIAL AND POLITICAL UNION

MANCHESTER, UK
OCTOBER 10, 1903

On October 10, 1903, Emmeline and Christabel Pankhurst hosted a meeting at their home. Four other members of the National Union of Women's Suffrage Societies were invited, all of them equally frustrated at the organization's failure to make any progress in winning the vote for Britain's women. That night, the six women formed the Women's Social and Political Union (WSPU), a group that would employ dramatic, often extreme, tactics to bring the issue of women's enfranchisement to the forefront of British politics.

At first, the WSPU adopted diplomatic strategies in attempting to win social reform, but after a women's suffrage bill failed to pass through Parliament in 1905 WSPU members became determined to use whatever tactics were necessary to achieve their goal. All of the other social reforms that they had previously campaigned for were dropped, and winning the vote for women became the organization's sole focus. With a swelling membership of women, dubbed 'suffragettes' by a national newspaper, the WSPU began demonstrating and picketing Parliament in 1906. Before long, WSPU members were being arrested and imprisoned, winning publicity and public support.

The following years saw campaigning become more intense. The WSPU newspaper Votes For Women was founded in 1907 and women's conferences were organized. Local branches of the WSPU sprung up across the country. By now, the organization's strategies were becoming increasingly militant. Imprisoned suffragettes went on hunger strike, WSPU members were involved in violent clashes with the police, and a campaign against property began, which saw churches, stately homes, and government buildings smashed and burned. In 1913, a suffragette protester called Emily Davison died beneath the hooves of the king's horse at the Epsom Derby.

In World War I, however, the WSPU set aside its differences with the British establishment, renaming its newspaper Britannia and encouraging women to work to support the war effort. In 1917, the House of Commons passed the Representation of the People Act by a huge majority, at last giving the vote to women – or at least, those who owned property and who were over the age of 30, and the WSPU was disbanded. A year later, it became illegal in Britain to exclude women from jobs because of their gender, and then finally, in 1928 – the year that Emmeline Pankhurst died – the Equal Franchise Act gave women the vote on the same terms as men.

Above: An illustration dating to 1908 depicting a suffragette march in London.

Left: Police scuffle with (from left to right) Emmeline Pankhurst and her two daughters, Christabel and Sylvia, as they try to enter Buckingham Palace to present a petition to the King.

Overleaf: Emmeline Pankhurst, one of the founders of the Women's Social and Political Union, speaks to a large crowd in Trafalgar Square, London.

AT A GLANCE

The formation of the Women's Social and Political Union in 1903 heralded a tireless, and often violent, campaign for female enfranchisement in Great Britain. Partial success was achieved by some women being entitled to vote at the General Election of 1918; full suffrage came in 1928. The organization's tactics were adopted by women's groups around the world, notably in the United States where the Nineteenth Amendment, giving women the vote, was passed in 1920. In Germany, women were enfranchised in 1918 and the French finally extended the vote to women in 1944.

TAKE-OFF AT KITTY HAWK

NORTH CAROLINA, USA
DECEMBER 17, 1903

Above: Bicycle mechanics Wilbur and Orville Wright, developers of the world's first practical aircraft.

Left: The famous Wright 1903 Flyer hangs from the ceiling of the National Air and Space Museum in Washington, DC.

Overleaf: Orville Wright glides over Kitty Hawk during glider tests.

AT A GLANCE

The 120-foot, 12-second flight Orville Wright made in 1903 ushered in the world of powered flight, because his machine was the first ever to use a practicable control system. Passenger flight, which is now taken for granted, and the supremacy given by air power in wars, both owe their beginnings to his brief hop above the sands at Kitty Hawk in a wood and fabric biplane braced with wires.

A primitive toy helicopter powered by a rubber band, a present from their father in 1878, prompted the young brothers Wilbur and Orville Wright to dream of powered, manned flight. Their mechanical curiosity led them first to design and build a printing press and then to run a bicycle repair shop, from which they manufactured their own bike design. In the 1890s they became fascinated with the pioneers of glider flight, and in 1899 began to carry out their own experiments.

Wilbur and Orville knew that the technology to build successful motorized flying machines already existed – more than 20 powered flights had been made in the 19th century. The missing element, they believed, was reliable control by the pilot. So in a series of gliders they concentrated their efforts on devising safe and effective ways of changing direction.

Their great innovation was to steer by banking (tilting the plane sideways when turning, like a bike). Rival flyers kept their plane wings level while steering with a rudder, but the Wrights had observed birds twisting their wings and banking, and used a system of wires to reproduce the effect by warping the wings of their gliders.

All their trials took place on the beach at Kitty Hawk in North Carolina, which had the benefit of constant Atlantic winds for take-off and flight, and soft sands for sudden landings. In 1902, after more than 700 glider flights, they perfected a revolutionary three-axis system for controlling yaw (flat rotation), pitch (tilt up and down forward–backward) and roll (banking).

They then turned to the question of power and devised an early version of a fuel injection engine. They even carved their own propellers, which proved to be up to 82 per cent efficient (modern props have a maximum efficiency of 85 per cent).

On December 17, 1903, there was a cold, strong headwind. Wilbur ran alongside their plane, the Wright Flyer, while Orville piloted that first attempt, reaching a height of 20 feet and proceeding at a stately 6.8 miles per hour, for 12 seconds. This flight, covering 120 feet over the ground, was shorter than the wingspan of a Boeing 747.

The Wright brothers made three more flights that day, finishing and climaxing with Wilbur's 59-second flight over 852 feet of ground. After the last flight, a gust of wind caught the plane and rolled it over several times, wrecking it. The Wright Flyer never flew again, but after that day, humankind could start to dream of the stars.

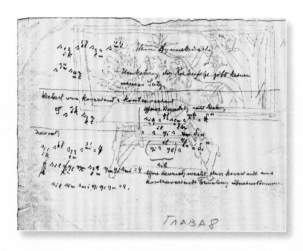

Above: Hand-written equations and drawing by Albert Einstein.

Right: Albert Einstein as a young man. He developed the Theory of Special Relativity while still in his twenties.

Below: Einstein and his revolutionary theory.

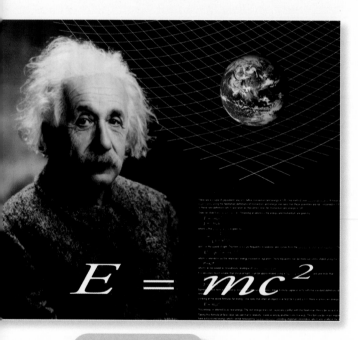

AT A GLANCE

Albert Einstein's Special Theory of Relativity was published in 1905, and it changed the way we look at our universe. Based on the premise that motion is relative and that matter cannot exceed the speed of light, it is expressed by the famous equation $E = mc^2$.

EINSTEIN PUBLISHES HIS THEORY OF RELATIVITY

SWITZERLAND
1905

Albert Einstein was an obscure clerk in the Swiss Patents Office when, in 1905, he published four papers in the prestigious magazine '*Annalen der Physik*' (Annals of Physics). One of these papers, now known as the Special Theory of Relativity, has changed the way we look at our universe.

Born in Germany in 1879, Albert Einstein was the son of a manufacturer of electrical instruments. The family moved to Italy and then to Switzerland. Albert renounced his German citizenship to avoid military service, and studied mathematics and physics at the Polytechnic of Zurich, graduating in 1900. Unable to find a teaching post, he accepted a job at the Patents Office in Bern. He worked as an evaluator of electromagnetic devices, and the knowledge he gained led him to come up with his theories of relativity. In 1905, he received his doctorate from the University of Zurich.

That same year, his Theory of Special Relativity brought him to the attention of the world. This and subsequent ground-breaking work such as his theory of General Relativity saw him hailed as the father of modern physics; he became one of the most famous and recognizable scientists in the world. Einstein's genius was not limited to physics; he also published papers on politics and philosophy. He is quoted as saying: 'the true sign of intelligence is not knowledge but imagination'.

The Special Theory is based on the premise that motion is relative, and also that matter cannot exceed the speed of light; the nearer matter approaches that speed, the more massive it becomes. This is expressed in the famous equation $E = mc^2$, E being energy (measured in joules), m mass (measured in kilograms), and c the speed of light (measured in meters per second). Einstein also proposed that the closer an object gets to the speed of light the more time, *as far as that object is concerned*, slows down.

Although Einstein had been influenced by other scientists like Isaac Newton, Henri Poincaré and James Clerk Maxwell, his work was a radical departure from tradition. Physicist Max Planck was the first to recognize the significance of Special Relativity, and his support led to its wider acceptance.

Einstein incorporated gravity into the theory, to arrive at General Relativity in 1915. This went beyond Newton's laws of gravity and introduced a universe of warped space and time, from which have sprung the ideas of black holes, wormholes and white holes. His work on the photoelectric effect won him a Nobel Prize in 1921.

Fleeing Germany in 1933 to escape the Nazis, Einstein became an American citizen in 1940, and he resided in New Jersey till his death in April 1955.

AT A GLANCE

Henry Ford's Model T was the world's first mass-produced motor vehicle. The car was affordable for the ordinary consumer, and it ushered in the era of the automobile – as well as kicking off a long line of Ford automobiles that continues over a century later.

Left: Henry Ford at the wheel of a Model T, with passengers John Burroughs and Thomas Edison (in back seat).

Below: The Ford Piquette plant in Detroit, Michigan, was the birthplace of the Model T.

Overleaf: Model T Fords chassis on the production line of the Ford Plant in Highland Park.

ROLLOUT OF THE MODEL T FORD

DETROIT, MI, USA
SEPTEMBER 27, 1908

When the first Model T Ford was built at the Piquette Plant in Detroit, Michigan, on September 27, 1908, it was the start of a revolution in worldwide transport. The Model T was the first mass-produced motor vehicle constructed on an assembly line and using identical parts. The car was affordable, and was built for the ordinary consumer.

Born in 1863, Henry Ford was a prolific inventor and engineer whose early fascination with watches developed into a talent for repairing steam engines. His experiments with designing and building automobiles led to the founding of the Ford Motor Company in 1903. The Model T was the culmination of a series of prototypes developed by the company.

Also known as the Tin Lizzie and the Flivver, the Model T was designed by Childe Harold Wills, Joseph A. Galamb and Eugene Farkas. The position of the steering wheel was standardized on the left for American cars, and the Model T was easy to drive and maintain. Ford created a nationwide network of dealers and coordinated an extensive advertising campaign for its launch.

In 1910, production moved to Highland Park, Detroit. By 1914, one automobile was rolling off the production line every 93 minutes. Ford was selling more cars than all its competitors put together, and every year the price of a Model T was reduced.

As only black paint dried quickly enough, the Model T was available in just that color in the early years. Henry Ford was famously quoted as saying, 'Any customer can have a car painted any color that he wants so long as it is black.' Although design modifications were made to the Model T, the car remained essentially the same until it ceased production in 1927. By then the company's rivals had achieved greater comfort and stylistic innovations, forcing Ford to abandon his concept of an unchanging model.

In his autobiography, Henry Ford summed up the Model T's contribution to motoring, 'I will build a car for the great multitude. It will be large enough for the family, but small enough for the individual to run and care for. It will be constructed of the best materials, by the best men to be hired, after the simplest designs that modern engineering can devise. But it will be so low in price that no man making a good salary will be unable to own one – and enjoy with his family the blessing of hours of pleasure in God's great open spaces.'

PEARY FIRST TO THE NORTH POLE

ARCTIC OCEAN
APRIL 6, 1909

Above: Matt Henson, who reached the North Pole with Admiral Peary helps, President Eisenhower locate the spot on the globe during a visit to the White House in 1954.

Left: Robert Peary, standing with Eskimo dogs onboard the Roosevelt *after his return from the North Pole.*

Below: A painting of Commander Robert Edwin Peary on one of his journeys to the Arctic.

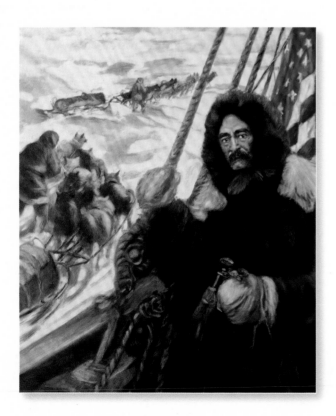

American navy engineer Robert Peary was hailed as the first to reach the geographic North Pole. The crowning achievement of Peary's final Arctic expedition took place on April 6, 1909.

Rear Admiral Peary's fascination with the Arctic was long-standing. He made several expeditions there, the first in 1886 when he explored Greenland by dog sled. Other missions in the 1890s saw him return with three large meteorites found in the area. Peary developed an innovative approach to polar exploration; he was the first to study and adapt the survival techniques of the native Inuit people who he employed as hunters and dog drivers on his expeditions. He also pioneered the deployment of support teams and reserves of supplies.

Expeditions in 1898–1902 and 1905–1906 cemented Peary's fame, but both of them ended short of the North Pole when Peary and his crew were forced to turn back. In 1899, Peary had eight toes amputated because of frostbite. Nevertheless, his discoveries and mapping of the region during the 1898–1902 trek earned him the gold medals of the American Geographical Society and Royal Geographical Society of London, UK.

The persistent Peary tried again, this time travelling farther by sea before setting out to cross the ice on foot. But yet again, after several weeks of arduous trekking, weather conditions left the exhausted explorers with no option but to turn back – just175 miles short of their goal.

Peary's final attempt to reach the Pole began when he sailed with a 23-strong team from New York in July 1908. Support parties went ahead to break the ice and carry supplies for the main party of six, consisting of Peary, fellow American Matthew Henson and four Eskimos. The last support team turned back on April 1, and Peary finally reached the North Pole on April 6, 1909.

Returning to America, Peary was confronted by the claim that his former ship's surgeon, Dr Frederick E Cook, had reached the Pole in 1908. Peary disputed the claim, and it was later rejected by an independent panel of Danish explorers.

Peary's achievement was recognised by the US Congress and by geographical societies around the world, but doubts have since been cast on it. Studies of his diary and other documents suggest that he may have only reached a point 30–60 miles short of the Pole; the absence of a trained navigator may have resulted in navigational errors. Nevertheless, we remember Peary, who died in 1920 at the age of 63, as discoverer of the North Pole.

Above: French pioneer Louis Blériot, the first person to fly across the English Channel.

Right: Blériot, accompanied by his wife, surveys where his monoplane came to rest on a Dover hillside, winning him a £1,000 prize.

Below: Louis Bleriot (left), with fellow flight pioneer Charles Lindbergh in 1927.

LOUIS BLÉRIOT FLIES THE CHANNEL

CALAIS, FRANCE–DOVER, ENGLAND
JULY 25, 1909

When French aviator Louis Blériot flew across the English Channel on July 25, 1909, he became the first person to complete a flight across a large body of water in a heavier-than-air machine. This crucial moment in the story of aviation came less than six years after the Wright brothers had achieved their record for manned, powered heavier-than-air flight – lasting for nearly a minute, covering over 850 ft along the ground – in December 1903 at Kitty Hawk.

The British *Daily Mail* offered a £1,000 reward for the first successful cross-channel flight, the latest in a series of prizes offered by the newspaper for aviation feats. Blériot had two rivals: the favorite, Hubert Latham, was a Frenchman, while Count Charles de Lambert was a Russian aristocrat and a protégé of Wilbur Wright. Latham was the first to attempt the crossing, but in his flight on July 19 his plane developed engine trouble and he ended by ditching in the sea six miles short of Dover. Meanwhile, de Lambert had injured himself during a test flight, so was out of the contest.

An engineer and inventor, Blériot had been building aircraft since 1903. He had created the world's first monoplane, but this, like most of his early prototypes, was unstable in flight. His most successful monoplane models were the Blériot VII and XI, but a problem with the VII left Blériot with a badly burned foot and also meant that only the XI was available. The channel crossing was to be its maiden flight.

On July 25, as Latham slept, Blériot took to the air at 4.30 a.m. Although he had been told the weather conditions were safe, he quickly found himself in difficulties. He was being escorted by a French navy destroyer, but soon lost sight of the ship. Flying in thick fog without the aid of a compass, Blériot had no alternative but to fly blind, steering as straight and level as he could. The 21-mile trip from Calais to Dover took around 37 minutes, and a rain shower cooled the engine so much that it was in danger of stalling. Sighting the English coast and a French reporter waving the tricolor flag of France to show him where to touch down, Blériot performed an awkward landing. Although this damaged his plane's undercarriage, Blériot was uninjured and the landing was judged a success. So Blériot was awarded the prize, and instant celebrity followed.

He continued to design and build aircraft throughout World War I. Louis Blériot died in August 1936.

Above: A photograph of Roald Amundsen taken in 1906 during a stay in Alaska.

Right: Norwegian explorer Roald Amundsen on the ice during his journey to the South Pole.

AT A GLANCE

Norwegian explorer Roald Amundsen was first to reach the South Pole in 1911, about a month before the rival British party headed by Captain Robert Scott. While Scott won posthumous glory, he was beaten to the prize by Amundsen, who saw his name given to several places in Antarctica.

AMUNDSEN, FIRST TO THE SOUTH POLE

ANTARCTICA
DECEMBER 14, 1911

Norwegian explorer Roald Amundsen led the first successful expedition to the South Pole, reaching his goal on December 14, 1911, 35 days ahead of the rival British party, headed by Captain Robert Scott. The Norwegian's success was announced to the world in March 1912 when he arrived in Australia.

Amundsen was one of the greatest explorers of his time. He found inspiration in the crossing of Greenland by his fellow Norwegian Fridtjof Nansen in 1888 and the lost British Arctic expedition of 1845 led by John Franklin. In 1903, Amundsen achieved the first successful navigation of the Northwest Passage, along Canada's northern coast between the Atlantic and Pacific Oceans, a feat which had defied explorers since the first recorded attempt, in 1497. He had intended to try for the North Pole next, but financial problems delayed him, and, on learning that Americans Frederick Cook and Robert Peary had both already laid claim to reaching it, Amundsen switched his sights to Antarctica.

His expedition left Christiania (now Oslo), Norway, on June 3, 1910, with the publicized sailing plan of calling in at Madeira, Buenos Aires and then the Arctic. It was not until the ship reached Madeira that Amundsen informed his crew of the change in destination. At the same time, he sent a telegram to Robert Scott, whose expedition to the South Pole was already under way, notifying Scott that he had competition.

Establishing his Antarctic base camp at a large inlet called the Bay of Whales, Amundsen and an eight-man team embarked for the Pole on September 8, 1911, but severe weather forced them to turn back. A five-man team with four sleds and 52 dogs departed on October 19, reaching the Antarctic Plateau nearly two months later. The success of the expedition was largely due to careful planning allied to Amundsen's extensive experience. The use of highly trained Greenland sled dogs also played an important part.

In contrast, Scott's expedition suffered from lack of foresight. His establishment of a base camp at Ross Island gave him 60 miles further to travel than Amundsen. Furthermore, Scott had refused to change his strategy when made aware of Amundsen's competing expedition.

The Englishman's doomed attempt, during which all his men perished, tended to overshadow the Norwegian triumph. It was celebrated as a heroic failure, and Scott was hailed as a iconic example of mankind. Since the 1970s, however, the myths surrounding Scott have been increasingly challenged by historians, and Amundsen's achievement in reaching the southernmost point in the world has been restored to its rightful place. Amundsen died in 1928 while on a rescue mission, ironically at the North Pole.

SINKING OF THE *TITANIC*

NORTH ATLANTIC
APRIL 14, 1912

Above: An emergency cutter lifeboat carrying a few survivors from the Titanic, *seen floating near the rescue ship* Carpathia *on the morning of April 15, hours after the disaster.*

Left: The Titanic *sails away from the dock prior to her ill-fated maiden voyage.*

AT A GLANCE

The loss of the 'practically unsinkable' Titanic in 1912 has passed into folklore and has inspired books, films and museum exhibits to commemorate it. The only silver lining from the loss of over 1,500 people was the revision of safety standards that had until then allowed ships to run the gauntlet of iceberg fields and other navigational hazards in the belief that they could survive almost any collision.

It's hard to imagine the shock and terror of the passengers of the RMS *Titanic* on that freezing April night when at long last they realized that the ship, having struck an apparently inconsequential iceberg, was doomed to sink. There had been a party atmosphere about the journey – the maiden voyage of the biggest, most luxurious ship in the world at the time. Confident celebration had been the order of the day. But such confidence was misplaced.

Although the *Titanic* was 882 ft 9 inches (269.1 metres) long by 92 foot (28 metres) wide, it was in fact, far from invulnerable. For example, the rudder was too small to steer such a large ship while it was steaming at full speed, and this was normal practice in the ice fields, where it was felt that any iceberg big enough to sink a ship would be spotted in ample time to take evasive action. Furthermore, only two of the three propellers could be put into reverse, also inadequate for such a massive ship. Ironically, in the event, the order to reverse given by Captain Edward Smith, the ship's master, reduced the rudder's effect even more.

The *Titanic,* as trade journals reported in advance of its departure, was 'practically unsinkable' thanks to its electrically controlled system of watertight bulkheads dividing it into 16 compartments below the waterline. The ship was designed to withstand up to any two compartments, or the first four, being flooded; it was appallingly bad luck that because the ship had slewed to avoid the iceberg, its side hit the berg with such force that it struck the plates of the hull across five compartments. Even then, the damage might have been limited had the rivets securing the plates not been substandard; it was the rivets, not the iron sheets, that gave way, opening up gaping holes for the icy North Atlantic to pour into.

Of the 2,223 passengers and crew on board, only 706 survived. Even if all the lifeboats launched had been filled to capacity, there were nothing like enough of them, and most victims died from hypothermia after around 15 minutes of immersion in the dark, numbing waters. Among so many sad stories, one of the saddest was that of Nils Pållson, a Swede waiting on the quayside in New York for the arrival of his wife Alma and their four young children, who were travelling in third class; he lost his whole family.

The *Titanic* had complied fully with all the safety regulations of the day, which subsequent government enquiries decided were thoroughly out of date. The enduring legacy of the sinking was the complete revision of those standards. The enormity of the disaster and the loss of life in the face of the optimism generated by the maiden voyage of this iconic vessel have ensured our continuing fascination with the tragedy a century later.

ASSASSINATION OF ARCHDUKE FRANZ FERDINAND

SARAJEVO, SERBIA
JUNE 28, 1914

Above: The assassination of Franz Ferdinand in Sarajevo as depicted by I.B. Hazelton.

Right: An illustration of soldiers arresting Gavrilo Princip, assassin of the Archduke Franz Ferdinand in Sarajevo.

AT A GLANCE

The opportunist assassination of Archduke Franz Ferdinand of Austria in June 1914 lit the touch paper on the First World War. When Austria declared war on Serbia, their respective allies, the stage was set for the map of Europe to be redrawn.

June 28 had long been a significant date in the Serbian national calendar, being the anniversary of the Battle of Kosovo in 1389 which had resulted in Serbia's loss of independence. Early in the 20th century, Serbian separatists of the Black Hand Organization planned to use the date to strike a blow for their cause, and a visit in 1914 by Archduke Franz Ferdinand to inspect troops in Sarajevo presented them with a golden opportunity. After the suicide of his cousin Rudolf in 1889, Franz Ferdinand had become heir to the imperial crown of the Austro-Hungarian Empire.

His assassination had been meticulously planned. Six men were stationed along the route of the Archduke's morning motorcade through Sarajevo. Although the first two lost their nerve, the third threw a grenade – but it failed to kill Franz Ferdinand because he batted it away with his arm. It exploded in front of the following car, and the thrower of the bomb was quickly captured. The sound of the explosion, however, convinced the remaining three conspirators that their efforts would no longer be required.

After lunch, the distressed Archduke decided that he and his wife would visit in hospital those injured by the grenade. By chance, his car passed a café just as Gavrilo Princip, one of the three remaining assassins, emerged from it and recognized him. Still armed with a pistol, Princip ran towards the vehicle and fired twice: the first bullet struck Franz Ferdinand in the neck, and the second hit his wife Sophie in the abdomen. As they both collapsed, the Archduke begged his duchess, 'Don't die! Don't die! Stay alive, for our children!' The car raced to the governor's residence, but the couple died within 15 minutes of each other.

Austria-Hungary, outraged, declared war on Serbia. Then Germany and Italy – the two other members of its military partnership known as the Triple Alliance – backed Austria-Hungary. Imperial Russia declared its support for Serbia, and was joined by Britain and France, Russia's allies in their partnership, the Triple Entente. Italy eventually chose to join the Entente forces.

The Great War which followed transformed the map of Europe. Russian losses during the war fueled the Russian Revolution and the rise of the Soviet Union. At the end of the war, the Austro-Hungarian Empire was dismantled, the Balkan borders were redrawn and the punitive Treaty of Versailles led directly to the rise of Hitler, and so to the Second World War and the Cold War. All these changes were triggered by an opportunistic bullet hitting an accidental heir.

Above: Created by Bernard Partridge, this poster typifies the British and the US (to a lesser extent) outrage felt at the sinking of a civilian vessel.

Right:: The liner **Lusitania** *pictured in New York prior to her transatlantic crossing.*

AT A GLANCE

In 1915 the sinking of the British Lusitania *shocked the world. En route from New York to Liverpool it was torpedoed and sunk by a German submarine. Many people died, including over 100 US citizens. Although explicit warnings had been given, the brutality of this attack was unexpected; it hardened feeling against Germany, eventually leading to US involvement in World War I.*

SINKING OF THE *LUSITANIA*

IRELAND
MAY, 1915

The *Lusitania*, a British passenger liner, was sailing from New York to Liverpool in May 1915 when it was sunk by a German U-boat submarine. Prior to this event, the German government had published an article in New York newspapers warning that all vessels flying the flag of Britain or her allies were in danger of destruction if they entered the war zone. But not everybody heeded this advice. This fast modern liner, owned by Cunard, was hit by a torpedo, and it sank. Including passengers and crew, 1,198 people died, accounting for more than half of those on board. Significantly, 128 American citizens died, victims of a war in which they were not involved. This event caused great ill-feeling towards Germany and was instrumental in America entering the war two years later.

As the liner approached the coast of Ireland, coming to the end of its journey, the U-boat struck. A torpedo hit the side of the liner and the 'greyhound of the seas' was doomed. There was mass panic on board. The lifeboats proved cumbersome, some even falling on top of the passengers on deck. Lowering the lifeboats into the sea proved almost impossible due to the speed the liner was travelling at, and many overloaded lifeboats tipped their occupants into the sea.

In America, condemnation was swift and unforgiving. It was argued that attacking a non-military vessel broke international agreements. The Germans countered this argument by saying that it was common knowledge that the liner was carrying explosives to help the British war effort. The US authorities denied this. The truth can only be guessed at. Many survivors told of hearing two great explosions, whereas the U-boat's Captain Schwieger logged only one torpedo as having been fired. Some maintain that the second explosion was caused by an illegal cargo of high explosives.

In Britain there were hopes that the USA would now enter the war, but its president, Woodrow Wilson, was more restrained in his views. He did insist, though, that Germany must apologize and cease its attacks on commercial vessels whatever flag they were flying. The Germans agreed. However, in August 1915 a German submarine torpedoed the British liner SS *Arabic* with the loss of 44 lives, including three US citizens. This confirmed that the sinking of the *Lusitania* had not been an isolated incident, and the USA's entry into the war was now inevitable.

FIRST DAY OF THE BATTLE OF THE SOMME

NORTHERN FRANCE
JULY 1, 1916

Above: British machine gunners fire during the Battle of the Somme.

Left: British troops would go 'over the top' to almost certain death.

AT A GLANCE

The futility of trench warfare was underlined by the British Somme Offensive of 1916 which, thanks to a catalog of errors and a lack of the information needed to make decisions, saw nearly 20,000 men lose their life in a single day, with no ground gained to show for their sacrifice. It was the worst loss ever sustained by the British army, and remains a sobering statistic today.

The Somme Offensive of 1916 was conceived as a counter-attack intended to breach the lines of the German Army, which had occupied northern France since 1914.

Defenders of the campaign argue that it was essential to prepare the ground for the subsequent defeat of Germany, and that it was a useful learning exercise in tactical and operational issues – in effect, a handy lesson in how not to do it. The campaign, however, failed in its objectives, and on the first day alone 20 per cent of Britain's entire fighting force was killed, the worst loss ever sustained by the British army.

On that single day, an estimated 19,240 British servicemen died. Britain's total losses for the day, including those wounded, missing or captured, ran to about 57,470. To that horrifying total should be added the 7,000 losses of the smaller French force involved, and another 10,200 of the German front line.

Germany had been expecting a major counter-offensive. Its army had been virtually unchallenged since the invasion, and now commanded high ground on which it was securely dug in. The German trenches were deep and wide, and created effective cover against the week-long barrage which preceded the infantry attack. The British bombardment had been made even less effective by their lack of heavy artillery, the inaccuracy of the British gunners and the wrong shells having been provided: even if the shells had landed on target, only 900 tons of the 12,000 fired were capable of damaging the enemy defenses.

Worse yet, the Garman barbed wire had not been destroyed – broken and tangled, it was an even more lethal trap than before. British troops had been told that thanks to the bombardment all they would have to do would be to walk over to the German lines. But in fact the Germans were still in a commanding position, and most of the soldiers who died were trapped by the wire and killed quickly – if they were lucky – by machine guns.

Poor communication also took its toll. One British officer mistook a German flare for a British signal indicating success, and deployed his reserves, the 801 men of the 1st Newfoundland Regiment. Just a few men of that volunteer force returned unscathed; nearly 300 were wounded, and 500 died – almost an entire generation of men from that Canadian province.

After ten days of fighting, the French had advanced about six miles into German-held territory, whereas the British had made no significant advance. Five months later, by the end of November, despite repeated assaults, this position had hardly changed, and the losses on both sides at the end of the Battle of the Somme had amounted to about 1.2 million men.

ATTACK ON THE WINTER PALACE

PETROGRAD, RUSSIA
OCTOBER 25, 1917

Above: A crowd of workers and soldiers gather in front of the Winter Palace to hear Lenin speak.

Left: Soldiers prepare in Palace Square as the Russian Revolution gathers momentum.

Military setbacks in the First World War and economic hardship at home were fueling resentment and dissatisfaction among the Russian people. In February 1917, after a wave of strikes that had been violently suppressed, Tsar Nicholas II was forced to abdicate. A new provisional government was formed by members of the Duma, the Russian Parliament, with its seat in the former tsar's Winter Palace in Petrograd (which had been called St Petersburg until the First World War, and is now once again known by that name). The working classes favored a system of workers' councils, called Soviets. There followed a tense Period of Dual Power, during which the provisional government ruled while reluctantly acknowledging the influence and power of the Soviets.

In April 1917, however, Vladimir Ilyich Ulyanov – Lenin – returned to Petrograd from exile in Switzerland; his arrival galvanized support for the radical Bolshevik factions within the Soviets. After a power struggle within the Soviets, the Bolsheviks won, forming the Soviet workers' militia, the Red Guards (the future Red Army).

The government's determination to continue the war with Germany, and its failure to address the country's economic crisis, led to a new wave of strikes across the country. In August the Red Guards thwarted a military coup, and the Bolsheviks' status as defenders of the people was confirmed. They were seen as the only organized opposition which had not compromised in their dealings with the government – and Lenin knew their time had come.

The first revolutionary action was a Bolshevik uprising in Tallinn (now in Estonia) on October 23, 1917. Two days later, Red Guards took over government offices in Petrograd with little opposition, while government ministers retreated to the Winter Palace. They cobbled together an inadequate defense force of Cossacks and soldiers from the Women's Battalion and waited for the inevitable. A blank shell fired from the battleship Aurora signaled the final assault on the Palace, and it fell in the small hours of the following morning.

The power struggle which followed the overthrow of the provisional government led to five years of civil war across Russia. Only in 1922 was the Soviet Union finally created. But the storming of the Winter Palace in 1917 had been, like the storming of the Bastille at the start of the French Revolution, a symbolic overthrow of the old order. When the Bolsheviks' control over Russia was consolidated, and the traditional European powers decayed after two world wars, the stage was set for the Soviet Union to emerge as a 20th-century superpower.

AT A GLANCE

In the same way as the storming of the Bastille in 1789 had represented the French claim to freedom, so the storming of the Winter Palace in 1917 symbolised the end of the Russian monarchy and the establishment of a new order, which became the Union of Soviet Socialist Republics. This would endure more or less unchanged until the last decade of the 20th century.

Above: A British tank advances towards enemy trenches in France.

Right: British tanks move slowly but surely towards the front line.

Below: A British tank rolls over a trench during the Battle of Cambrai in 1917.

AT A GLANCE

The introduction of the tank to battlefield warfare in the later stages of the First World War revolutionized the way future conflicts would be conducted. The tank's combination of defensive armor, offensive firepower and mobility added a new dimension to ground warfare that would be exploited even further in wars to come.

FIRST TANK BATTLE

CAMBRAI, FRANCE
NOVEMBER 20, 1917

The Romans had started it, with their *testudo*, then in the 1500s Leonardo da Vinci had sketched a proposal for an armored war machine; and since the 1830s the idea had been bandied about – in 1855, an engineer had drawn plans for one for use in the Crimean War. But the terrain created by trench warfare in the First World War made the rapid development of tanks an urgent priority. Early British prototypes were tested during the later phases of the Somme Offensive. Rushed into service, they were liable to break down; only nine of the 49 Mark I tanks deployed at the Somme in 1916 reached the German lines. More seriously, perhaps, their use in that battle gave away to the enemy the secret of their existence.

But the trials did provide useful information for subsequent improvements to their reliability and effectiveness. A little over a year later, at Cambrai, large numbers of tanks were incorporated into a battle plan for the first time: they were to be used in a full-scale assault on the strongly defended German positions of the Hindenburg Line in northern France.

381 Mark IV tanks from 12 battalions were involved, and immediately proved their worth, breaching the German defenses and advancing up to five miles into enemy-held territory – a greater advance in six hours than the Allies had achieved in the three months before. Furthermore the casualty rate – 4,000 on that first day – was half that of the recent action at Passchendaele.

Mechanical difficulties persisted, and at the end of the first day 180 tanks were out of action, only 65 of them destroyed by German fire. More tanks were lost when a canal bridge which their unit had successfully taken collapsed under their weight, making further progress on that front impossible.

Germany was quick to reinforce, resisting further British advances and eventually driving them back almost exactly to their lines before the battle. After two weeks of grueling stalemate, both sides had lost around 45,000 men and gained almost no ground.

However, at Cambrai the point had been made that even well defended trenches could be overcome in an attack by tanks, with far fewer casualties than by infantry alone. Public opinion would never again accept human losses on the scale of the War to End All Wars. The art of war was changing; since then, wars have increasingly been fought with modern technology on both sides rather than with the unprotected bodies of men ordered to face mechanised defence systems.

Above: John Logie Baird, pictured in his workshop in 1942, demonstrating color television images using a cathode ray tube.

Right: Baird demonstrates his television apparatus, known as the Televisor, to an enthralled audience on June 16, 1926.

JOHN LOGIE BAIRD DEMONSTRATES TELEVISION

LONDON, UK
JANUARY 26, 1926

While Scottish engineer John Logie Baird's technology was outstripped by later developments, his first successful transmission of primitive grayscale moving images to a small audience represents the dawn of the age of television.

While Baird is widely viewed as the pioneer of television, his work was preceded by that of other inventors, notably that of the German Arthur Korn, who in October 1906, transmitted a still black-and-white photograph over 1,100 miles (1,800 km), and Paul Gottlieb Nipkow, who invented the scanning mechanism known as the Nipkow Disk. While Baird used this technology in his own experiments, he developed and expanded on the Germans' work and, by 1924, had succeeded in transmitting a moving silhouette across his workshop in Hastings, UK.

Soon after, he was told to leave the premises (he electrocuted himself with a 1,000-volt shock) and he relocated to rooms in Frith Street, Soho, London (where a Blue Plaque now commemorates him). There, he continued work on refining his apparatus, and on October 2, 1925, managed to transmit a moving grayscale picture of a ventriloquist's dummy, the first time such a feat had been achieved. The picture was extremely rudimentary. Made up of just 30 vertical lines, it was refreshed five times per second, though over the following months Baird managed to attain a rate of 12.5 images per second.

On January 26, 1926, he demonstrated his achievement to a party of 50, including members of Britain's scientific organization, The Royal Institution, and a journalist from The Times newspaper. After showing them the transmitter and explaining its mechanism, Baird transmitted images of the dummy and of a business associate speaking.

Over the following years, he went on to transmit his images over greater distances, between London and Glasgow in 1927 and across the Atlantic in 1928. He also pioneered color television, demonstrating the first ever color television pictures as early as July 1928. In 1930, he successfully began broadcasting sound simultaneously. However, while early commercial broadcasts were all made using the equipment he had developed, by the 1930s a superior electronic system was pioneered by other companies, including EMI-Marconi. In 1937, the BBC made its last broadcast using Baird's system.

In his later career, Baird made many more contributions to the development of his invention, including pioneering work on the cathode ray tube, and the invention of a 3-D television set; in 1944, he demonstrated electronic color television. He remains best known, though, for introducing the world to the first recognizable television images, an innovation that transformed the way people live and which, perhaps more than any other, defines the modern age.

AT A GLANCE

In the attic rooms of his small laboratory in Soho, London, John Logie Baird demonstrated the first grayscale moving television images to an invited audience on January 26, 1926. While the system he invented later became obsolete, it was used for a decade, and the Scottish inventor is credited with introducing the world to television.

Above: A factory worker oversees the production of fiber optic cable. Carrying data as pulses of light, fiber optics now form the core of information networks around the world.

Right: Doctors and surgeons today routinely use fiber optic-based equipment to look within the human body.

AT A GLANCE

Clarence W. Hansell's description, in 1926, of bundled glass rods that could carry images marks the beginning of an era in which fiber optics have brought about unprecedented progress in information technology as well allowing the development of revolutionary new surgical techniques.

PRINCIPLES OF MODERN FIBER OPTICAL IMAGING DESCRIBED

ROCKY POINT LABORATORY, LONG ISLAND, USA
DECEMBER 30, 1926

The technologies of the modern world, as we know them, would not be available to us without the bundles of hair-thin conduits that weave their way around the globe. Yet what may seem to be a modern invention has a history stretching back to 1854 when a British physicist called John Tyndall began experimenting with light and water, showing that light could be bent along a conductive stream.

His work was taken up by other scientists and inventors, notably two Viennese doctors who, by 1888, were using curved glass rods to bring light into the human body. Then the idea for using bundles of fibers to carry data rather than light was pioneered by two people, almost simultaneously, in 1926. In Britain, John Logie Baird, inventor of television, proposed using transparent or hollow rods bundled together to transmit images, while in the USA an idea similar to the fiber optics we know today was described by Clarence W. Hansell, a scientist working at the RCA Radio Transmission Laboratory at Rocky Point, Long Island. An inventor whose patents are outnumbered only by those of Thomas Edison, Hansell patented his idea not only in the USA but also in the UK, pipping Baird at the post.

Four years later, a German medical student, Heinrich Lamm, built a device using glass fibers that he hoped would revolutionize surgery, and succeeded in transmitting an image. Later advances included Holger Møller's cladding of the glass fibers to lessen interference, as well as breakthroughs in reducing the width of fibers, the creation of ultra-transparent glass, and the revolutionary invention, in 1986, of fiber optics cables that did away with the previously indispensable electronic amplifiers. These cables could carry a far greater amount of information.

Since the first fiber optic phone lines were installed in Britain and the USA during the mid 1970s, cables have spread around the globe carrying massive amounts of digital information over thousands of miles. Without fiber optics there would be no high-speed broadband internet or high-definition digital TV. Fiber optical cables are also routinely used by medics as tools to peer into the human body and perform laser surgery, while many other professions use the cables to investigate dark or hard-to-reach places. They are used to wire sensitive machines in which electromagnetic interference could cause malfunctions, such as submarines and aircraft, for a variety of military uses, and as sensors to measure temperature, pressure, and vibration. It is no exaggeration to say that the invention of fiber optics has brought about, not one, but several revolutions.

Above: A diagram showing the interior layout of Charles Lindbergh's Spirit of St. Louis *airplane.*

Right: Charles Lindbergh standing beside the Spirit of St. Louis.

Below: An American stamp commemorates Lindbergh's trailblazing flight.

AT A GLANCE

Charles Lindbergh's achievement in flying across the Atlantic solo in 1927 demonstrated the potential of air transport to shrink the globe. It also inspired many Americans to take to the air as private pilots.

LINDBERGH FLIES THE ATLANTIC SOLO

PARIS, FRANCE
MAY 21, 1927

In 1919, Raymond Orteig, French owner of the Lafayette Hotel in New York, offered a prize of US $25,000 to the first pilot to fly between Paris and New York, in either direction. Aviation was entering a golden age of aeronautical advances, spurred on by public fascination with the new form of transport and by prizes such as that dangled by Orteig.

In 1909, only six years after the Wright Brothers' record-breaking flight, Louis Blériot had won the £1,000 offered by the British *Daily Mail* for the first flight across the English Channel. Just a month after Orteig's prize was announced, two British aviators, Alcock and Brown, flying from Newfoundland in Canada to Ireland, had collected the same newspaper's £10,000 reward for the first flight across the Atlantic. Their success, in just under 16 hours, had only been possible because Brown had climbed out onto the wings to chip ice off the engines while Alcock piloted the plane.

Despite the need for a two-man team, Charles Lindbergh was determined to win the Orteig Prize with a solo effort. By the time, eight years later, he took off from Roosevelt Field outside New York on May 20, 1927, six other airmen had died in their attempts at the prize. But Lindbergh was a courageous and skilled flyer, an airmail pilot and former stunt-flying barnstormer. Overcoming fog, ice, exhaustion, disorientation, storms at altitude and waves at sea level, he landed nearly 34 hours later at Paris's Le Bourget airfield, hailed by a crowd of 200,000. His cramped monoplane, *Spirit of St. Louis,* was half the length of Alcock and Brown's converted First World War heavy bomber, with only two-thirds of the wingspan, and his flight had lasted twice as long as theirs.

Above all, he was the first man to fly solo across the Atlantic – a feat which captured the public imagination, gave him instant fame, and helped transform flying from a military activity and a thrill-seeker's entertainment into a form of mass transport. On his return to New York, Lindbergh's tickertape parade was watched by four million people. In the course of the year-long tour of the United States which followed, it is estimated that 30 million people – a quarter of the population – turned out to see him.

Lindbergh became a passionate advocate of aviation for commerce and travel. In the six months after his achievement, pilot license applications in the USA rose threefold, and the number of licensed aeroplanes in the country increased by a factor of four. By 1929, there were 30 times more air passengers than in 1926, before Lindbergh's flight. Charles Lindbergh's spirited adventure had ushered in the Air Age.

FIRST TALKING PICTURE

NEW YORK, USA
OCTOBER 6, 1927

Above: Al Jolson in The Jazz Singer, *the first feature film 'talkie'.*

Left: A huge crowd waits outside Warners' Theater in New York to see The Jazz Singer.

Warner Bros chose to premiere *The Jazz Singer* on October 6, 1927, the eve of *Yom Kippur*, the Jewish holiday at the center of the movie's plot. In it, the son of a Jewish cantor is torn between his religious duties, the hopes of his parents and the secular stage; in the end he cancels a jazz performance to sing the *Kol Nidre* in the synagogue.

It was not the first sound film; two Warner releases in 1926 had included music and sound effects. Nor was it the first talkie; Fox had released short drama and news reels in May 1927 using the Movietone sound format. But it was the world's first full-length feature film with audible dialogue – a full two minutes of it in a running time of nearly an hour and a half.

Most of the dialogue in the film still needed to be read by the audience on captions as usual. But the film contained 11 songs. Warner Bros favored the Vitaphone recording system, which meant that every song and dialogue sequence was on a different reel, each accompanied by a soundtrack on disc. The projectionist – surely the unsung star of the movie – had to thread 15 reels and cue up 15 discs with split-second accuracy in the course of each 89-minute showing.

The first words spoken by the film's star, Al Jolson, 17 minutes into the movie, were his catch phrase, "You ain't heard nothin' yet." Loud excitement from the audience greeted this and each new section of dialogue. At the end of the film the crowd spilled onto the street chanting "Jolson! Jolson! Jolson!" It was clear to everyone that a new film era had begun.

The Jazz Singer was a phenomenal success. Although it had cost Warner over $400,000 to produce, it grossed over $2,500,000, almost $1,000,000 more than the studio's previous highest earner. Warner received a special Academy Award for the pioneering film, and it was clear that the public wanted more, so Warner moved fast and in July 1928 released the first all-talking feature film, *Lights of New York*.

The rush by every studio to convert to sound production is affectionately and accurately portrayed in the 1952 film *Singin' in the Rain*. Within two years of the *Jazz Singer* premiere, silent films were no longer being produced. Silent film stars whose voices did not record well found themselves out of work. And the stage version of *The Jazz Singer*, on tour at the time of the film premiere, closed when its $3 seats could not compete with the 50c ticket queues at the movie theaters.

AT A GLANCE

The year of the silent movie gave way to the talkies in 1927 when Al Jolson's The Jazz Singer *hit the screens. Its hour and a half required extreme dexterity from the projectionist to line up the sound track discs, but within a decade Hollywood as we know it was up and running.*

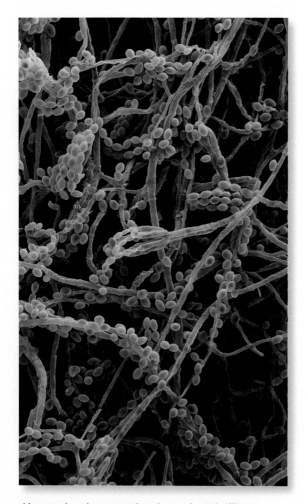

Above: A microscopic view of penicillium *mould spores, from which the antibiotic penicillin is derived.*

Right: Dr Alexander Fleming, the man who discovered penicillin, pictured in his lab in Paddington, London.

AT A GLANCE

A chance occurrence in Alexander Fleming's laboratory in 1928 led to his discovery of one of medicine's most widely used and useful antibacterial agent. Penicillin is now taken for granted, but has saved millions of lives in eight decades.

ALEXANDER FLEMING DISCOVERS PENICILLIN

PADDINGTON, LONDON, UK
1928

It took a series of chance events to facilitate the discovery that would kick-start 20th-century medicine. When Scottish biologist Alexander Fleming took a two-week break in 1928, he left his work unattended at St Mary's Hospital Medical School in Paddington, London. Upon his return, the contents of his discarded culture plate displayed a culture at work that would go on to be known as penicillin.

Fleming had been pursuing his own theory that nasal mucus could fight bacteria. He had been growing micro-organisms and attacking it with the bodily fluid, which contained the antibacterial enzyme lysozyme.

On returning from his holiday, he discovered that a plate of staphylococcus bacteria that he had left untreated had mould growing on it – and a clear ring surrounded the bacteria showed that they had been destroyed. The plate having been left in the open air had allowed the mould to flourish, releasing a property called *penicillium notatum*, which was fighting the staphylococcus on the plate. While Fleming had been on holiday, a significant scientific event was taking place in his absence.

Instantly realizing the importance of his discovery, Fleming quickly went about determining what this antibacterial agent was. He named the active element penicillin; it was a landmark moment in medicine, as bacterial diseases such as tuberculosis and typhoid fever were at the time going untreated and generating high fatality rates. The potency of this new substance could save millions of lives.

Though credited with the discovery of penicillin, Fleming found it hard to cultivate and, with little initial interest from the scientific community, he decided in 1940 to halt his efforts to develop it as a drug. It was shortly before this, in 1939, that Australian pharmacologist Howard Florey led a team that continued Fleming's work and ultimately led to its mass production.

Florey and his team were able to purify penicillin in amounts that allowed them to carry out experiments on mice and, later, humans that proved its antibacterial effects. The world of science finally took notice, and penicillin was mass produced in the USA. By the time the Second World War ended in 1945, penicillin had been used to treat millions of injured soldiers.

Florey, Fleming and biochemistry expert Ernst Boris Chain were awarded the Nobel Prize for medicine in 1945 for their roles in the discovery and application of penicillin. And millions of lives might not have been saved if Fleming had been a little tidier.

Above: *A headline announcing the stock market crash of October 29, 1929.*

Right: *Panicked stock traders crowd the sidewalks outside the New York Stock exchange on the day of the market crash.*

Overleaf: *After the Wall Street Crash of 1929, the U.S. was plunged into the Great Depression. This photograph shows 'Hooverville' in Seattle, a shantytown populated by the unemployed and destitute.*

AT A GLANCE

The Wall Street Crash of 1929, in which share prices slumped due to panic selling by investors heralded the Great Depression, which afflicted the USA for most of the 1930s. Shares took a quarter of a century to regain their 1929 price levels, and the human cost – probably as long-lasting – was considerably greater.

WALL STREET CRASH

NEW YORK, USA
OCTOBER 29, 1929

After the horrors of the First World War, a giddy optimism overtook most of the world. The Roaring Twenties was a time of hedonistic excess and prosperity which made people feel financially invincible, almost immortal. From 1923, share prices rose steadily for six years.

Profit on the stock market seemed to be a sure thing, and if you didn't have the money to invest in speculation there was always a stockbroker to lend you some 'on a margin'. At the height of the boom, brokers were prepared to lend two-thirds of the value of shares to new investors – and by 1929 the level of loans (more than $8.5 billion) exceeded the amount of US currency in circulation. It was an overstretched bubble ready to burst.

On September 3, 1929, the Dow Jones Index, peaking at 381.17, began a long, stumbling, painful decline. It finally bottomed out nearly three years later, on July 8, 1932, at 41.22, 89 per cent lower than at its peak. Shares would not return to their 1929 levels until 1954. What had started as a slight reverse on September 4, 1929, continued for a month before the market staged a faltering recovery in mid-October. But confidence had been fatally shaken by the fall, and in late October panic set in. As prices crashed, investors sought to sell their shares as quickly as possible to minimize their losses.

One terrible day has become immortalized as Black Tuesday. In that single day, October 29, 1929, the Dow Jones fell by 12 per cent, and a incredible 16 million shares were traded at the stock exchange – a record unbeaten until 1968. But Black Tuesday set another record; the value of the stock market fell by $14 billion.

One in six American households (belonging to the 16 per cent of the population who played the market) were directly affected by the crash. But worse was to come. Debate still rages about the precise connection between the Wall Street Crash and the Great Depression of the 1930s – but basically, when people lose money they stop buying, so manufacturers stop producing and employers stop hiring people. So there was mass unemployment and bankruptcies in America, affecting virtually everybody in the country, with knock-on effects throughout the world.

The US banking system itself collapsed, leading to reforms in 1933 which separated the roles of commercial lending banks from those primarily involved in investment. The idea was that never again would greed and conflicts of interest be able to create the conditions for such a disastrous financial meltdown.

GANDHI COMPLETES SALT MARCH

DANDI, INDIA
APRIL 5, 1930

Above: A bronze monument in Delhi commemorates Gandhi's 1930 Salt March to Dandi.

Left: Mahatma Gandhi , third from the left (head down), on his famous march to make salt, in defiance of the British monopoly.

Mohandas Karamchand Gandhi will be forever associated with India's fight for independence against the British Raj. He was instrumental in India's eventual victory, and his salt march to Dandi in 1930 was seen as the defining moment in the struggle. Known as Mahatma, 'great soul', Gandhi was India's spiritual leader and chief political activist during its battle for autonomy, and it was his philosophy and practice of *satyagraha* that was integral to the success of the salt march and to the defusing of the conflict that had been grumbling on for decades.

Satyagraha means non-violent action, primarily through civil resistance. Gandhi urged his followers, rather than becoming violent and rioting – thus making the problems worse – to quietly disobey the rules and stay true to their own principles.

He rejected claims that this was just passive resistance, stating that the goal of satyagraha was 'to convert, not to coerce, the wrong-doer'. For Gandhi, success was people helping their antagonists to discover the obstruction they have raised, so that everyone can work together to remove it and come to an amicable and mutually respectful resolution. This was his main tool in trying to remove the colonial authority of the British Raj over India.

He had already been imprisoned by the British for attempting to inspire insurrection in 1922, but a few years later he returned to the limelight, focusing on the Empire's new taxation laws on salt, which put this vital substance out of the reach of most Indians. He planned to march from his home in Sabarmati to Dandi, with the intention of producing his own salt. The 241-mile (390-km) trek drew worldwide press attention, and many Indians joined him on the way. He reached Dandi 26 days later, on April 5, 1930, reaching down to grasp his own symbolic handful of salt. Nationwide civil resistance followed, with millions of Indians producing their own salt or purchasing it tax-free. Over 60,000 were arrested, including Gandhi; the conflict went on for a year until agreement was reached: release of the prisoners for suspension of civil resistance.

This was a pivotal point in the long march towards independence, with the planet watching; the salt satyagraha of 1930 would become known as one of Gandhi's highest achievements. It wasn't, however, until 1946 that the salt tax laws were abolished, and a year later, in August 1947, that India finally became an independent nation.

Gandhi lived to see India's independence, but at a prayer meeting in New Delhi in 1948 he was assassinated by extremist Nathuram Godse. Gandhi had been one of the world's greatest modern thinkers, a man who had led his country to self-government by peaceful means.

AT A GLANCE

The example in civil resistance set by Mahatma Gandhi in 1930 in defying a tax on salt would sow the seeds that resulted in India receiving its independence from the British Empire in 1947. Salt, a commodity esential to all, was used as a metaphor for freedom, and both goals were achieved by non-violent means.

Above: Owens betters the Olympic record with his time of 21.1 seconds during a 200-meter heat.

Right: The start of the 100 meters at the 1936 Olympic Games in Berlin.

AT A GLANCE

Black athlete Jesse Owens dominated the 1936 Olympic Games in Germany, winning four gold medals. Yet his achievement was all but ignored by the authorities in his native United States, where segregation was still rife – ironically, since the USA disapproved of Hitler's Aryan ideals.

JESSE OWENS, OLYMPIC CHAMPION

BERLIN, GERMANY
AUGUST 3, 1936

When the Olympic Games was held in Germany in 1936, Adolf Hitler saw it as a chance to display a 'resurgent' country. In reality, Germany had a dark interior, tainted by scientific racism and the focus on the 'Aryan race' – but African-American athlete Jesse Owens upset the applecart when he won four gold medals, including the prestigious men's 100 meters.

The 22-year-old Owen had already set sprinting world records while a student at Ohio State University. But, as for many black people in America, life was far from easy for him; he lived in a segregated society, needed to work at multiple jobs to pay his way through college, and was denied a scholarship despite his athletic prowess.

For all the United States' racial problems, however, it was Germany who later came to the fore with its persecution of anyone who did not fit with Hitler's views for the country. But the Second World War was still three years away, and the Olympics had been awarded to Berlin five years before, in 1931. The world turned up to watch, albeit slightly apprehensively.

The USA had considered boycotting the games due to the already well publicized Nazi administration, but finally agreed to attend. Its argument that sport should not be bound up with politics and discrimination was justified, yet it was considered hypocritical coming from a country with its own racial problems. Berlin and the surrounding areas were 'cleaned up' in an attempt to allay the suspicions of the visitors; anti-Semitic propaganda was concealed, and any 'unwanted' natives were hidden in camps. Ironically, Owens whilst in the fascist country did not have to comply with segregation, enjoying the same rights as his white counterparts. He even became the first black man to receive sports sponsorship, when a young German businessman named Adi Dassler persuaded him to wear his Adidas footwear.

In the 100 meters, Owens fended off a late challenge from previous world record holder Ralph Metcalfe, to win the gold. During the next five days Owens won three more gold medals: in the long jump, the 200 meters and the men's relay.

Owens' achievement was a monumental one, and it seriously dented Hitler's vision of Aryan superiority. But amidst claims that Hitler had snubbed Owens at the games, Owens pointed out it was actually his own country that had slighted him; despite his achievements he heard nothing from President Roosevelt.

Owens returned to the USA a hero, but he got into financial difficulties, and when he pursued commercial opportunities his amateur status was rescinded. He died in 1980 aged 66, but his legacy lives on as the man who showed it is the individual, not nationality, creed or race, that defines a person.

Above: Photographed in July 1945, the Gloster Meteor was the first jet-engine fighter aircraft to take to the skies, and was used by the British Royal Air Force during the final months of World War II in Europe.

Left: Frank Whittle explains the features of his jet engine to journalists at a press conference on May 31, 1948.

AT A GLANCE

The successful testing of Frank Whittle's jet engine on April 12, 1937, marks the moment that jet propulsion became a viable reality. Within four years, It was the first aircraft equipped with a jet engine would take to the skies, it was the forerunner of the military and commercial craft that would take humankind into a new epoch of flight.

FRANK WHITTLE TESTS THE FIRST JET ENGINE

RUGBY, UK
APRIL 12, 1937

A daredevil pilot with a gift for mathematics and engineering, Frank Whittle is widely regarded as the 'father of jet propulsion'; the pioneer of engines that would lead to a revolution in air travel.

Whittle first joined the Royal Air Force in 1928 at the age of 15, but was dismissed two days later after failing the medical. Having undertaken a punishing fitness regime, he reapplied under a false name and started as a mechanic. His career progressed steadily, though not without incident; he was sent for officer training by an officer who was impressed by his mathematical talents, but Whittle gained a reputation for theatrical flying that nearly saw him court-martialed. He shone in all his courses, and in 1928 he wrote a graduation thesis examining theories of jet propulsion and suggesting that jets might be combined with a normal piston engine to take aircraft to unprecedented speeds.

Aged 21, Whittle became an RAF flying instructor but continued to develop his idea, dropping the piston in favor of a full jet turbine engine. In 1929, he submitted his plans to Britain's Air Ministry – who turned them down as impracticable. Nevertheless, Whittle took out a patent and continued to promote his design. In 1934, he began an engineering course in Cambridge, and was approached by two RAF men, Rolf Dudley-Williams and James Collingwood Tinling, who had seen Whittle's design and offered to act on his behalf to find money to take it further. On January 27, 1937, Power Jets Ltd was created and a workshop was set up in an old factory in Rugby. With £20,000 available from an investment bank, work on a prototype began. Whittle, still a serving RAF officer, acted as Technical Consultant.

The first jet, named the WU, or Whittle Unit, was tested on April 12, 1937. Based on the laws of motion described by Isaac Newton in the 17th century, it demonstrated the principles still in use today; a turbine providing compressed air to a combustion chamber, with forward thrust achieved by the engine's powerful exhaust. Although it was considered a success, the test revealed some problems with the engine, and further refinements were made at a new site in Lutterworth, Leicestershire.

On May, 15, 1941, after a few short flights to test the engine, the Gloster E.28/39 jet-engined aircraft, also known as the Gloster Whittle, took to the air at RAF Cranwell in Lincolnshire. Its short, but historic, flight of 17 minutes marked the beginning of a new age in aircraft design. In July 1944, the Gloster Meteor, the first British jet fighter, went into active service in combat, and after World War II had ended, jet engines were embraced and refined by civil aviation companies, resulting in larger aircraft and faster, cheaper international air travel.

Above: Aerial View of Crude Oil Refinery.

Left: Two men view the site of the Arabian American Oil Company's first successful oil well in Saudi Arabia at Dharan.

LARGEST SUPPLY OF CRUDE OIL FOUND IN 20TH CENTURY

SAUDI ARABIA
MARCH 1938

Oil is the most actively traded commodity on the planet and has a huge impact on the world's economy. So when a huge supply of crude oil was found in Saudi Arabia it was very big news indeed.

Until the 1930s, the kingdom of Saudi Arabia had no real interest in oil; its economy had relied on pilgrimages to the holy sites of Mecca and Medina, the two most sacred cities in the Muslim religion of Islam. The kingdom had been created by Abd-al-Aziz ibn Saud in 1932 after he had spent three decades reclaiming the land he believed belonged to his family, the House of Saud.

The United States saw the untapped potential of newly formed Saudi Arabia's 830,000 square miles of land, and approached ibn Saud about the possibility of drilling for oil in what was now the largest country in the Middle East.

The King hoped they might find water, and so authorized giant company Standard Oil of California to explore a desert bordering the Persian Gulf, in the northeast of the country, in 1933. Four years of drilling yielded no results and it was beginning to look like a futile exercise until, in March 1938, the eastern province was chosen for the seventh attempt to discover oil. They struck more oil than had ever been seen in history.

What the Americans found would be called the Ghawar Field – 1.3 billion acres of crude oil spanning 173 miles. It is estimated that this oil field alone would account for more than half Saudi Arabia's oil production.

Six years later, the originally US-controlled oil company was renamed Arabian American Oil Company, commonly known as Aramco, and it was fully nationalized by the Saudis in 1980. Saudi Arabia had become the most oil-rich country on the planet, and as such held an incredible amount of bargaining power in the world's marketplace. Oil accounts for over 90 per cent of Saudi's exports; it is estimated to possess over 250 billion barrels in reserve, and still extracts 5 million barrels per day.

That day in March 1938 was the making of a country. No longer having to rely on tourism and pilgrimage to scrape an economy together, Saudi Arabia found itself winning the global equivalent of the lottery and becoming one of the most important nations in the world.

AT A GLANCE

The opportunism of the USA was the catalyst for the discovery, in 1938, of the largest supply of crude oil ever found, in the newly created country of Saudi Arabia. This country's ownership of the planet's most actively traded commodity made it, during most of the 20th century and the early part of the 21st, the most oil-rich country in the world, increasing exponentially both its political importance and its wealth.

Above: Nazi Panzer tanks forge through Belgium in May 1940, conquering the country in less than three weeks.

Right: German troops travel past Cleopatra's Needle in Paris, June 1940, following the Nazi invasion of France.

Below: Ju-87 Stuka dive-bombers helped push the Allies back from northern France to the Channel coas.t

AT A GLANCE

Learning from the lessons of World War I's stalemate trench warfare, Germany employed a combination of aerial bombing and highly mobile artillery to blaze a trail across Europe in 1940, causing the British army to retreat across the English Channel from Dunkirk. It would take the Allies four years to regain the lost ground and turn the tide of the war.

NAZI BLITZKRIEG ON THE WESTERN FRONT

THE NETHERLANDS, BELGIUM, LUXEMBOURG, FRANCE
MAY 10, 1940

The Nazi invasion of Poland in September 1939 caused the United Kingdom and France to declare war on Germany. But during the first few months after that, the European nations held back – this period known as the Phoney War – waiting to see whether Adolf Hitler intended to conquer any more territories.

The answer came with his invasion of Norway and Denmark in April 1940. The Phoney War finally ended on May 10, when the Nazis launched Operation Yellow (*Fall Gelb*), the blitzkrieg against the Netherlands, Belgium and Luxembourg. Together with France, Norway and Denmark (and, later, Germany itself) the battle zones in these countries were known as the Western Front of World War II.

Blitzkrieg is German for 'lightning war' and its use took the Allies by surprise. Tanks advanced rapidly across open country, but the new dimension came from above, in the demoralizing and crippling bombing raids on major cities and supply points. The Nazis used these techniques rapidly and decisively, giving their enemies little chance to recover or strike back.

The blitzkrieg avoided the prolonged trench warfare of World War I. Also, the concept of highly mobile troops combined with aircraft had the advantage of not contravening the Treaty of Versailles, which had at the end of World War 1 strictly limited the size of the German army. Now, the Nazi advance, spearheaded by the immensely powerful Panzer Mark III tanks, sliced its way into the Netherlands, forcing its surrender within five days. Luxembourg held out for only 48 hours. The fall of Belgium took just 18 days.

The attack on the Low Countries was partly a diversionary tactic. Hitler's main target was France, and the invasion, code-named Operation Red (*Fall Rot*), began on May 13. German armored units pushed from Belgium through the densely forested Ardennes region before moving quickly towards the English Channel. The Allied forces, consisting of the British Expeditionary Force alongside French and Belgian troops, were overwhelmed. After an unsuccessful counterattack at Arras, the Allies were forced to retreat to Dunkirk, from where 338,226 soldiers were evacuated over a nine-day period between May 26 and June 4.

France fell to Germany within seven weeks, sending shockwaves around the world. An armistice was agreed on June 25, with most of France occupied, but part of the south remaining as the Free Zone. It was a stunning victory for Germany, achieving in less than two months what four years of trench warfare in World War I had failed to do.

Above: Russian tanks roll towards the battle front on June 22, 1941, the first day of the German drive to defeat the USSR.

Right: Women dig anti-tank trenches near Moscow to confound Hitler's Operation Barbarossa.

AT A GLANCE

Hitler's strike against Russia, Operation Barbarossa, in June 1941, opened a second front in the European war. But the combination of inhospitable Russian winter and terrain plus the opposing Red Army, on their home ground and used to the conditions, proved impossible for the Germans to overcome. When the Germans failed to take Moscow after a long-drawn-out battle, Barbarossa was doomed to failure.

OPERATION BARBAROSSA – HITLER INVADES RUSSIA

USSR
JUNE 22, 1941

The German offensive against the USSR, codenamed Operation (*Fall*) Barbarossa, was the largest military operation of all time, with more than 4.5 million troops invading along a 1,800-mile front, with 600,000 motor vehicles and 750,000 horses. The assault began on June 22, 1941.

Hitler intended to conquer Russia using the blitzkrieg technique which had been so successful on the Western Front. The Germans confidently expected that the USSR would fall as easily as France. The result of six months' detailed planning, Operation Barbarossa aimed to conquer the European part of the Soviet Union, up to the A–A line between the cities of Archangelsk and Astrakhan.

Although Hitler had long nurtured the ambition to invade the Soviet Union, his intentions had been masked by a non-aggression treaty, the Molotov–Ribbentrop Pact, signed shortly before Germany invaded Poland in 1939. This agreement had surprised the world because of the visible mutual hostility and the ideological differences between Germany and the USSR. A trade pact followed in 1940, but the two countries still remained suspicious of each other. The Soviet Union was invited to enter the Axis Pact with Germany, Italy and Japan, but negotiations broke down, making war between them more likely.

Hitler believed that the Russian Army was in a weakened state. Meanwhile, German propaganda claimed that Operation Barbarossa was a necessary pre-emptive strike against a dangerous foe. Then the German campaign in the Balkans spilt over into war with Russia. Yet, despite the massing of Axis troops on the border between German-controlled Romania and Russia during February 1941, the attack took the Soviets by surprise; the Russian leader, Stalin, had not believed that Germany would open up the war on a second front.

The Nazis made significant gains during the early part of the operation, capturing some important economic areas like the Ukraine – but they fatally underestimated the stoic endurance of the Soviet Red Army. The Nazis had been so confident they would secure victory before the onset of the harsh Russian winter that they had failed to prepare for it, and so the freezing weather and poor road conditions contributed to the ultimate failure of their campaign.

By October 1941 the Germans had got close to the Russian capital, but then they lost the two-month Battle of Moscow. The decisive moment arrived when a Red Army counterattack on December 5 forced the Nazis back and crippled Operation Barbarossa. But even so, the war on the Eastern Front continued, with the Germans attacking Stalingrad in 1942, and, at the northern end of the battle line, the siege of Leningrad which dragged on until 1944.

ATTACK ON PEARL HARBOR

HAWAII
DECEMBER 7, 1941

Above: The battleship USS **Arizona** *sinks after being bombed by Japanese planes on December 7, 1941.*

Left: Sinking battleships after the Japanese bombing of Pearl Harbor include USS **California** *(right foreground) and* **Oklahoma***.*

Inset: Mitsubishi dive-bombers on deck of a Japanese carrier before their attack on Pearl Harbor.

AT A GLANCE

Japan's undeclared air attack on Pearl Harbor impelled the USA into involvement in the Second World War, and so this was a pivotal moment in the conflict. Over 2,300 people were injured or killed there – but four years later Japan suffered the US nuclear attacks on Hiroshima and Nagasaki.

Until 9/11, it was December 7, 1941, that was the date no American alive at the time would ever forget. The Japanese attacks on the US naval base in the Hawaiian port of Pearl Harbor caused devastating casualties and propelled the United States into the Second World War.

Tensions between the USA and Japan had been building for some time, escalating in the 1930s due to Japan's treatment of neighboring China. As a result of Japan's invasion of French Indochina at the turn of the 1940s, the USA cut its oil exports to Japan. This forced the Japanese to look for their supplies to Indonesia – at the time ruled by the Dutch – and to the US-owned Philippines.

As an attempt to invade the Philippines would obviously result in a strong US counterattack, the Japanese decided to immobilize the US forces before attempting to overrun the islands, and the nearest US base to the Philippines was Pearl Harbor.

Japan sent a message to the USA informing them of their intention to cease negotiations. This was due to arrive before the attack, but because of communication failures and decryption errors, the message did not arrive until after the attack had begun.

The attack came as a complete surprise to the USA; both countries had been well aware of the potential for conflict, but the USA had believed the Japanese would go after the Philippines first, and had underestimated the Japanese military strength. American radar had actually spotted the Japanese fleet – but had misidentified them, thinking they were friendly.

Just before 8 a.m. on Sunday December 7, the Japanese attacked, with an air raid lasting nearly two hours. The death toll reached over 2,300, half of that from the battleship USS *Arizona*, which was destroyed by a Japanese bomb just minutes into the assault.

With the harbor laid waste, seven US ships destroyed and more ships seriously damaged, the United States policy of isolationism from the war had to be re-assessed. The next day, President Roosevelt addressed the nation, and less than an hour later the USA declared war on Japan.

In 1945, German forces surrendered in May, and the war with Japan ended in August with the atomic bombs on Hiroshima and Nagasaki.

Overleaf: The battleships U.S.S. West Virginia (foreground) and U.S.S. Tennessee sit low in the water and burn after the Japanese surprise attack on Pearl Harbor.

Above: The battered city of Stalingrad as it looked during its siege by German forces in 1942 and 1943.

Left: Prisoners are marched through the snowy streets of Stalingrad after the German defeat by Soviet forces in February 1943.

Inset: A huge World War II memorial to the defenders of Stalingrad on Mamayev Hill, scene of some of the fiercest fighting.

GERMAN SURRENDER AT STALINGRAD

USSR
FEBRUARY 2, 1943

The Battle of Stalingrad was one of the bloodiest in history, with casualties estimated at more than 1.5 million. The battle involved more participants, military and civilian, than any other. The levels of bloodshed and brutality were unparalleled. The decisive victory it gave Russia, however, marked a major turning point in World War II, with the German army suffering its first major military setback. It was the start of the Soviet counter-offensive which contributed to Germany's unconditional surrender in 1945.

After being repulsed from Moscow in December 1941, the German army regrouped and waited until spring 1942, when they would not be hindered by the severe winter weather, to launch their second offensive in Russia. Capturing Stalingrad was important to Hitler because it was a major industrial centre whose location on the Volga river was vital for transportation. If the Nazis controlled Stalingrad, they could cut off the fuel supplies to the Russian military – and Hitler relished the propaganda coup that would come from seizing the city named after Stalin, the Soviet leader.

The German army began its push into southern Russia on June 28, 1942, meeting little opposition at first, and reaching the outskirts of Stalingrad by the end of July. Stalin, well aware of the crucial nature of the battle, ordered that anyone capable of holding a rifle should do so, and the Russians took him at his word, and prepared to defend their city at all costs.

The Luftwaffe's bombing reduced much of Stalingrad to rubble. German troops gained control of up to 90 per cent of the city from time to time, but they were never able to eradicate the last pockets of resistance in the city center, on the west bank of the Volga; the Germans were better at coordinated, combined mass assaults than the hand-to-hand, house-to-house skirmishing which they faced in Stalingrad. The fighting dragged on for months, into the same bitter Russian winter conditions had already defeated the Nazis, earlier that same year.

Taking advantage of this, Stalin launched a counter-attack, codenamed Operation Uranus (Операция Уран), in November 1942. A pincer movement, it trapped the Nazi troops inside the city, cutting them off from their supplies. Besieged for three bitter months and unable to break out, the surviving Germans, starving, frozen and desperate, surrendered in February 1943. In doing this their commander, Field Marshal von Paulus, had disobeyed Hitler's order to fight to the last man and take his own life rather than be captured, and so he incurred Hitler's wrath. It was from this point on that the army generals started to lose confidence in Hitler.

Above: Omaha Beach pictured on D-Day as Allied forces made landfall and the tide of war in Europe turned irrevocably.

Right: American troops disembark on one of the Normandy invasion beaches on June 7, 1944, the day after D-Day.

Overleaf: Winston Churchill speaks to some to troops who led the assault on D-Day.

Below: General Dwight D Eisenhower (left) confers with his deputy, Britain's Field Marshal Bernard Montgomery (right).

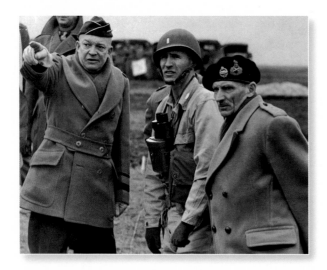

D-DAY LANDINGS TURN THE TIDE OF WAR

NORMANDY, FRANCE
JUNE 6, 1944

World War II in Europe entered its final phase with the landing of Allied troops in German-occupied France. Beginning in the early hours of June 6, 1944, Operation Overlord was masterminded by US General Dwight D. Eisenhower (Ike), as Supreme Commander of the Allied Expeditionary Force. The Allied forces were composed of British, US and Canadian units together with representatives of the Free French. Known as the 21st Army Group, they were commanded by Field Marshal Viscount Montgomery of Alamein (Monty), the British general famous for his victory at El Alamein in Egypt in 1942.

After a day's delay because of bad weather, the landings took place along a 50-mile strip on the coast of Normandy. This comprised five beaches, codenamed Gold, Sword, Juno, Omaha and Utah. There were two phases to the assault, starting with an air attack shortly after midnight followed by an amphibious landing at 6.30 a.m.

The invading force was massive, consisting of some 5,000 ships and 13,000 aircraft from the United States Air Force alone. Two temporary harbors, known as Mulberries, were constructed for use until the existing harbors could be captured. During the first day of the operation, 175,000 Allied personnel went ashore.

German resistance was determined, particularly on Omaha and Utah, the beaches attacked by the US troops. But the Allied forces soon established a beachhead, supported by airborne assaults using paratroopers and glider-borne soldiers. From there, they gradually fanned out into the French countryside. During the fighting, the Allies sustained approximately 10,000 casualties, whilst it is estimated that the Germans suffered up to 9,000.

Within four weeks, more than a million Allied troops had landed in Normandy, and the German army was pushed back towards the River Seine. Some 100,000 Germans surrendered at Falaise. Then, with the invasion of southern France, victory for the Allies grew closer.

Paris was liberated in late August, and the Allies moved towards the Netherlands and the Rhine Valley, although they suffered occasional setbacks such as the failure to capture the bridges at Arnhem in Holland. When the Germans counterattack was repulsed at the Battle of the Bulge, the Nazis' last hope of success on the Western Front had gone.

With the Russians advancing from the east, the war was nearly over. American and Russian forces converged on the banks of the River Elbe, and two days later, on April 30, 1945, Hitler committed suicide in his bunker in Berlin. The Germans surrendered unconditionally on May 7, 1945, and the war in Europe was over.

Codenamed Operation Overlord, the Allied landings in northern France in June 1944 signaled the beginning of the last phase of the war in Europe. After the landings, British, US and Canadian forces pushed towards Paris and then towards the Netherlands: Russian forces moved in from the east, and Hitler's days were numbered.

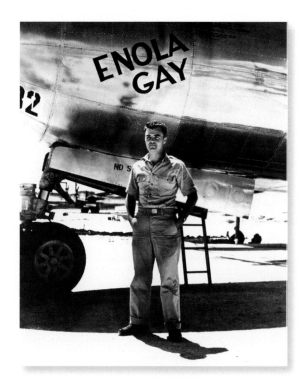

ATOM BOMB DROPPED

HIROSHIMA, JAPAN
AUGUST 6, 1945

The Second World War had raged for six years, the death tolls for the countries involved running into tens of millions. The planet had never seen such death and destruction, but in 1945 it appeared an end was in sight. On August 6, the USA dropped the world's first atomic bomb on the Japanese city of Hiroshima.

The Allies had won the battle against the Axis countries of Germany and Italy, which were imploding: Italy had surrendered in 1943, and Germany had signed an unconditional surrender early in 1945, ending the war in Europe. But Japan refused to give up.

During the war the USA had begun the top secret Manhattan Project, aimed at equipping the country with nuclear weapons. Born out of the fear that Nazi Germany was doing the same, the project began on a small scale but quickly escalated into a major industry, employing over 100,000, people including some of the foremost scientists on the planet.

On July 16, 1945, they tested the first atom bomb in Los Alamos, New Mexico – the same day as US President Harry Truman, Britain's Winston Churchill and the Soviet Union leader Josef Stalin met in Potsdam to discuss the fate of a defeated Germany. The three leaders ordered the surrender of Japan, threatening 'utter destruction' if the Japanese did not comply. Japan ignored the ultimatum.

At 8.15 a.m. on August 6, the Enola Gay, a B-29 Superfortress bomber aircraft, dropped the world's first atomic bomb onto humans, in Hiroshima. Picked for its importance as an army depot, the city was obliterated in a giant mushroom cloud of smoke, an image that would go down in history.

The bomb had 2,000 times more power than any other explosive ever used in the war, and killed a reported 166,000 people, the majority of them civilians. Those who did not die from the original blast perished from flash burns or radiation sickness, which affected many in the city for years after. The immediate blast radius was one square mile, with flash fires ravaging a further four.

Just three days later the US dropped a second bomb, this time on Nagasaki, a strategic Japanese port. The city was completely destroyed, with another 80,000 deaths.

With two vital cities wiped out and the threat of more atom bomb attacks, Japan surrendered unconditionally five days later, on August 14, although the document was not signed until September 2. The war was over, but peace had come at an appalling cost; the world now knew of a weapon so powerful that it could destroy all human and animal life on the planet.

Above: Colonel Paul W Tibbets stands next to the Boeing B-29 he piloted on its historic bombing mission over Hiroshima.

Left: A mushroom cloud rises over Nagasaki on August 9, 1945, as the USA drops a second atomic bomb. Japan surrendered five days later, ending the war.

Inset: Only a few buildings were left standing in Hiroshima after the destruction wrought by the US atomic bomb.

AT A GLANCE

With Italy and Germany defeated, the Allies decided on nuclear bombing to end Japanese resistance and win the Second World War in 1945. Hiroshima and Nagasaki were the cities chosen for the strikes that ended that conflict – but which also started the Cold War between the West and Russia, who both had the atomic might to destroy humanity.

Above: Viceroy of India Lord Mountbatten meets with various Indian leaders to devise a plan to partition the country.

Right: Prime Minister Nehru addresses a mass meeting of Hindus and Muslims in Delhi in a plea to end fighting, October 1947.

Below: The border city of Amritsar was a main crossing point for people migrating between India and Pakistan.

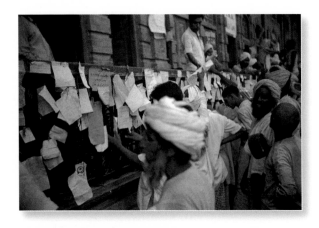

AT A GLANCE

When Britain granted India independence on August 15, 1947, the process also led to the foundation of Pakistan. This new country was formed from the two principal Muslim regions, in the east and the west, with the remaining territory still belonging to India – mainly Hindu and Sikh – separating them. This untidy compromise was followed, in 1971, by East Pakistan becoming the independent nation of Bangladesh.

PARTITION OF INDIA

INDIA/PAKISTAN
AUGUST 15, 1947

India had been governed by Britain since 1612, originally by the British East India Company, and after 1858 as a British colony. At that time, India was made up of a number of large provinces directly administered by the British, together with over 500 princely states which the British ruled indirectly through their Indian sovereigns, who had sworn allegiance to Britain.

Early in the 20th century, the country's largest political party, the Indian National Congress, had launched the struggle for a free state. India's spiritual and political leader, Mahatma Gandhi, was an advocate of independence, believing in non-violent opposition to British rule – but he was opposed to partition. The INC party leader, Jawaharlal Nehru, was also a key figure in the independence movement, and went on to become independent India's first Prime Minister.

In 1906, the All India Muslim League had been formed as a new political party by Muslims dissatisfied by the Hindu domination of the Indian National Congress. At the party's convention in 1930, writer/philosopher Allama Iqbal had proposed a separate region for Muslims, and although the party's president, Muhammad Ali Jinnah, had initially favored a united India, by 1935 he had become convinced that division on religious lines was necessary.

In January 1946, after a series of mutinies amongst British Indian forces, bloody Hindu/Muslim riots broke out in Calcutta (now Kolkata) and spread throughout the country. These events spurred Britain's new Labour government into action. Deciding that Britain could no longer control India, the prime minister, Clement Attlee, announced that independence was to be granted and the country was to be divided.

The newly-appointed viceroy of India, Lord Mountbatten, was given the task of drawing up the map of a partitioned India. Under the Mountbatten Plan, the predominantly Hindu and Sikh areas formed the new India, whilst areas with a Muslim majority comprised Pakistan. The latter was split into East and West, separated geographically by India, and the princely states were allowed to decide which country to join. In the following months, millions of refugees migrated across the newly-drawn borders, resulting in scenes of unprecedented violence and the loss of about half a million lives.

The Indo–Pakistani War of 1947 was fought over the former princely state of Jammu and Kashmir, which had a Hindu leader but a Muslim majority. This war was the first of four post-partition conflicts, three of which were over Kashmir; the last conflict, in 1971, saw East Pakistan become the independent nation of Bangladesh.

FIRST FASTER THAN SOUND FLIGHT

CALIFORNIA, USA
OCTOBER 14, 1947

The prestige of breaking the sound barrier in a manned aircraft went to Chuck Yeager in 1947. So the combat warplanes of the 1950s and beyond went supersonic, and were powered by turbojets rather than rockets – but during the rest of the 20th century it was only a single commercial aircraft, Concorde, that was able to bring the benefit of these speeds to civil aviation.

AT A GLANCE

Left: Charles E. Yeager, Major Gus Lundquist and Captain James Fitzgerald (left to right), stand before the XS-1 at Muroc Air Force Base, California.

Below: President Truman awards the Collier Air Trophy, aviation's highest honor, to scientist John Stack, Chuck Yeager and Lawrence D. Bell, president of Bell Aircraft Corporation.

In the aftermath of the atomic bomb, the United States continued their mission to be the most pioneering and innovative country on the planet. On October 14, 1947, they flew the first aircraft to break the sound barrier.

It had all begun in March 1945, five months before the obliteration of Hiroshima and Nagasaki. The National Advisory Committee for Aeronautics – which later, as NASA, became the organization that sent men to the moon – commissioned three aircraft titled XS-1 (experimental supersonic) to gather information about transonic and supersonic flight.

Abbreviated to X-1, the aircraft looked more like a machine-gun bullet than an airplane, and first took to the skies via gliding flights in January 1946. The first powered flight was by Chalmers Goodlin towards the end of the year, but he was removed from the program after his wage demands and calls for hazard pay were deemed to be excessive.

Enter Charles 'Chuck' Yeager; under the new control of the United States Air Force, World War Two pilot Yeager was selected as the new pilot of the X-1 project. He named the aircraft Glamorous Glennis after his wife who he had wed in February 1945.

The 23-year-old nearly dropped out of his historic flight that day. A horse-riding accident had left him with broken ribs, but he persevered despite being in so much pain that he could barely walk. Yeager later said, "If it became physically impossible to climb into the X-1, then I'd scrub the mission. If I could get into the pilot's seat, I knew I could fly."

Get in the cockpit he did, and the X-1 was launched from a B-29 bomber over California in an eerie comparison with the atomic bombings two years previously. The rocket aircraft was the first to reach supersonic speeds, recorded at Mach 1.06 – 807 mph.

According to Yeager, he travelled faster than sound for 18 seconds. He reflected on the event and its significance for the USA, saying: "It opened up space for us and put us ahead of the rest of the world in aeronautical knowledge."

It was another race won for the USA, both figuratively and literally. The USA would go on to record many more achievements, the highlight undoubtedly landing men on the moon. But for now they could be content with being the fastest nation in the world.

STATE OF ISRAEL IS PROCLAIMED

TEL AVIV, ISRAEL
MAY 14, 1948

Above: Members of the newly created state of Israel gather to hear Prime Minister David Ben-Gurion read the Declaration of Independence.

Left: Arab soldiers shell Jewish forces striving to recapture the vital supply route from Tel Aviv to Jerusalem.

AT A GLANCE

The division of Jews and Arabs into the states of Palestine and Israel proved controversial in 1948 and remains so today. The bid to expand Israel's borders won UN approval, but subsequent peace agreements have failed to suppress both resentment and terrorist acts.

Zionism, the movement calling for an independent Jewish state, gained momentum in the late 19th century, with a wave of Russian Jews migrating to their traditional homelands in Palestine. After the collapse of the Ottoman Empire in 1917, Britain took control of the region, and the British Prime Minister Balfour lent his support to the idea; but Arab objections during the 1920s and 1930s stalled moves to create the state.

At the end of the Second World War, the revelations about the Holocaust aroused greater international sympathy for the cause. But the Arabs remained violently opposed to the proposed partition of Palestine, a country in which they had been for many centuries the majority and saw as their own. Britain went to the newly formed United Nations, which ruled in favor of the division of the country.

Britain, whose mandate to rule in the area was due to expire on May 15, 1948, refused to implement the new scheme. It regarded the UN solution as unworkable, since the majority Palestinian population was to be left only 46 per cent of the original territory. But the Jewish settlers took up arms, and seized control of the area assigned to them; on the eve of the departure of the British, the Jewish leader, David Ben-Gurion, proclaimed the new state of Israel in a ceremony in Tel Aviv's Art Museum.

As the British marched out of Israel, forces from Egypt, Jordan, Syria, Lebanon and Iraq invaded it in support of the Palestinians. But the Jews of Israel not only defended themselves but seized further territory, expanding Israel's original borders by 50 per cent. The fighting ended in 1949 when the UN sanctioned this expansion; hundreds of thousands of Palestinians fled their homes, becoming refugees in the remnants of Palestine controlled by Jordan and Egypt.

After the Second World War, many people had seen the creation of a separate Jewish state as a moral imperative. But imposing a minority Jewish population from outside onto the long-settled Arab people of the area was always going to create problems, and not just in the region itself. For example, the strong US support for Israel (declared by President Truman only 11 minutes after Ben-Gurion's proclamation) drew the USSR into opposition as suppliers of armaments to the Arab League.

Israel further increased its territory during the Six Day War in 1967 and established military supremacy in the region. But in the early years of the 21st century, despite peace agreements with Egypt in 1979 and the Palestine Liberation Organization in 1993, Israel's existence continues to trigger acts of war and terrorism both within and beyond the Palestinian homelands.

Left: German police and American soldiers face Soviet soldiers at the border between Allied- and Soviet-controlled Berlin in 1948.

Right: Residents of Berlin wave to an American airlift plane approaching Tempelhof Airfield.

BERLIN BLOCKADE BEGINS

EAST GERMANY
JUNE 24, 1948

At the end of the Second World War the Allies (France, Britain, United States and Soviet Union) occupied the defeated Germany and divided the entire country, and its capital, Berlin, into four administrative zones. The four powers were united in wanting to ensure that Germany's military capacity and ambitions could not be revived, but they disagreed about the role the country should have in post-war Europe.

The Western Allies wanted Germany to be fully integrated into Western Europe, so that, as they said, they could 'keep a watchful eye' on it. The Soviet Union was, however, concerned that a country so strongly supported by the capitalist West might destabilize the communist bloc in eastern Europe. Soviet leader Josef Stalin felt sure, too, that the US recovery program for Europe, the Marshall Plan, was a ploy to disguise a Western attempt to infiltrate his post-war buffer zone of communist states in eastern Europe, so he did not go to the European talks in early 1948 which resulted in the formation of West Germany.

Berlin was located deep in the Soviet sector of Germany, through which all supplies for the city had to be transported. Stalin saw the city as a bargaining chip in his political ambitions; so overnight on June 23–24, the Soviet Union blocked all road, rail and river routes into and out of the city. Without deliveries, the 2.5 million inhabitants of West Berlin had food for only five weeks.

The Western Allies were taken by surprise. The USA recommended a show of military strength – which might have provoked a new war – but British Foreign Minister Ernest Bevin successfully argued for an airlift into the city. Part of the post-war settlement of Berlin had been the allocation to the Western Allies of three air corridors between West Germany and Berlin, and Bevin reasoned that the Soviets would not dare shoot down planes on a humanitarian mission.

From haphazard beginnings, the airlift became a visible demonstration of the West's political determination, industrial capacity and military co-ordination. At its height, up to 1,000 planes were airborne at any given time, one landing in West Berlin every three minutes, delivering 8,000 tons of freight a day.

The blockade was the first skirmish in the Cold War; its imposition led to the formation of NATO in April 1949, and alerted Europe to the potential threat of a powerful USSR. Meanwhile Stalin, thwarted, was forced to lift the blockade on May 12. And Germany remained divided, the dividing line forming part of the new Iron Curtain across Europe, until the fall of communism led to the country's reunification in 1990.

AT A GLANCE

When the Soviet Union attempted to isolate the city of Berlin, deep in East Germany, from Western supplies in 1948, the response of France, Britain and the United States was to supply the former German capital by air. Stalin's aggressive stance failed to intimidate the Allies, and Berlin, like Germany itself, remained divided between East and West for another 42 years.

Above: The United Nations General Assembly commemorated the 30th anniversary of the Universal Declaration of Human Rights in 1978.

Right: Eleanor Roosevelt, René Cassin and RSS Gunawardene celebrate the tenth anniversary of the Universal Declaration of Human Rights.

AT A GLANCE

The Universal Declaration of Human Rights arose directly from the horrors of World War II and is the first global expression of rights to which it is considered all people are entitled. Its 30 articles have since been elaborated in international treaties, regional human rights instruments and national constitutions and laws.

UNIVERSAL DECLARATION OF HUMAN RIGHTS ADOPTED

PALAIS DE CHAILLOT, PARIS, FRANCE
DECEMBER 10, 1948

Having just witnessed a second devastating world war, the United Nations General Assembly, established in 1945, adopted the Universal Declaration of Human Rights (UDHR) in 1948 as an attempt to outlaw oppression and discrimination. The document set down in writing for the first time a recognition by the international community that individual human rights and fundamental freedoms applied to everyone.

Pressure for such a bill of rights had been growing during the course of the war. In his 1941 State of the Union address, US President Franklin D. Roosevelt had called for the protection of what he termed the 'essential Four Freedoms': freedom of speech, freedom of conscience, freedom from fear and freedom from want. This became the slogan of a movement that sought to make human rights part of the conditions for peace at the end of the war. And after Roosevelt died in 1945, his widow Eleanor played a major role in fulfilling his vision.

The Universal Declaration had to reflect in its 30 articles the different values and traditions of the 58 member states of the United Nations. It was a common statement of mutual aspirations, a shared vision of a more equitable and just world. Its success is reflected by its virtually universal acceptance, and the Universal Declaration is today the best known human rights document in the world, having been translated into nearly 250 languages. It also serves as a model for numerous international treaties and declarations, and is incorporated in the constitutions and laws of many countries.

The text was drafted in just under two years from January 1947 by an eight-member drafting committee. This was chaired by Eleanor Roosevelt and included John Peters Humphrey (Canada), René Cassin (France), P.C Chang (China) and Charles Malik (Lebanon). They revised the draft declaration in the light of replies from member states before submitting it to the General Assembly. It was unanimously adopted, apart from eight abstentions, on December 10th, a date since celebrated annually as Human Rights Day.

For the first time in history, the international community had embraced a document considered to have universal value – 'a common standard of achievement for all peoples and all nations'. In 1966 the General Assembly also adopted two detailed covenants which complete the International Bill of Human Rights.

Above: Philip Staples (left), President of the Franklin Institute, presents the Franklin medal to Edwin Hubble in 1939.

Left: The Hale Telescope inside the Palomar Observatory, San Diego County, California.

HUBBLE FIRST USES THE HALE TELESCOPE

PALOMAR MOUNTAIN, USA
JANUARY 26, 1949

The Hale Telescope on Palomar Mountain was the last in a series of giant advances in telescope design by American astronomer George Ellery Hale. He had already founded observatories at Yerkes in Wisconsin and at Mount Wilson outside Los Angeles, both of which had made great improvements to the way space was observed from Earth.

At Mount Wilson, Hale had designed a 60-inch reflector telescope (an earlier Hale Telescope) which 'saw first light' (was first used for observation) in 1908. It was the largest telescope in the world until Hale built a second one nearby, the 100-inch Hooker Telescope. This saw first light in 1917, and it remained unsurpassed in size and quality for 30 years.

In 1919 Hale appointed Edwin Hubble to the staff at Mount Wilson, and Hubble's observations there of what became known as the Red Shift – the light-borne Doppler Effect produced by the rapid retreat of distant galaxies – provided firm evidence that the universe is expanding. His discovery, in 1929, became known as Hubble's Law, and it confirmed Lemaître's 'primeval atom' theory of 1927, later renamed the Big Bang.

Meanwhile, by 1928 it had become clear that they were going to need a bigger telescope. Hale won $6 million of funding from the Rockefeller Institute for a new telescope with a massive 200-inch reflector. The giant mirrored-glass parabolic bowl was made of Pyrex, a new material at the time, and innovative solutions were required not only for its manufacture but also for the support of this immensely heavy piece of equipment.

The original reflector bowl weighed 20 tons. Grinding and polishing it accurately (to within 2 nanometers) took 13 years and reduced its weight by five tons. The 1930 technique devised to coat the Pyrex in mirroring is still used today when it is periodically resurfaced.

The construction of the Hale Telescope at Palomar spanned major world events including the Great Depression and the Second World War. Hale, dying in 1938, did not live to see his greatest work come into service; it saw first light on January 26, 1949, when Hubble used it to make observations of a nebula, now known as Hubble's Variable Nebula, which he had first studied through the telescopes at Yerkes and Mount Wilson.

The Hale Telescope remained the largest telescope in the world for 27 years, and its high resolution was unbeaten until 1993. It was vital in studying the nature of quasars, and it is still a key research instrument for astronomers. Hubble's work with it was honored in the naming of the Hubble Space Telescope.

AT A GLANCE

The work of American astronomer George Ellery Hale and his protégé Edwin Hubble added much to our understanding of the universe around us. The Hale Telescope, inaugurated by Hubble in 1949, was the largest telescope in the world for 27 years and is still in use today.

Above: Captured North Korean prisoners are marched at gunpoint after Inchon was secured by the USA.

Right: Smoke rises from shelled buildings in Inchon after the US bombardment.

Below: General Douglas MacArthur accompanies US troops during their attack on Inchon, September 1950.

AT A GLANCE

In the brief, bloody Korean War, the USA strove to stem the spread of communism by whatever means necessary. It was the precursor to a longer and even more costly conflict in Vietnam. The Korean War achieved nothing, either territorially or ideologically, and peace has never formally been declared.

BATTLE OF INCHON

SOUTH KOREA
SEPTEMBER 15, 1950

In June 1950, a series of skirmishes along the 38th parallel in partitioned Korea erupted into a full invasion. The North Korean People's Army (NKPA) raced southwards, catching South Korea off guard and capturing its capital, Seoul, after only three days before pressing on to the key south-eastern port of Pusan.

A rearguard action by hurriedly assembled United Nations forces (chiefly from Britain, Australia and America) delayed the invading army and stopped them at the Pusan peninsula, the only part of South Korea never to fall under communist control. US General Douglas MacArthur secured the port, then conceived a daring counter-attack.

Inchon, a large port north-west of Seoul, had a well-protected harbor and was heavily defended by the NKPA. It was the last place they would expect a massive amphibious landing – so on September 15 this MacArthur masterstroke, led by the US Marines, took the communists completely by surprise.

The US forces took Inchon with minimum loss of life, cutting North Korean supply and communications lines and triggering a chaotic retreat. The liberation of Seoul was a much harder and bloodier battle, but with the enemy in disarray MacArthur was able to pursue them almost to the Chinese border in the far north of the country. But there, he in turn was caught out, unprepared for the massive intervention by the Chinese Army supporting the North Koreans.

Now it was the UN forces that retreated in disorder, to positions south of Seoul. But by the end of April 1951 they had fought their way back to a line more or less along the 38th parallel, where it had all begun. Two years of virtual stalemate followed whilst an armistice was discussed. It came into force in July 1953, when a demilitarized zone between the two countries was established, but peace in Korea has never been formally declared.

The decisiveness of the Battle of Inchon was a rare occasion in a brutal war which saw great loss of life (an estimated four million military and civilian) and achieved almost nothing. The war itself was the result of an unwelcome, arbitrary and unilateral division of Korea imposed by a joint US/Soviet committee onto the formerly Japanese territory. Having been separated, each side sought reunification on its own terms, and the USA was drawn into the conflict by its over-riding post-war foreign policy of containing the spread of communism at all costs. The Vietnam War was just around the corner.

DISCOVERY OF THE STRUCTURE OF DNA

CAMBRIDGE AND LONDON, UK
FEBRUARY 21, 1953

It has long been understood that physical characteristics are passed on from generation to generation. Recognizing which gene is responsible for which trait has become the holy grail of the life sciences in the early 21st century. If genes are the building blocks of life, then deoxyribonucleic acid, DNA, is the instruction manual for assembling those blocks.

It's a relatively simple molecule, compared for example to protein, the other component of our life-defining chromosomes; DNA has only four sub-groups compared to protein's 20. Discovering how those sub-groups are structured was a vital first step in unlocking the genetic codes contained within them.

In the early 1950s, two teams of British scientists were racing to solve that problem. At Imperial College, London, Rosalind Franklin and Maurice Wilkins found a way to photograph DNA using X-ray diffraction. One image they produced clearly showed a spiral structure, a helix. Based on this visual evidence and on data about DNA established by many independent researchers, Francis Crick and James Watson of Cambridge University set about building a theoretical structure for the molecule.

Using metal rods and balls, they produced a model in the form of two intertwined, interconnected spirals, a double helix which satisfied all the known information about DNA. Crick and Watson announced their discovery on February 28, 1953, a week after they had completed their model. A month later, articles by Franklin, Wilkins, Crick and Watson appeared side by side in the influential science journal *Nature*.

Subsequent experiments confirmed the truth of Crick and Watson's theoretical model, and in 1962 Crick, Watson and Wilkins received a Nobel Prize for their discovery. Only living scientists are eligible for the prize, and Franklin had died in 1958; but neither Crick nor Watson cited her ground-breaking work in their Nobel lectures. Only Maurice Wilkins acknowledged her contribution.

With the structure of DNA established, all efforts turned to cracking the genetic code itself. Once that had been achieved, scientists set about mapping the genome, first in fruit flies (which have only 8 pairs of chromosomes) and eventually in humans (who have 46).

The discovery of the structure of DNA has led to significant insights into the development of species and indeed of life itself, and to an understanding and potential cure for genetic disorders. DNA forensics is now routinely applied to solving crimes. But with the benefits come ethical risks, and society is still wrestling with the moral dilemmas posed by our ability to engineer both animal and vegetable species genetically.

Above: Dr Francis Crick (left) and Dr James Watson (right) at a Molecular Biology Symposium.

Left: A computer-generated image of a strand of DNA.

AT A GLANCE

The genetic code represented by DNA, discovered in 1953 by a group of British scientists, has revolutionized various aspects of life from solving crime to changing the characteristics of living creatures. Some believe it has also opened an ethical Pandora's box that may never be closed.

CONQUEST OF EVEREST

NEPAL/TIBET BORDER
MAY 29, 1953

It was only in 1856 that Peak XV, as it was then known to Westerners, was confirmed as the world's highest mountain. That year, calculations by the staff of Andrew Waugh, the British Surveyor General in India, proved that it was higher than the previous title holder, Kangchenjunga. The announcement had been delayed for four years while the team checked and rechecked their sums.

Although it was the policy of the Survey to retain local names wherever possible, Waugh never discovered this mountain's traditional names, Chomolungma and Sagarmatha, because Nepal and Tibet were at the time closed to Westerners – Waugh's staff had been carrying out their observations from a distance of more than 170 miles. So he named it after George Everest, his predecessor as Surveyor General. George Everest pointed out that his name could not be written in Hindi or pronounced by the local population; nevertheless in 1865 the British Geological Society formally adopted Mount Everest as the name of the world's highest place. Its generally accepted height, 8,848 m (29,029 ft) includes a 3.5 m (11 ft) allowance for snow and ice.

The first known expedition to the mountain was led by George Mallory in 1921. He aimed to explore the region for possible routes to the summit, and returned in 1924 for a serious assault. It was Mallory who, when asked why he was so intent on climbing Everest, replied, "Because it's there." He died in the attempt that year. His body was recovered 75 years later, but debate still rages about whether or not he had reached the summit before he died.

Other early attempts included a flight over Everest in 1933 by two Westland Wallace biplanes in an effort to drop a British flag onto the summit. It was funded by Lady Lucy Houston, an eccentric millionaire and former chorus girl.

The expedition led by John Hunt in 1953 was the ninth British outing. Hunt nominated two pairs of climbers from his team to make the final assault. The first pair were defeated by exhaustion just 100 m (300 ft) from the top. But at 11.30 a.m. on May 29, the second pair, New Zealander Edmund Hillary and Nepali Sherpa Tenzing Norgay, stepped onto the summit of Mount Everest and into the record books. They buried some sweets and a cross in the snow, took a few photos and came home.

News of the achievement reached Britain on the morning of Queen Elizabeth II's coronation. She promptly knighted Hunt and Hillary, and awarded the George Medal to Tenzing – and Tenzing, who did not know the date of his birth, adopted May 29 for all his subsequent birthdays.

Above: Tenzing Norgay (left) and Edmund Hillary pose triumphantly at their camp after their return from the peak.

Left: Mount Everest as seen from the Rongbuk Monastery in China.

AT A GLANCE

The conquering of Everest in 1953, then known as the world's highest peak, by Tenzing and Hillary is still, over half a century later, the most famous mountaineering feat in history. The fact that it coincided with Queen Elizabeth's coronation cemented it in history as a great British achievement that brightened up the drab postwar years, and in many people's minds heralded a new and great Elizabethan era.

Above: Senator Joseph R. McCarthy replies to Ed Murrow's televised attack, April 1954.

Right: Journalist Ed Murrow on the set of See It Now, *his television program which was aired on CBS from 1951 to 1958.*

EDWARD MURROW ATTACKS SENATOR JOSEPH McCARTHY

CBS TELEVISION NETWORK, USA
MARCH 9, 1954

In the immediate post-war years, American foreign policy was dominated by a single over-riding concern – to stop the spread of communism. Amongst most ordinary Americans, an atmosphere of concern and suspicion gradually deteriorated into one of intolerance and fear. For a few years it seemed that America's sense of liberty and justice had been lost in a blind panic; and that panic was encouraged and exploited by Edgar Hoover, director of the FBI, together with a junior Republican senator from Wisconsin, Joseph McCarthy.

The FBI's role in this panic was covert, and so it was the senator who gave his name to its public face: McCarthyism. Employees, particularly in government, education and the media, were rigorously interrogated, sacked on the merest whiff of sympathy with communism, blacklisted, and encouraged to give up the names of other supposed communist sympathizers. There was some evidence of communist infiltration ... but the McCarthy witch-hunt destroyed the lives and careers of many innocent people and their families. The invasive mistrust of colleagues had more in common with the secret police society of East Germany than with the Land of the Free.

Although most of America was swept up in the hysteria, there were resisting voices. Edward Murrow was a respected television journalist who had made his name with radio broadcasts to America from Europe during the Second World War. He had a reputation for fair and honest reporting, and he ran a weekly 30-minute slot called *See It Now* on the US television channel CBS. A 1953 edition of the program had exposed unfair McCarthyist dismissals within the air force. Expecting that McCarthy would now turn his guns his way, Murrow decided to devote his broadcast of March 9, 1954, to attacking the senator. Murrow used McCarthy's own words to deliver a damning picture of the senator and the threat to civil liberties that he posed.

Murrow's was not the first rallying cry against McCarthyism. Arthur Miller's 1953 play *The Crucible*, ostensibly about the Salem witch-hunt of the 1690s, had been a thinly veiled attack on it. But it was Murrow's broadcast that marked the start of McCarthy's fall from grace. Calls to CBS after the Murrow program were 15 to 1 in support of his view, and McCarthy's response, in his right-to-reply TV appearance, did not come over well. Irrational outbursts about the integrity of the armed forces further undermined his position, and by the end of the year McCarthy had been formally censured for conduct unbecoming a member of Congress. US abiding mistrust of communism, however, remains.

AT A GLANCE

With the USA and the Soviet Union bent on a superpower arms race, Senator Joseph McCarthy's one-man mission to seek out communist sympathizers in the nation's midst was over-zealous. His campaign caught many innocent people in the crossfire until Ed Murrow's intervention started to turn the tide.

Above: Sir Roger Bannister pictured in 2004 holding the running shoes in which he had broken the four-minute mile.

Right: Roger Bannister crosses the finish line on May 6, 1954, becoming the fastest human ever recorded over that distance.

AT A GLANCE

Roger Bannister's breaking of the four-minute mile barrier represents one of history's defining sporting moments. Long thought to be impossible, his achievement has become an enduring symbol of winning against overwhelming odds.

ROGER BANNISTER BREAKS THE FOUR-MINUTE MILE

OXFORD, UK
MAY 6, 1954

A medical student who later went on to become a leading neurologist, Roger Bannister had an athletic career vastly different to those of today's leading competitors. In fact, he first began running in 1946 at the late age of 17, having never set foot on a track before, and even in those less professional times his training was far from rigorous. Nevertheless, Bannister showed promise, and was picked as having Olympic potential for the 1948 games, though he did not feel himself sufficiently prepared to run and turned the opportunity down.

Over the following years, Bannister continued to train sporadically but ran well in various athletic meetings although he failed to win any prestigious medals. In 1950, disappointed by his performances, he began to train in earnest. His improvement was dramatic. On December 30, he came first in a mile race with a time of 4:09.9, which he bettered in 1952 with a time of 4:08.3. At the Amateur Athletic Association meet on July 14 of the same year he improved his personal best even further, completing the mile in 4:07.8, and winning first place.

In the 1952 Helsinki Olympics, Bannister came fourth in a tightly run 1500-meter final, with a British record-setting time of 3:46.3, but almost quit running after what he thought of as a failure. However, he decided on a new ambition: to become the first to break the four-minute mile. While this speed was widely thought to be impossible, in fact there was no real basis for the belief. At the time, the world record holder, Gunder Hägg, was just 1.3 seconds over four minutes, and the time had been quickly falling from 4:14.4 at the beginning of the 20th century. And, as Bannister well knew, his great rival, the Australian John Landy, was also close to achieving the 'impossible'. Nevertheless, the myth cast a long shadow, and anyone who shattered it stood to win international acclaim.

By May 1953, Bannister had reduced his time to 4:03.6. By the end of that year, Landy had reached 4:02 and through the early months of 1954 the Australian looked poised to break the four-minute barrier at any moment. Fearing it might be his last chance, Bannister lined up at the starting blocks at a British AAA meet at Iffley Road Track, Oxford, on May 6, 1954. It was a windy day, and he had almost pulled out in order to conserve his energy, but the wind dropped just in time and at the last moment he decided to compete.

As the results were read out, with Bannister standing exhausted on the track, the crowd roared. At the age of 25, he had completed the mile in 3:59.04, smashing the world record and the impossible four-minute barrier. Despite the fact that Landy beat Bannister's time by more than a second just 46 days later, Bannister's achievement stands today as one of the greatest moments in sporting history and is a testament to human triumph.

ELVIS PRESLEY RECORDS 'THAT'S ALL RIGHT' (MAMA)

SUN STUDIOS, MEMPHIS, USA
JULY 5, 1954

When Elvis Aaron Presley arrived at the Sun Studios at 706 Union Avenue in the summer of 1953 to record two songs as a present for his mother, he lit the touch paper on a musical and cultural revolution that continues to this day.

Elvis moved with his parents, Gladys and Vernon Presley, to Memphis at age 13, and was a fan of the city's black-dominated live music scene, secretly frequenting clubs on Beale Street. Sun Records boss Sam Phillips had already recorded bluesmen like Howlin' Wolf, and had long sought a 'white boy who could sing black'; Presley would soon fuse white country with black blues to create rock'n'roll.

It happened when, during a break in an otherwise unproductive session on July 5, 1954, the trio made up of singer Elvis Presley, guitarist Scotty Moore and bassist Bill Black spontaneously struck up an Arthur Crudup blues number, 'That's All Right (Mama)' in a break between takes. The energy with which they mixed country and blues was duplicated on an uptempo reading of Bill Monroe's bluegrass classic 'Blue Moon of Kentucky', and the two songs were released as a single on July 17, 1954.

Reaction in the Memphis area was enthusiastic, even though many listeners were surprised to learn that the voice they were listening to was not that of a black singer. Elvis was no mean performer, and the band's weekly slot on the *Louisiana Hayride* radio show helped them gain fame in the local area. Drummer D. J. Fontana was added, and when Colonel Tom Parker, a wily old pro, became Presley's manager things started moving fast.

Elvis's contract was sold to RCA in late 1955 for $35,000, and his new label promoted his music first nationally and then internationally. TV appearances, a movie debut in *Love Me Tender*, even being drafted into the US Army in March 1958, all added to the legend as Parker pulled the strings. And while public appearances were put on hold for seven years from 1961 as movies and married life took precedence, Elvis had already inspired a generation to pick up a guitar, widening the generation gap.

Elvis Presley was the first and greatest star of the rock'n'roll era, and continued to exert an appeal that for his many millions of fans more than withstood the widespread popularity of Beatlemania, Motown and psychedelia. He remained an icon even after his death from heart failure in August 1977 at his palatial house, Graceland.

Above: The Sun Studios in Memphis, Tennessee, where Elvis Presley first recorded.

Left: Elvis Presley appearing on the Ed Sullivan Show in 1956.

AT A GLANCE

Elvis Presley is credited with creating rock'n'roll, a new music that was adopted by young people bored with postwar austerity and keen to seize opportunity and live life to the full. Just as James Dean portrayed their dreams on the big screen, Presley gave them the soundtrack by which to live and love – and the teenager was born.

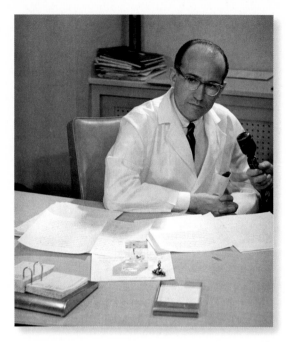

Above: Polio researcher Dr Jonas Salk giving a press conference in 1960.

Right: US President Eisenhower commends Jonas Salk on the fifth anniversary of the doctor's development of a vaccine for polio, 1960.

Inset: A cryo-electron micrograph of the polio virus.

SUCCESSFUL POLIO VACCINE ANNOUNCED TO THE WORLD

UNIVERSITY OF PITTSBURGH, PA., USA
APRIL 12, 1955

Poliomyelitis is a virus that attacks the nervous system and usually occurs in children, causing deformation and paralysis. In the first half of the 20th century this disease affected hundreds of thousands worldwide and was considered a global epidemic. But all that changed in April 1955 when a cure was announced to the world.

The United States appeared to be a hotbed of the disease, which usually struck in the summer months. By the early 1950s, warmer weather was greeted each year with great anxiety, as yet more children and adults would be left dead or crippled by polio outbreaks. Even the late US President Franklin D. Roosevelt was believed to have been left paralyzed by the ailment.

The public reaction of sheer terror to this child-afflicting sickness meant that scientists around the world were racing to discover a cure, a vaccine that would reduce the increasing rate of death and paralysis and one that would herald a breakthrough in modern medicine.

The man who succeeded in this was US virologist Jonas Salk. After others had performed vaccination trials using live versions of polio which resulted in death and crippling, Salk believed protection could be achieved using deactivated forms of the virus. He predicted that by using the non-harmful version of polio, the human body would learn to reject the live form if and when it attacked. With large-scale outbreaks in 1952 and 1953 in the USA, the pressure was on for a resolution.

He had successfully created his vaccine in 1952, but the years of testing that followed prevented its immediate use. But it was in 1955 at his laboratory at the University of Pittsburgh that he was able to announce that the world's first effective vaccine for polio had been discovered.

It was the culmination of a three-year testing program, firstly on animals and later – and most crucially – on humans. Immediately, large-scale immunization programs for children were implemented across the country, and Salk was heralded as a savior.

Years later the virus had been effectively eradicated in the USA and most of the developed world, with cases drastically reduced to just a few thousand; a remarkable turnaround in just half a century.

AT A GLANCE

The epidemic disease known as polio was a danger to all, a fact underlined by news that even US President Franklin D. Roosevelt had suffered from it. The work of US scientist Jonas Salk in using a deactivated form of the virus to immunize children it saved generations from the scourge of this crippling disease.

ROSA PARKS REFUSES TO GIVE UP HER SEAT

MONTGOMERY, ALABAMA, USA
DECEMBER 1, 1955

Above: Rosa Parlos (centre) accompanied by her attorney, Charles D. Langford (right), on her way to jail following her arrest on charges of violating city segregation laws.

Overleaf: Civil rights pioneer Rosa Parks addresses a crowd celebrating the 25th anniversary of the signing of civil rights legislation.

Left: Rosa Parks in 1956, when the Supreme Court ruling banning segregation on Montgomery's public transport vehicles took effect.

AT A GLANCE

Rosa Parks's symbolic refusal to give up her seat for a white person in 1955 was used by civil rights campaigner Martin Luther King Jr as a focal point for protest. The struggle lasted a year, but was the first thread in the unraveling of segregation in the USA.

'No one can understand the actions of Mrs Parks unless he realizes that eventually the cup of endurance runs over, and the human personality cries out, "I can take it no longer." ' So wrote Martin Luther King Jr in 1958. Three years earlier he had been a relatively unknown minister at the Dexter Avenue Baptist Church in Montgomery, Alabama – but then Rosa Parks said No.

When Parks, voluntary secretary of the Montgomery Chapter of the National Association for the Advancement of Colored People (NAACP), refused to vacate her bus seat for a white man after the 'white' section had been filled, she wasn't the first to do so in the segregated South. But that evening she had had enough. She became a focus for all the overflowing anger of the black community at the racist system of segregation which prevailed on buses and in other institutions across the southern states of the USA. "When that white driver stepped back towards [me]," she recalled, "I felt a determination cover my body like a quilt on a winter night."

The driver called the police, who arrested her for breaking the segregation laws. At her trial and conviction four days later, the black community began a boycott of the city buses which held solid for 381 days. In all weathers its 40,000 black commuters chose to share cars, take black-run taxis or walk (sometimes up to 20 miles), until their demands for black bus-drivers, common courtesy and bus seats on a first-come basis were met.

A new organization, the Montgomery Improvement Association, was formed to co-ordinate the boycott. Its president, a recent arrival in the neighborhood, was the young Martin Luther King Jr. His new position put him literally in the line of fire: churches were burned and his home bombed by segregationists during the boycott.

The NAACP won its legal challenge in the Supreme Court and segregation on buses was declared unconstitutional, and the boycott was called off the next day, December 20, 1956. But snipers opened fire on buses, and on King's home, which they also bombed again. King's leadership of the boycott had placed him at the head of the Civil Rights Movement, a powerful voice for its supporters and a dangerous target for its enemies.

Looking back, Rosa Parks commented, "People always say that I didn't give up my seat because I was tired, but that isn't true. No, the only tired I was, was tired of giving in."

Above: Statesmen of six European countries sign the European Common Market Treaty in 1957.

Right: France's Robert Schuman (right), a strong advocate of European union, greeting West German Chancellor Konrad Adenauer.

AT A GLANCE

In the aftermath of the Second World War, world leaders were keen to form alliances that would minimise the chance of another conflict and at the same time encourage economic regeneration through trade. Britain's ties with the Commonwealth left the British outside the European Economic Community, which it eventually joined in 1973. By 2010 its original membership had swelled to 27 countries thanks in part to the admission of former communist states.

TREATIES OF ROME

ITALY
MARCH 25, 1957

Winston Churchill, speaking in the neutral Swiss city of Zurich in 1946, called for 'a kind of United States of Europe' to be set up. The nations of Europe, exhausted by two world wars, were determined to put structures in place that would create a lasting peace.

The first step was the formation of West Germany, incorporating the larger part of the defeated nation into the economic life of the Western world. Then the Treaty of Paris in 1951, drawn up between Italy, France, Belgium, Luxembourg, West Germany and the Netherlands, formed the European Coal and Steel Community, a cross-border marketplace for those industries. It had been proposed a year earlier by the French foreign minister Robert Schuman as a means of making war 'not only unthinkable but materially impossible'.

This limited experiment in international cooperation was successful enough for the same six nations to extend the agreement. In 1957 they signed not one but two treaties in Rome. One set up Euratom, the European Atomic Energy Community, to develop mutual interests in nuclear power. The other, the one commentators mean when they talk about the Treaty of Rome, created the European Economic Community. The EEC was very much a trade-based organization, and became known as the Common Market.

Britain had declined to join the organization because they felt loyal to the many non-European countries that were members or former members of the British Empire or Commonwealth. Although Britain soon saw that it was missing out on EEC benefits, its applications for membership were repeatedly blocked by the French president, Charles de Gaulle. He wanted the EEC to become a third superpower, along with the USA and the USSR, and he objected to British ties with the USA. It was only after his death that Britain was able to negotiate entry to the EEC, which it achieved in 1973.

As the EEC expanded, so did its political aims. The first elections for the European Parliament took place in 1979. Border controls between many of its members were ended by the Shengen Agreement in 1985, and the community dropped the word 'economic' in 1986, becoming the European Union (EU). The fall of communism in 1990 saw the community's rapid expansion eastwards. Then in 2002 the common currency of the Euro was first introduced; by 2010, 16 out of 27 EU member states were using it.

Most of the participating countries consider they have reaped an economic benefit so far as commerce is concerned. While debate about the extent of European political union remains far from peaceful, military war between members of the EU is, as Schuman envisaged, unimaginable.

THE LAUNCH OF SPUTNIK 1

TYURATAM, KAZAKHSTAN
OCTOBER 4, 1957

Above: A back-up version of Sputnik 1 (right) and a replica of Sputnik 2 in a Moscow museum.

Left: Sputnik 1 resting on a metal stand before it was sent into space. The four projecting rods are the satellite's antennae.

Below: This diagram compares the relative orbits of Sputnik 3 and the three orbiting US satellites, Explorer I, Vanguard I, and Explorer III.

AT A GLANCE

The quest for national prestige led the USA and the Soviet Union, the world's nuclear superpowers, to push the boundaries and attempt to put a satellite into earth orbit. Sputnik 1 won the first round of the Space Race for the USSR, and the Russians also put the first man into space, three and a half years later.

The launch of the satellite Sputnik 1 is generally celebrated as the start of the space race between the USA and the Soviet Union. Whatever the motivation, the rush to reach milestones in extraterrestrial exploration drove the two governments to inspiring voyages of discovery in science and space unimagined 30 years before. Although huge amounts of government money have been spent on the projects, the benefit to humanity from technologies first developed for the exploration of space is already incalculable, and although future exploration is subject to political whim, its potential is as vast as the universe.

The first rival steps in the Space Race were arguably taken not in 1957 but in the summer of 1955, within ten days of each other. On July 29 that year, the USA announced that one of its key scientific events planned for the International Geophysical Year, 1957–58, would be the launch of an artificial satellite; and on August 9, the Soviet Union gave an identical go-ahead for the Sputnik program.

In the USA, the job of development was given to the US Naval Research Laboratory. But while they were working on a test vehicle for the first stage of their Vanguard launch rocket, news reached them of the successful launch by the USSR of Sputnik 1 on October 4, 1957. The blow to US pride echoed round the globe. To add insult to injury, Russia encouraged the world's radio operators to record the satellite's beep-beep signal as it passed 150 miles overhead every 96 minutes.

Sputnik 2 soon followed, carrying Laika the dog into space on November 3. The catastrophic failure of two US Vanguard launches over the next four months only deepened US gloom, and the US navy was embarrassed even more when the US army's rival Explorer 1 (hastily revived after the triumph of Sputnik 1) became the USA's first artificial satellite, on February 1, 1958. The eventual success of Vanguard 1, on March 17 that year, was swiftly overshadowed by the launch of Sputnik 3 two months later.

Vanguard 1 was the first solar-powered satellite, and the US navy may take comfort in the fact that it has outlived all its predecessors; it transmitted for seven years, and in 2010 it is still up there while its predecessors have dropped out of orbit and burnt up on re-entry. Sputnik 1's conventional batteries powered its information-laden beeps for a mere three weeks, and it fell back to Earth, mission accomplished, on January 4, 1958.

ORAL CONTRACEPTIVE PILL APPROVED

USA
MAY 9, 1960

After being tested in Puerto Rico and Haiti in 1956, the oral contraceptive pill was approved by the US Food and Drug Administration on May 9, 1960. It went on sale in the USA in the spring of 1961 under the brand names Enovid and Norlutin, the price for a four-week supply being $10.

The Pill, as it universally became known, has been described as the most significant medical advance of the 20th century. It was developed by American biologist Dr Gregory Pincus, who had been approached in 1953 by family planning pioneers Margaret Sanger and Katherine McCormick. He was able to build on the research of Frank Colton, a chemist at the Searle Company, and in 1957 the Pill was released as a treatment for gynecological disorders.

The first version contained the hormones estrogen and progestin, which were synthetically produced to mimic the body's natural hormones and suppress ovulation. In the early years, the Pill contained around 50 mcg of estrogen, and this has since been reduced to around 30 mcg due to health concerns. Progestin levels have been reduced to a tenth of their original level.

The Pill allowed women greater sexual freedom. Within five years, 40 per cent of married US women under age 30 who used contraception were using the Pill. But its influence grew still further in the early 1970s when the age of majority was reduced to 18 years. Young, single women could now 'go on the Pill', and within a couple of years, 73 per cent of all single women age 18 and 19 using contraception were using the Pill.

The Puerto Rican study had been monitored for adverse side effects; one in five women reported nausea and/or weight gain. Preliminary findings showed a reduction in breast and uterine cancer, but health worries persisted: after congressional hearings on the Pill's safety, the US Food and Drug Administration was prompted in 1970 to order drug manufacturers to provide information about possible risks and side effects with each prescription package; these warnings were a first for any prescription drug.

In the USA, the number of users fell in the early 1980s from around 10 million women to around 8.4 million because of the concerns. Research suggested possible links between use of the Pill and breast cancer, strokes, heart attack and blood clots. Some of the concerns were linked to the hormone levels in the pill; these have now been lowered again.

Above: Dr Gregory Pincus, the man regarded as the inventor of the contraceptive pill.

Left: A pack of birth control pills, as used by millions of women around the world.

AT A GLANCE

The development of an oral contraceptive pill, preventing pregnancy by suppressing ovulation, has been described as the most significant medical advance of the 20th century. It gave women the ability to control their fertility and inevitably opened the doors to increased sexual activity, for better or worse. The Swinging Sixties was on the horizon …

Above: How the US nation viewed the first televised presidential debate between Vice President Richard Nixon and Senator John F. Kennedy in 1960.

Right: Presidential nominees Kennedy and Nixon meet, prior to their first debate.

Below: A large crowd gathered to greet Kennedy as he arrived in Chicago for his televised debate.

FIRST TELEVISED PRESIDENTIAL DEBATE

CHICAGO, USA
SEPTEMBER 26, 1960

Republican Vice President Richard Nixon and his Democratic opponent, Senator John F. Kennedy, took part in the first ever televised US Presidential debate in 1960. It took place in the Chicago television studio of WBBM-TV and was carried by all major US television and radio stations.

Questions were posed by representatives of the TV channels NBC, CBS, ABC and Mutual, with Howard K. Smith of CBS acting as moderator. The one-hour show saw both candidates score points, Nixon claiming that Kennedy's proposed spending program would cost the taxpayers billions of dollars while Kennedy accused the vice president of 'paying only lip service' to the concept of increasing the minimum wage to a dollar an hour. Kennedy also attacked Nixon's plans for building more schools and health care for the aged, as being inferior to his own.

The show attracted over 66 million viewers out of a population of 179 million, making it one of the most-watched broadcasts in US television history. Yet most viewers polled after watching the show said their voting intentions had not been changed. But when the election on November 8 was won by Kennedy by a narrow margin, the televised debate was thought to have made the difference in what was an extremely close election.

Kennedy, 43 years old to Nixon's 47, was considered more televisual. He had recently returned from vacation and was tanned and relaxed, his navy suit standing out better than Nixon's grey, which blended into the background. Nixon himself had a somewhat haggard appearance due not only to his refusal to wear television make-up but also to fatigue; he had recently been hospitalized for a knee operation and, according to one commentator, appeared 'unshaven, tired and sweaty' under the lights.

It was not until 1976 that a second series of televised presidential debates was held during the election campaign, this time between Jimmy Carter and Gerald Ford. Since then, these televised debates have been a regular feature in the hustings, as have vice-presidential debates. The UK adopted the format for the first time in 2010, when leaders of the Labour, Liberal Democrat and Conservative parties all took part in a three-way debate.

AT A GLANCE

The first ever televised US Presidential debate took place in 1960 between Richard Nixon and John F. Kennedy. While its effect on the result could not be measured, from this moment on the new medium of television played an ever-growing part in presidential elections. Candidate-centered television campaigns were launched, and it became important for politicians to be well versed in the arts of communicating via the camera.

MRBM FIELD LAUNCH SITE
SAN CRISTOBAL NO 1
14 OCTOBER 1962

ERECTOR/LAUNCHER EQUIPMENT

TENT AREAS

EQUIPMENT

ERECTOR/LAUNCHER EQUIPMENT

2 MISSILE TRAILERS

CONSTRUCTION

KHRUSHCHEV AGREES TO REMOVE MISSILES

CUBA
OCTOBER 28, 1962

AT A GLANCE

One and a half decades of superpower posturing came to a head in 1962 when the USA and the Soviet Union focused on the Caribbean island of Cuba, where Soviet missile sites had been established, and stared each other down; the first one to blink might possibly ignite a worldwide nuclear conflict. However, the standoff was resolved, the missiles were removed and an uneasy détente was established.

In 1961 the USA made an effort, with an invasion of US-trained Cuban exiles, to overthrow Cuba's communist regime, but failed embarrassingly. The exiles, landing at the Bay of Pigs on the island, were defeated within three days by the USSR-backed Cuban army.

It was a humiliation which former US President Eisenhower had predicted would 'embolden the Soviets to do something that they would otherwise not do' – and 18 months later the Russians began to install nuclear missiles on the strategically important island of Cuba. It was a response to continuing US harassment of the island on land and by sea, as well as the installation of US missiles in Turkey, in easy striking range of Moscow.

US U-2 reconnaissance planes first spotted the new missile sites in Cuba on October 15, 1962, and a week later President Kennedy announced a naval blockade of the island to prevent the arrival of further warheads. He declared that any attack launched from Cuba on any target would be considered an attack on the USA, and liable to a counter-attack on the USSR.

For two weeks the world held its breath as troops massed in Florida, the nearest mainland point to Cuba. The US military commanders, as hawkish as ever, had argued for a pre-emptive invasion of Cuba, and Kennedy assured them that if Cuba shot down any US spyplanes he would authorize an attack on the missile sites. It seemed a very real possibility that the USA and the USSR would soon be at nuclear war with each other. According to the media, this had the overwhelming support of Americans, but it resulted in anti-war demonstrations around the world.

In the end, the Soviet ships turned back without trying to breach the US blockade. The Soviet leader, Nikita Khrushchev, offered to remove the missiles in return for a promise that the USA would not invade Cuba. But while Kennedy was discussing this offer with his staff, news arrived of the shooting down of a US spy plane over Cuba, triggering fresh demands on Kennedy for a military assault. He, however, correctly deduced that it was an isolated action by a rogue Soviet officer, and instead of ordering a retaliation accepted Khrushchev's terms.

The Cuban missile crisis led directly to the establishment of a hotline between the White House and the Kremlin, and to the quiet removal three months later of US missiles in Turkey. It was a landmark of common sense in Cold War diplomacy. Two superpowers had stepped back from the brink, and the world breathed again.

Inset: An aerial photograph of MRBM Field Launch Site No. 1 in San Cristobal, Cuba, taken by US Intelligence forces in October 1962.

Left: The Soviet freighter **Anosov** *leaves Cuba with eight ballistic missiles on board as the crisis eases.*

Above: Leaders of the March on Washington link arms as they move along Constitution Avenue. Martin Luther King is seventh from right.

Right: Thousands of people gather at the Lincoln Memorial and around its reflecting pool to hear featured speakers at the conclusion of the March on Washington.

Overleaf: A section of the 200,000 people who came to Washington, D.C. to demand civil rights.

Below: Martin Luther King Jr gives his famous 'I Have a Dream' speech in front of the Lincoln Memorial.

AT A GLANCE

Martin Luther King's 'I have a dream' speech, delivered from the steps of the Lincoln Memorial in the US capital in 1963, inspired a generation and encapsulated the cause of racial equality. It has been voted top American speech of the 20th century.

MARCH ON WASHINGTON, DC

USA
AUGUST 28, 1963

In 1963, US President John F. Kennedy's government was working towards passing a civil rights bill meant to bring the USA into the modern world by creating racial equality in society, employment and education. But even though it was eight years after Rosa Parks had said No, entrenched prejudices still held sway in certain states, especially in the Deep South.

A civil rights march on the nation's capital, Washington, DC, planned for August 28, 1963, was intended to show support for the proposed bill and raise awareness of the inequalities still suffered by millions of black people in the USA at the time.

The figurehead was clergyman Dr Martin Luther King Jr, but in reality the march was a collective effort made by many different factions of the civil rights movement. It was chiefly organized by Asa Philip Randolph, chairman of civil rights faction The Brotherhood of Sleeping Car Porters. But not all civil rights campaigners were on board, most notably Malcolm X, head of religious faction The Nation of Islam, who did not participate in the march and strongly criticized it, saying that white participation in it was counterproductive.

The event went ahead regardless, with over 250,000 people converging on Washington, DC, in the largest public protest in the USA's history. The march ended at the Lincoln Memorial, where there were speeches from leaders and music from artists sympathetic to the cause, including folk singers Bob Dylan and Joan Baez.

The highlight of the event was an emotive and inspiring sermon-style speech by Martin Luther King that was picked up by US television and the international media. The most quoted line was: 'I have a dream that one day this nation will rise up and live out the true meaning of its creed. We hold these truths to be self-evident, that all men are created equal'.

The Kennedy civil rights bill was passed in 1964, outlawing segregation and allowing all men and women in the USA to vote. And while racism might not have been eradicated, the bill paved the way for change, ultimately resulting in the election of America's first black president, Barack Obama, in 2009.

The 1963 March on Washington was a pivotal moment in not just US but world history. Martin Luther King, like President Kennedy, died a violent death and never saw the full fruits of his struggle, but the change in American society that he helped create was undeniable.

ASSASSINATION OF PRESIDENT KENNEDY

DALLAS, TEXAS, USA
NOVEMBER 22, 1963

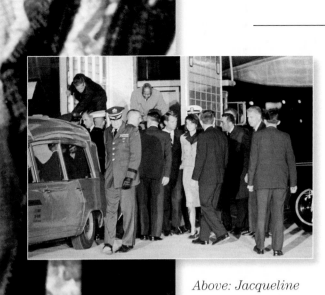

Above: Jacqueline Kennedy watches as her husband's body is placed in an ambulance at Andrews Air Force Base.

Left: President Kennedy, First Lady Jacqueline Kennedy, and Texas Governor John Connally ride in the motorcade in Dallas, moments before the President and the Governor were shot.

AT A GLANCE

The assassin of the 35th president of the USA has still not been definitively identified, despite the fact that the event was captured on film. What is certain is that the charismatic 46-year-old who had defeated Richard Nixon in the 1960 US presidential election still had much he wanted to achieve.

When President John F. Kennedy was assassinated in Dealey Plaza in downtown Dallas in 1963, the bullets ricocheted around the world. It caused the death of a postwar optimism and innocence which had flourished in the economic prosperity of the 1950s. That bullet, in taking the life of the USA's virile and youthful leader, also affected millions who admired him. In the days that followed, most of the world felt stunned.

People simply could not believe that anyone would want to kill such a popular figure, and that disbelief has expressed itself ever since in the many conspiracy theories – often conflicting with one another – that have arisen almost from the moment JFK was hit. One gunman or two – the Mafia – the FBI – the CIA – pro-Castro Cubans, anti-Castro Cubans – even Vice President Lyndon B. Johnson … all these and more have been the focus for elaborately conceived 'solutions' to the murder.

The official version of events is that a single gunman, Lee Harvey Oswald, fired on the presidential motorcade from his place of work, the Texas School Book Depository, overlooking the plaza. Oswald was a mentally unstable ex-Marine who had defected to the Soviet Union and then returned to the USA where, seven months before Dallas, he had tried to assassinate a retired US major-general. Oswald denied involvement in Kennedy's assassination, and the truth may never be known: he was shot dead two days later by Jack Ruby, a Dallas nightclub owner who, it is said, took it upon himself to avenge the USA's loss.

At least five separate investigations into the shooting of President Kennedy have taken place since then. The Warren Commission was the first, set up by newly sworn-in President Johnson a week after the event. It found that Oswald had acted alone in committing the crime – but a 1979 enquiry by the House Select Committee on Assassinations lent weight to the possibility that a second gunman was involved, who fired (and missed) from a grassy knoll on the other side of the car.

To this day every witness statement, every audio or video recording, and every artifact of evidence from the scene is examined and re-examined in the hope of new insight into the who and why of JFK's assassination. In 1981 one author even had Oswald's body exhumed.

Above: Host Ed Sullivan speaks with the Beatles on the set of his television show at CBS studios in Manhattan.

Right: Paul McCartney and John Lennon pose holding their guitars on the set of **The Ed Sullivan Show** *at the CBS television studios in Manhattan.*

AT A GLANCE

Just as Elvis Presley had dominated the Fifties music scene so the Beatles bestrode the Sixties. It took just one appearance on American television by these four young men from Liverpool to conquer the country where rock'n'roll had been born less than a decade earlier. And unlike Elvis, they were screened below as well as above the waist.

BEATLES APPEAR ON THE ED SULLIVAN SHOW

NEW YORK, USA
FEBRUARY 9, 1964

Pop sensations the Beatles had burst out of the northern UK seaport of Liverpool to top the UK charts with their first two albums in 1963, their first full year as Parlophone/EMI recording artists. Their concerts attracted screaming teenage girls, resulting in what the British press called Beatlemania. It took a single TV appearance in February 1964 to provoke similar hysterical scenes in the USA.

Things had been slow to start Stateside, the situation not helped by a small label, VeeJay, being granted the rights to early releases before Capitol Records (EMI's American arm) realized that they'd signed away a goldmine. The 'Fab Four' made their first live US TV appearance in February, 1964 on The Ed Sullivan Show, which had been running since 1948 and had helped break Elvis Presley nationally in 1956. While Elvis (filmed only from the waist upwards to avoid the risk of upsetting some viewers) had created the Fifties' highest viewing figures, the Beatles would eclipse even him.

They appeared for 13 minutes, singing five songs – 'All My Loving', 'Till there Was You' and 'She Loves You' in the first half, followed by 'I Saw Her Standing There' and 'I Want To Hold Your Hand'. It was the first of three contracted shows, for which they were paid $10,000. Presley's manager Colonel Parker sent a telegram of good wishes that was read out by Sullivan. The show was watched by 73 million viewers, a staggering 40 per cent of the US population.

From Elvis onwards, the flow of music between the USA and Britain had been one-way; now it had suddenly changed direction. The Beatles accounted for 60 per cent of all records sold in North America during February 1964 – a statistic unlikely ever to be repeated – and The Ed Sullivan Show later gave similar exposure to the Searchers, Gerry and the Pacemakers, the Dave Clark Five and other members of the 'British Invasion' that followed in the Beatles' wake.

As the Beatles' earlier singles followed no 1, 'I Want To Hold Your Hand', up the chart, April 1964 saw all top five positions occupied by the group. They played only two dates at Washington Coliseum and New York's Carnegie Hall plus another Ed Sullivan Show, but they returned in August to tour the States to tour more widely. Right across the country, UK-style Beatlemania inevitably ensued.

The year ended with 'I Feel Fine' atop the Billboard charts; this song was the group's sixth American chart-topping single of the year. They retained a strong following in the country for years, well past their last live date in San Francisco in August 1966. Ed Sullivan's TV show continued until 1971, its host dying three years later.

FIRST HEART TRANSPLANT

CAPE TOWN, SOUTH AFRICA
DECEMBER 3, 1967

In 1967 an operation was carried out in Cape Town, South Africa, that revolutionized surgery as we knew it, and started the ball rolling on a procedure that would save millions of lives. On December 3, Christiaan Barnard completed the world's first full heart transplant.

Barnard was a surgeon from Beaufort West, South Africa, who had travelled to the USA as a 34-year-old postgraduate in 1956, specializing in cardiac surgery. He returned to South Africa two years later, to the Groote Schuur Hospital teaching facility where he began his career with a residency, assembling its first cardiac team.

He prepared for the milestone procedure by performing South Africa's first kidney transplant, in October 1967. He was already seen as one of the country's top surgeons, and with several completed heart transplants on animals the next step was clear.

The patient was chosen; Louis Washkansky had incurable heart disease and, at 54, was still relatively young. With the end in sight, he had no hesitation in agreeing to the operation. His donor had to come through tragic circumstance, in the form of Denise Darvall, a young woman killed in a road accident.

Barnard's 30-strong team, including his brother Marius, took five hours to complete the transplant from Darvall to Washkansky, but at its conclusion the heart was beating with no mechanical assistance. Tragedy struck just 18 days later, however, as Washkansky died from severe pneumonia; his fragile immune system could not resist the infection so soon after the procedure.

Despite this, the transplant was considered a huge success, as Washkansky's new heart continued to beat unaided right up until his death. Further attempts were longer-lasting, with one patient, Dirk van Zyl, living on for 23 years after his 1971 operation, to the age of 68.

Since the first surgery, thousands of people have undergone successful heart transplants, though a lack of donors has kept the number from rising faster. British surgeon Sir Terrence English performed the world's first heart and lung transplant in 1984.

Above: Surgeon Christiaan Barnard shows an X-ray image of Louis Washkansky's chest taken during the historic first heart transplant.

Left: Members of Christiaan Barnard's surgical team perform open-heart surgery in the theater where the Washkansky operation was carried out.

Below: Louis Washkansky, the middle-aged grocer who accepted the heart of Denise Darvall.

AT A GLANCE

The actions of Christiaan Barnard and his team of surgeons in South Africa in 1967 set a new benchmark in surgical procedures. In transplanting a working heart from one human being to another it furthered our ability to prolong life, and it was a truly world-changing achievement.

213

PARIS RIOTS AND GENERAL STRIKE

FRANCE
MAY, 1968

Above: A young man helps an injured woman during a student riot in Paris in 1968. Police brutality against the protesters evinced a huge wave of sympathy for their cause across France and throughout the rest of the world.

Left: Students hurl bricks at police on the streets of Paris on May 7, 1968.

Overleaf: A policeman faces demonstrators in Paris, May 1968. During that month, millions of angry students and workers took to the streets to protest against the restrictions of the conservative government of Charles de Gaulle.

AT A GLANCE

Fuelled by left-wing politics and the revolutionary atmosphere of the sixties, the cataclysmic student-led events in France during May 1968 almost brought down a government, heralding a shift in French society away from the conservative ways of the past and into a new, more liberal, era.

The events that would lead to mass violence on the streets of Paris, and two-thirds of the French workforce going on strike, began on March 22, 1968, at the Parisian University of Nanterre. Students appealing for a more liberal regime at the university took over an administration building and the police were called. Although the demonstrators left peacefully, many were later threatened with expulsion, and after weeks of growing tensions the university was shut down on May 2.

The students' cause was taken up by their peers at the nearby Sorbonne University and, on May 6, 20,000 young people marched through the streets of Paris, protesting the closure of Nanterre. They were met by police armed with batons and tear gas. Barricades were thrown up and the students and their supporters responded by throwing paving slabs. Hundreds were arrested, but by the following day their numbers had been swelled by thousands more students and young people. Meeting at the Arc de Triomphe, the demonstrators demanded that their fellows be released, charges dropped, and the schools reopened. When told that the government had agreed, they returned to their campuses – only to find them still full of police.

On May 10, massive crowds gathered again on the Rive Gauche and, after talks with government representatives broke down, rioting began in earnest. Once again the police reacted with a heavy hand, and France recoiled as hundreds of their young people were seen to be arrested and dragged away bleeding. On May 13, a general strike called in sympathy with the students coincided with a million people gathering. So the French prime minister, Georges Pompidou, promised to release all demonstrators and reopen the universities. But it seemed that France was aflame with revolutionary zeal. Students declared the Sorbonne a 'people's university', while in industry, 10 million French workers were on strike. The French president, Charles de Gaulle, went into hiding while his supporters organized a counter-demonstration on the streets of Paris.

The civil unrest ended as abruptly as it had begun. De Gaulle announced that elections would be held on June 23, and demanded an end to the strikes. Police occupied the Sorbonne again, many left-wing organizations were outlawed and de Gaulle was triumphant in the elections. Nevertheless, it seemed that the British and American sixties revolution had been effected in France in a single month. The traditional French morality and paternalistic society gave way to a more modern France where equality, sexual liberation and human rights gained precedence over authority, religion and patriotism. Now almost legendary, the events have since been immortalized in film and literature, and are seen as one of the great revolutionary moments of the 1960s.

STONEWALL RIOTS

GREENWICH VILLAGE, NEW YORK CITY
JUNE 28–29, 1969

In the decades following World War II, the persecution of homosexual and transgendered men and women in the USA reached a peak. Suspected homosexuals were precipitately fired from government jobs and ejected from the military, while the FBI kept secret files on private individuals. The police relentlessly enforced anti-gay laws, raiding bars and arresting anyone who could not produce identification or whose clothing did not conform to gender expectations. Many were later 'exposed' in the press. It was widely believed that homosexuality was a mental disorder, and those who 'suffered' got sent to mental hospitals.

All this changed after Saturday June 28, 1969, when police raided a Mafia-run gay club in Greenwich Village, New York City, at 1.20 am. Over the years such raids had become commonplace, and the Stonewall Inn at 51 & 53 Christopher Street had been raided on average once a month since it had opened in 1966.

It had about 200 customers that night and, as the police sealed the exits, it soon became clear that this was not going to be a normal raid. Many would not hand their identification papers over, and the transvestites refused to go quietly. The situation soured further when policemen began groping lesbian customers while frisking them. As usual, anyone not arrested was told to leave, and a large crowd of them began to gather by the door, swelled by passers-by. As the police began acting more aggressively, the crowd began applauding those who were being handled roughly. Soon a chant of 'We Shall Overcome' had started and shouts of 'Gay Power!' were heard. When a lesbian was hit with a nightstick, the crowd exploded into full-scale rioting, throwing cans, bottles and bricks as the police took refuge inside.

The number of rioters grew to over 600 as homosexuals and sympathizers joined the fray. Police attempted to arrest as many as they could, and furious fighting broke out while other demonstrators formed singing chorus lines to mock the officers, who responded by rushing them with nightsticks. By 4 am, the police had been forced to withdraw.

The next night, thousands flocked to the Stonewall Inn. Rioting broke out again, and those involved recalled later that it was as if a dam had burst after years of being restricted to secret expression of sexuality. Within months of the riots, gay liberation groups appeared across the USA, and in other countries as well. New magazines were soon being published demanding equality for homosexuals, and on the first anniversary of the riots Gay Pride marches were held in New York, Chicago and Los Angeles. The next year, many other cities followed suit. Around the world gay men and women, as well as transsexuals and the transgendered, began to proudly demand full civil rights, a process that has fundamentally shifted perceptions of homosexuality across the Western world.

Above: The scene of the historic riots is now commemorated by a plaque.

Left: The Stonewall Inn, where gay liberation began, has been recently renovated and is now a Greenwich Village landmark.

AT A GLANCE

The Stonewall Riots in Greenwich Village, New York City, in 1969 saw the customers of a gay bar react violently to police oppression enforcing laws designed to persecute homosexuals. The riots proved to be a spark that caused an inferno: in their wake, gay, lesbian, bisexual, and transgendered people around the world formed organizations to demand equality and respect.

Above: Astronaut Neil Armstrong leaves a footprint on the surface of the Moon at Tranquility Base.

Right: Buzz Aldrin stands beside an American flag at Tranquility Base on the surface of the moon during the Apollo 11 *mission.*

Overleaf: Buzz Aldrin heads back to the Lunar Module Eagle *having deployed an array of scientific testing equipment.*

AT A GLANCE

One man's first steps on the moon ended the sixties on an optimistic note, allowing the USA to forget Vietnam and the Kennedy assassination, and celebrate the achievement of winning the 'Space Race'. Neil Armstrong and his crew made history, even if subsequent decades have seen the focus of exploration switched elsewhere.

MAN LANDS ON THE MOON

JULY 20, 1969

It was an event so unbelievable and significant that some claim it did not even occur, and conspiracy theories persist to this day. But when the pictures of a man walking on the moon was shown live in 1969, the world watched in awe.

The United States and the Soviet Union had been involved in what had been dubbed the Space Race since the Soviet's launch of its Sputnik 1 *satellite* in 1957. Both nations wanted to be considered the planet's dominant force, on land and on sea, in the air and in space; the high point of that dominance would be landing the first human on the moon. With millions of dollars ploughed into the North American Space Administration (NASA), it was the USA that won the race, with the Apollo 11 mission launching on July 16, 1969.

Its crew was headed by former navy aviator Neil Armstrong, accompanied by fellow astronauts Michael Collins and Edwin 'Buzz' Aldrin. Their Saturn V rocket blasted off from the Kennedy Space Center in Florida just after 9.30 a.m., aiming to make history. Four days later, the lunar module Eagle, manned by Armstrong and Aldrin, detached from the Columbia command module that still contained Collins, and began its descent to the moon's surface. Their destination was a lunar plain known as the Sea of Tranquility. On reaching the surface, Armstrong reported, "Houston, Tranquility Base here. The Eagle has landed."

Six and a half hours after landing on the surface, Neil Armstrong became the first man to set foot on the moon. With 600 million eyes watching on Earth, he uttered the immortal words, "That's one small step for man, one giant leap for mankind."

Aldrin soon joined him and the pair spent time photographing the surface and the lunar module and taking soil samples for analysis before planting a US flag. They talked over a radio phone with President Richard Nixon, which he described as 'the most historic phone call ever made from the White House'.

The crew of Apollo 11 splashed back down on Earth on July 24, in the middle of the Pacific Ocean. Picked up by a US Navy vessel, they returned to land and spent three weeks in quarantine. They emerged to mass adulation and fame, the only three humans in history to have set foot on another body in space.

The Apollo program saw six more lunar landings completed in the next three years, before NASA's budget decreased and attention turned to other experiments. But it is the moment when a man took his first steps on the moon that linger in the memory.

Above: President Nixon meets with children wearing Mao Tse-tung buttons during his visit to China.

Left: President of the United States of America Richard Nixon and Premier of the People's Republic of China, Zhou Enlai, applaud a sports contest in China, during Nixon's historic 1972 visit to the country.

AT A GLANCE

President Nixon's unexpected overtures to China in the early seventies broke two decades of silence between the USA and China. It was an act which, together with his similar attempts at a rapprochement with the Soviet Union, earned the president a second term in the White House.

PRESIDENT NIXON VISITS CHINA

CHINA
FEBRUARY 21, 1972

It was an unexpected olive branch that would become a historic event. After two decades of acrimonious relations between the two countries, US President Richard Nixon took the surprise step of visiting the People's Republic of China, in a move that would begin the healing process between the two countries.

At his inauguration in 1968, Nixon proclaimed, "The greatest honor history can bestow is the title of peacemaker." But few then would have predicted his actions a few years later; on his election, Nixon, along with the whole of America, had been a determined opponent of communism, and the country was at odds with the Soviet Union because of it. With China a communist nation, there looked to be no amicable future between the two, either.

There were however a few factors behind Nixon's visit; the US general election was just months away, and his critics would argue that improving the long-running poor relations with China would be beneficial to his re-election campaign.

Also, the meeting between US and Chinese table tennis athletes Glenn Cowan and Zhuang Zedong, which had been covered in the press and adopted by the Chinese as an official diplomatic move by the USA, provided evidence of a thaw in relations between the two countries.

After the foundations had been laid by Nixon's national security advisor, Henry Kissinger, in a secret visit the previous year, the President landed on Chinese soil on February 21, 1972. The week-long visit provided a visual treat for the American media, with some of the first images of China being broadcast in nearly two decades. Behind the PR masterpiece, however, was the intention of creating a new alliance, punctuated by an immediate meeting with China's leader, Chairman Mao.

The conclusion of the visit saw the announcement and signing of the Shanghai Communiqué, which outlined the intention of the USA and China to create a stronger relationship, though the USA's ambiguous stance on the ownership of Taiwan would prevent a complete normalization of relations. Seven years later, full diplomatic relations were achieved between the two countries; this was announced in the Joint Communiqué on the Establishment of Diplomatic Relations of 1979.

The initial surprise of Nixon's visit to China was eclipsed by the seven-day media circus that followed, and the positive diplomatic outcome. Nixon described his visit as 'the week that changed the world.'

FIRST HOME VIDEO GAMES CONSOLE IS LAUNCHED

USA
AUGUST 1972

In 1951, television engineer Ralph H. Baer had a novel idea, suggesting to his employers at Lorel Electronics that the TV sets they were making could be used to display interactive games generated by a separate unit. His bosses dismissed the proposal, and Baer did nothing more about it for another 15 years until 1966, when he produced a paper that set out his idea more fully. At this time he was working as a chief engineer and designer at the military electronics company Sanders Associates; joined on the project by two colleagues from Sanders, Baer began to construct prototypes, finally building a machine called the Brown Box in 1968. Having applied for the first ever patent on a video game, Baer demonstrated his machine to leading television manufacturers in the United States. In 1969, he signed a contract with Magnavox.

Released in August 1972, the Magnavox Odyssey console came with two player control units, colored overlays that could be fixed over a TV screen, and 6 'game card' cartridges. The 12 games initially available included Tennis, Hockey, Simon Says, Haunted House and Roulette, although more were added to the range, including Shooting Gallery, which came with a light gun that players pointed at the screen to register a hit.

Priced at US$99, the original console enjoyed only modest success by today's standards, with many prospective customers put off by the assumption that only a Magnavox television could support it. Even so, it sold about 100,000 units and inspired other manufacturers to produce their own video games consoles, beginning a series of legal actions in which Magnavox successfully defended the patent. In 1978, the company released the Odyssey2 (known in Europe as the Philips Videopac G7000), an improved design that now included sound and games that didn't need separate scoresheets. While it was now in competition with second generation consoles, such as the massively successful Atari 2600 which introduced the world to Pac Man, by 1983 the Odyssey2 had sold a million units in the USA, and also inspired third-party developers to begin producing games cartridges, a trend that continues with today's games consoles.

Since then, the world has become hooked on video gaming, and consoles have become ever more sophisticated, their programmers leading the way in technological advances, just as racing car designers lead the way for the motor industry. In the few decades since Ralph Baer designed the innovative Brown Box, video gaming has become a multi-billion-dollar industry and produces games with graphics and interactivity levels that players of the Magnavox Odyssey could not have imagined.

Above: A young boy plays noughts and crosses on the Fairchild Video Entertainment System. Released in 1976, this was the first games console to feature plug-in cartridges. This meant that new games could be released and the user would not be limited only to those that were on the console itself, as was the case with all previous games consoles.

Left: Today's video games consoles demonstrate the staggeringly swift evolution of technology since Baer began experimenting with video games in the late 1960s. In this photograph, Pete Sampras demonstrates a tennis game for the motion-sensitive Wii console.

AT A GLANCE

Based on a prototype machine known as the Brown Box, designed by Ralph H. Baer, the Magnavox Odyssey2, released in the USA in 1972, began a video gaming revolution that has swept the world and now generates tens of billions of dollars each year.

US TROOPS LEAVE VIETNAM

VIETNAM
MARCH 29, 1973

Above: The last planeload of US troops out of Vietnam arrives home, March 1973.

Left: Alan L. Brunstrom, a recently released prisoner of war, greets his family on his arrival at Travis Air Force Base, California, 1973.

Below: American soldiers relax with their baggage as they await their flight home, March 1973.

After over 13 years, and in spite of determined opposition from large sections of the USA, in 1973 President Nixon finally declared his country's withdrawal from the conflict in Vietnam.

America's disillusionment with the war and how it was handled reached a climax in the aftermath of the Tet Offensive of 1968; the force of the communist attack had brought the realization that the conflict was far from over, as had been suggested earlier, and a beleaguered President Johnson did not run for re-election.

The escalation of the USA's involvement had fatally damaged Johnson's presidency, and it looked to continue with Nixon at the helm; the bombing of Cambodia in March 1969 and the number of US fatalities rising above 33,000 both had a strong negative effect on public opinion.

Despite the removal of 25,000 troops in June 1969, the exposing of the My Lai massacre five months later in which more than 500 innocent Vietnamese were killed by rampaging American troops, and then the Kent State Shootings of May 1970 in which four students were shot dead by the National Guard, only served to increase protestors' resolve. The US presence in South Vietnam continued to decrease steadily; at the turn of 1972 just over 130,000 troops remained.

The end of the war – as far as America was concerned – was in sight as that year came to a close. The Paris Peace Accords signed by North Vietnam and the USA on January 27, 1973, declared a ceasefire throughout southeast Asia (Vietnam, Cambodia and Laos); the USA would withdraw its remaining troops, and American prisoners of war would be returned. The agreement recognized the South Vietnamese government remaining in power under President Thieu, but also permitted North Vietnamese troops to remain in the South.

On March 29, 1973, two months after the peace agreement, Hanoi freed the remaining American prisoners of war and the last US troops left South Vietnam, but 7,000 employees of the US Department of Defense remained in South Vietnam to aid the ongoing battle. North Vietnam eventually took South Vietnam's capital Saigon in April 1975.

It was a blow for the US's policy of containment, but the conflict had raged for so long that priorities had shifted. Nixon had turned his attention to détente with the Soviet Union and China, a policy that had succeeded in getting him re-elected for a second term. He also achieved popular support for ending the longest war in the country's history.

AT A GLANCE

The Vietnam War had always been controversial, and President Nixon's decision to withdraw in 1973 finally recognized the fact that this particular part of the USA's global battle against communism could not be won. The majority of Americans agreed with him, some 50,000 US troops and nearly two million Vietnamese having lost their lives.

Above: Sheikh Ahmed Zaki Yamani, Saudi Arabia's Oil Minister, attends talks on the oil crisis, 1973.

Right: The sign speaks for itself – US motorists run on empty during the 1973 oil crisis.

AT A GLANCE

October 1973's oil crisis – the six-month embargo placed on exports by the Arab petroleum exporting counties – had a massive effect on the USA and it's allies' infrastructure. Peace efforts in the Middle East saw the ban lifted, but the West would never again control oil prices, as the balance of power had changed irrevocably. And despite subsequent attempts to find alternative sources of energy, the West still relies on oil.

OIL CRISIS

KUWAIT
OCTOBER 1973

The 1973 oil crisis began in October of that year when members of Organization of Arab Petroleum Exporting Countries (OAPEC), based in Kuwait, instigated an oil embargo against the USA and its allies in response to US support for Israel in the Yom Kippur war. The catalyst had been the request by President Nixon to Congress to put $2.2 billion towards emergency aid to Israel.

President Nixon asked US citizens to cut back on oil consumption to reduce the effects of the embargo: he asked gas stations to close voluntarily on Sundays, ordered a cutback on home heating oil deliveries and a 15 per cent cut in gas consumption, and reduced speed limits to 50 mph. He believed the combination of measures would reduce the shortfall in supply from 17 per cent to 7 per cent. In Britain, meanwhile, a three-day working week was adopted.

By February 1974, over half the gas stations in New York area had closed for lack of supplies, while lines up to six miles long were observed at stations that were open. The price of crude oil, which in October 1973 had risen by 70 per cent to $5.11 a barrel, rose to over $10 per barrel, Libya posting the record of $18.77.

The Nixon administration also began negotiations with Israel to pull back from the Sinai and the Golan Heights, territories it had claimed. The promise of a settlement between Israel and Syria persuaded Arab oil producers to lift the embargo in March 1974. But OPAEC members, who would earn more than $100 billion in 1974 thanks to the price increases, now realized the enormous power they held with their ability to set oil prices by rationing its supply.

Crude oil prices over the next two decades fluctuated, notably in 1979 when the Shah of Iran was deposed, and again after Iraq's invasion of Kuwait in the 1990s. The energy crisis led to greater interest in renewable energy sources such as solar and wind power. Yet even now in the early 21st century, the world's dependence on Middle Eastern oil remains heavy.

There was also a political shift by many Western nations towards a pro-Arab approach that led to tensions in military alliances with the USA, which remained strongly pro-Israel. While the 1973 crisis had been averted, it was clear that the countries that controlled the oil fields would have much more of a say in the Middle East's political complexion in the years to come.

Above: Nixon speaks with chief of staff H. R. Haldeman in the White House. Haldeman was later convicted for his role in Watergate.

Right: Richard Nixon departs in the Presidential helicopter from the south lawn of the White House on the day of his resignation.

NIXON RESIGNS

WASHINGTON, DC, USA
AUGUST 9, 1974

The Watergate Scandal in 1974 led to Richard Nixon becoming the first US president ever to resign from office, amidst a cloud of controversy. Watergate was a series of events that shocked the world and shook the USA to its foundations, fundamentally damaging that nation's faith in its political system.

The affair began in June 1972, when five men were caught breaking into the Democratic National Committee offices in the newly built Watergate complex in Washington DC. In January 1973, they were charged with conspiracy and burglary. All five, plus two others charged with assisting them, were found to have worked for agencies like the CIA, FBI and the US Marine Corps. Additionally, all seven were linked to the fundraising group Campaign to Re-elect the President, CRP, designed to keep Nixon in office.

Police investigations revealed the burglars were being bankrolled by the Nixon administration despite White House officials strenuously denying any involvement. Head of Nixon's re-election campaign John Mitchell had a fund to bankroll spying on Democratic activities, and the Watergate break-in was part of that. Two months later, in November 1972, Nixon was delighted to be re-elected President by a landslide majority.

But 1973 saw the net began to close around the Nixon administration. The US press – specifically the *New York Times* and *Washington Post* – highlighted the President's link to the break-in, dedicating many exclusive articles to the scandal with the help of a mystery informant known as 'Deep Throat'.

In April 1973, Nixon accepted the resignation of two of his closest aides, as well as Attorney General Richard Kleindienst. But efforts to cover up the break-in were blown apart at the committee hearings, when many of the recently departed aides implicated their former employers.

Key to their testimony was the claim that Nixon had recorded every conversation in his office since 1971. After a long battle, in which Nixon refused to hand over the tapes and even had independent prosecutor Archibald Cox dismissed, he was finally forced to hand them over, and he did this in July 1974.

The tapes exposed Nixon and his administration as being in league with the Watergate Five, and the Judiciary Committee recommended he be impeached for obstruction of justice, abuse of power and contempt of congress. Nixon, 61, resigned from office in August 1974, after a long drawn-out affair that tarnished not only the White House but the USA itself. He was granted a pardon by new president Gerald Ford, exempting him from prosecution, but he was a broken man.

AT A GLANCE

A June 1972 break-in at the Democratic National Committee offices led, two years later, to Richard Nixon becoming the first US President ever to resign from office after a series of lies and deceptions had failed to distance him from the crime. The nation's faith in its political system did not survive the trauma – and, despite a pardon from his successor, neither did Nixon's political career.

FOUNDING OF MICROSOFT

ALBUQUERQUE, NEW MEXICO, USA
1975

Above: Bill Gates and Paul Allen in 1983, after signing a contract to write MS-DOS for IBM. At that time, Microsoft had 100 employees.

Right: By 2005, Microsoft's main corporate campus in Seattle housed almost half of the company's 59,900 workers.

Founded by Bill Gates and Paul Allen in 1975, Microsoft expanded to become the third largest company on the planet, its products having helped create the personal computer (PC) as we know it, and with an estimated 500 million people around the globe using Microsoft products. Gates became the wealthiest man in the world.

Microsoft was founded in Albuquerque, New Mexico, after Gates had offered to produce a programming language system for an early computer known as the Altair 8800. Gates and Allen produced the program in weeks, and within five years the company was on its way to success. No industry was growing faster than computers, with technology progressing at a phenomenal rate, and Microsoft had arrived at the right time.

Their early years were spent providing their own computer operating system, MS-DOS, for hardware and software giant IBM, before Microsoft came into its own in 1983 with the release of its user-friendly word-processing program for a PC.

Word 1.0 was released in 1983, and the program changed the way the world used computers. It was a word processor that allowed the user to see what they were typing on the screen. After years of computers being a device that only trained operators could use, the user-friendly 'what you see is what you get' concept, with which Microsoft would become synonymous, opened up the PC to all.

Microsoft was now competing with other software companies like Macintosh and Corel, but then it began to leave its competitors behind. The first version of Windows was released in 1985, but it wasn't until Windows 3.0 five years later that Microsoft eclipsed its closest rival, Apple Macintosh. It went from strength to strength as the 20th century came to a close, constantly changing and becoming ever more complex with Windows 95, 98, and 2000. Now released on multiple platforms, Windows is claimed to be the number one computer operating system in the world.

Though Word and Windows are its two most successful products, Microsoft has been successful in other areas too; its Internet presence is characterized by its Internet Explorer browser, as well as the MSN network and Hotmail email system. In 2001 Microsoft branched into computer games consoles with the release of the X-Box. Since then it has released the console's successor, the X-Box 360, rivaling Sony's PlayStation.

From having just a handful of employees in New Mexico over three decades ago, Microsoft's expansionist marketing policy rocketed the company to the top, rewriting the way we use IT.

AT A GLANCE

The rise of Microsoft and the ubiquity of the personal computer went hand in hand. Its Windows operating system and Word word-processing package brought 'what you see is what you get' ease of operation to millions, making co-founder Bill Gates the world's wealthiest individual within less than a quarter of a century in business.

FALL OF SAIGON

SOUTH VIETNAM
APRIL 30, 1975

Above: North Vietnamese forces enter Saigon in 1975, completing the country's reunification.

Left: North Vietnamese troops seize the presidential palace in Saigon..

After over a century of conflict against a number of enemies, peace finally came to Vietnam: the fall of Saigon brought the end to the Vietnam War that had begun over 15 years earlier.

The battle for control of the country between the Republic of South Vietnam and the communist forces of North Vietnam had begun in 1959, with the USA heavily involved in accordance with their policy of communist containment.

But American support for US involvement in Vietnam had dwindled, leading to the withdrawal of its troops in 1973 after the signing of the Paris Peace Accords. Without the military support of its biggest ally, South Vietnam was now at a distinct disadvantage. The Watergate scandal had ousted President Nixon, and the new US government would not necessarily uphold the diplomatic assurances he had given to the South.

The US government said that they did not believe the South faced defeat, predicting they could hold out for at least a year. But in reality the South was on the ropes; a campaign of offensives from the North, named after communist icon and former president Ho Chi Minh, was going according to plan, and they were closing on the South's capital of Saigon.

The South's President Thieu resigned on April 21 after losing the confidence of his supporters. He was succeeded by Vice-President Tran Van Huong, who was himself replaced by Duong Van Minh six days later.

Minh had a less than a day in the hot seat before North Vietnamese troops stormed the outskirts of Saigon. As they continued to converge on the city, the USA, which had already been evacuating personnel since the beginning of the month, stepped up its efforts with Operation Frequent Wind, removing both US and South Vietnamese citizens thought to be at risk.

Saigon was in meltdown, with looting and rioting, and with its fall imminent Minh announced the South's surrender 'in order to avoid bloodshed' on April 30. Saigon was renamed Ho Chi Minh City. A year later, in July 1976, North and South Vietnam were reunified under communist rule, though April 30 has remained the national holiday.

It has taken decades for Vietnam to rebuild relations with other countries, even after the communist regime was relaxed in the eighties, but Ho Chi Minh City now appears as a sister city to beacons of modern capitalism like Lyon and San Francisco, a far cry from the capital of a defeated nation.

AT A GLANCE

The fall of Saigon, capital of South Vietnam, was inevitable from the moment, two years earlier, that President Nixon had withdrawn the US troops. The 15-year war came to an end having achieved little but loss of life (2,000,000 Vietnamese and 50,000 American), and the reunited country worked hard to rebuild relations with the outside world.

APPLE INC. IS FOUNDED

CUPERTINO, CALIFORNIA, USA
APRIL 1, 1976

Above: An Apple 1 computer, sold in kit form in 1976 for $666.66. Steve Wozniak and friend Steve Jobs produced assembled boards for a local shop.

Right: John Sculley (left), President of Apple Computer, talks with Apple co-founders Steve Jobs (center) and Steve Wozniak (right) as they introduce a new Apple computer at a 1984 conference in San Francisco.

AT A GLANCE

Apple computers were at the forefront of bringing the personal computer into the homes of the world. Initially regarded as more expensive or elitist than the standard PC, Apple's range of products now includes phones and mobile music systems.

Steven Jobs and Stephen Wosniak had been friends since 1971 when they were both working at Hewlett Packard. Wosniak was a self-taught electronics genius and by 1974, when Jobs was working as a technician at Atari, Wosniak had helped him design for the computer game *Breakout* an electronically efficient motherboard so tightly constructed that it could not be built by the assembly lines of the time.

In 1975 the two began to go to meetings of the Homebrew Computer Club in California. Wosniak was inspired by the latest generation of microcomputers to build his own, taking advantage of a cheap, newly available chip. When he demonstrated it at a Homebrew meeting, Jobs immediately saw the commercial potential of a pre-assembled motherboard and won 50 orders from their local computer store, The Byte Shop.

The motherboard complex, named Apple I, eventually sold around 200 copies. It had no keyboard or casing, but allowed hobbyists to use their TV as a monitor, and at $666.66, it gave the two Steves a healthy profit margin. They were able to give up their day jobs and concentrate on designing the Apple II, with better memory, graphics, a case and a keyboard.

The development of this more sophisticated Apple needed the sort of cash injection which Jobs and Wosniak, two college drop-outs, could not hope to attract alone. With the help of business angel Mike Markkula, they secured a bank loan of $250,000, and on April 1, 1976, Apple Inc. was born. They chose the name because it would be listed above the market leader Atari in the phone book.

The Apple II was released in 1977; it created and dominated the new home computer market, selling well into the 1980s. But the Apple III, designed to compete with the business market dominated by IBM, was less successful: it was prone to overheating and thousands were recalled.

It was the launch of the Apple Macintosh, with a 90-second commercial shown during the televised Superbowl XVIII in January 1984, which secured Apple's global status. Its new capacity for desktop publishing and computer animation made it the essential computer tool for the creative industries.

Both Jobs and Wosniak left Apple in the mid 1980s, Wosniak to pursue his interest in philanthropic work, teaching computer skills to schoolchildren, while Jobs bought and developed the cinema animation company Pixar. He returned to Apple in 1997, leading it into the new millennium with products such as the iMac and the ubiquitous iPod.

Above: Dr. Raymond Damadian (left) demonstrates his MRI scanner at a press conference on July 20, 1977.

Right: Today's MRI scanners use techniques developed by Sir Peter Mansfield and Paul Lauterbur, and play a vital role in modern medical diagnosis.

AT A GLANCE

Although the inventor's work was surpassed by rivals, the first use of an MRI scanner to produce an image of the human body, in 1977, marked an important step in the development of what has become a powerful tool in medical diagnosis.

FIRST MRI BODY SCAN OF A HUMAN BEING

BROOKLYN, NEW YORK, USA
JULY 3, 1977

The greatest leap forward in medical technology since the invention of the X-ray, Magnetic Resonance Imaging (MRI) creates computerized images of thin slices of the body. Credit for its invention is generally given to the British physicist, Sir Peter Mansfield and American chemist, Paul Christian Lauterbur, who won a Nobel Prize for their work in 2003. However, the award was protested by Raymond Vahan Damadian, who had put forward the idea of a magnetic resonance body scanner in 1969. During the early 1970s, Damadian, aided by teams of students, had worked at the SUNY Downstate Medical Center in Brooklyn, USA, to make his idea a reality, obtaining a patent in 1974. In 1977, they succeeded in creating the first MRI scan of a human with a machine they named Indomitable.

That first scan produced a fuzzy image of heart, lungs and chest, using a technique based on a phenomenon first observed by Professor Isador I. Rabi in 1937. He had noticed that atomic nuclei, when subjected to a magnetic field, absorb or emit radio waves. Damadian realized that because different types of tissue contained more or less water, different levels of hydrogen atoms were present, and so they took different amounts of time to stop giving off radio waves after being subjected to a magnetic field. And so the varying emission times could be mapped, to produce an image that showed up the different tissues inside the body.

Although it had potential, Damadian's machine was not destined to be used by the medical community. During the early 1970s, Paul Lauterbur had also been producing images of organic materials at Stony Brook University in New York, using the chemistry department's nuclear magnetic resonance machine. Published in the prestigious scientific journal, *Nature*, Lauterbur's work was taken up by Peter Mansfield of Nottingham University, UK. His contribution was the mathematical analysis of MRI radio signals, converting these into wsharp images. He also developed the 'echo-planar imaging' protocol which dramatically speeded up the MRI process and is now used in all machines.

It was Lauterbur and Mansfield's research that was adopted for the production of MRI scanners now found in hospitals around the world, though Damadian holds some patents and his work represents important strides in the technology. The work of all three men has been invaluable to medicine, helping improve the quality of countless lives around the world, and Damadian's successful demonstration in 1977 can be seen as the moment that the possibilities of MRI became obvious. Since then, the techniques pioneered by Lauterbur and Mansfield have become an important tool in hospitals, where they are very helpful in detecting cancerous tumors and in the diagnosis of heart disease and diseases of the central nervous system, such as Multiple Sclerosis.

Above: GPS receivers in cars translate the signal transmitted from satellites and channeled through a master control station into a map format that calculates a position based on exact longitude, latitude, and altitude. Directions are spoken aloud, allowing drivers to respond without taking their eyes off the road.

Right: A Boeing Delta II rocket carrying a cargo of GPS satellites lifts off from Cape Canaveral, Florida, in November 2006.

AT A GLANCE

The launch of the first experimental Global Positioning System satellite in 1978 marked the beginning of a program that has resulted in highly accurate global mapping data becoming available to anyone with a GPS receiving device.

FIRST GLOBAL POSITIONING SYSTEM SATELLITE LAUNCHED

VANDENBERG AIR FORCE BASE, CALIFORNIA, USA
FEBRUARY 22, 1978

During the first weekend of September 1973, a group of military officers met at the Pentagon in Washington, DC, and devised a plan for a satellite navigation system that could be used by the US military and government agencies. Named Navstar-GPS, which was later shortened to simply GPS, the system would involve between 24 and 32 satellites orbiting the Earth and broadcasting to a control station run by the US Air Force. Signals sent from the satellites could be picked up by GPS receivers to calculate and map a precise location on or near the Earth's surface.

The first experimental satellite, Block-I, was launched aboard an Atlas rocket from Vandenberg Air Force Base on February 22, 1978. Five other launches have since then taken place, seeding space around the planet with a constellation of 60 satellites, of which 29 are now in operation. The system reached operational capability in December 1993.

Although GPS was initially intended for the use of the US military, in 1983 Korean Air Lines Flight 007 entered Soviet airspace after a navigation failure. The Soviets believed the passenger flight to be on a spying mission and the airliner was shot down by interceptor aircraft, resulting in the deaths of 269 people, also heightening tension between the USSR and the US. In response, US President Reagan ordered that, once functioning reliably, the GPS system should be accessible by civilians in the hope that such a catastrophe would never be repeated. Nevertheless, for the first seven years of operation, the satellite information was transmitted in two bands: high quality for use by the US military, giving an accurate position to within 65 feet (20 meters) and a separate channel for civilians that gave a position to within 1,000 feet (300 meters). On May 1, 2000, on the command of US President Clinton, the higher quality signal was made available to everyone who used GPS.

Since then, GPS receivers have become used around the world by transport companies and many individual users, including motorists, sailors, pilots and hikers. Although the system is still maintained by the 50th Space Wing of the US Air Force, advances in technology – and the availability of the higher quality signal – have meant that the manufacture of small, affordable, accurate devices has become commercially viable. Many vehicles are now manufactured with GPS capability built in, giving an accurate position to within a few feet and allowing software to calculate and deliver a stream of directions on the move.

FIRST TEST TUBE BABY IS BORN

OLDHAM GENERAL HOSPITAL, GREATER MANCHESTER, UK
JULY 25, 1978

Above: Dr. Patrick Steptoe shows the suction device used to transplant a mature egg from the ovary of Mrs. Lesley Brown to a dish where it was fertilized with the sperm of her husband.

Left: Louise Brown, the world's first test tube baby, appears at age one on US television in 1979. Louise's mother Lesley holds her.

Below: Louise Brown, pictured with her parents in later life.

When a child first looks up at their parents and asks, "How was I born?" the reply is sometimes an awkward one, the stork initially being the most popular answer amongst those who find the truth difficult. But when Louise Brown asked her parents the same question, the answer was completely different.

Louise was the world's first 'test tube baby', that is, conceived in a laboratory and transplanted into her mother's womb. She would be the first of well over a million worldwide in the years following her birth in July 1978. Her parents, Lesley and John Brown, were the first to undergo *in vitro* fertilization, IVF. Lesley's fallopian tubes were blocked and she was unable to conceive naturally despite a decade of attempts, but gynecologist Patrick Steptoe and physiologist Robert Edwards had a solution after rapid advances in procedures for the extraction of human eggs.

Steptoe and Edwards fertilized Lesley's egg with John's sperm in a laboratory and inserted it into her womb. Though Lesley developed toxemia during her pregnancy, it was otherwise uneventful and she was able to deliver Louise via a caesarean section on July 25.

Despite Louise being of low weight – just 5lb 12oz – her birth was a success. As the world's media gathered around Oldham General Hospital, Steptoe announced, "All examinations showed that the baby is quite normal. The mother's condition after delivery was also excellent."

Louise's birth opened the door to more births via IVF, including that of her younger sister Natalie; she was born four years later in 1982, by which point there had been 40 more test tube babies. (Natalie went on to become the first IVF baby to have a child herself, when in 1999, aged 17, she gave birth to her daughter naturally.)

Louise went on to have a normal childhood, and married in 2004. Two years later she had her own child; son Cameron arrived in 2006, also a natural conception. The advert for IVF treatment could not have been any better. And while the success rate remains below 20 per cent, the course still produces 'miracle' babies and offers hope to millions of couples who cannot conceive normally.

AT A GLANCE

With many women unable to conceive for gynecological reasons, the arrival of in vitro fertilization in 1978 was truly an innovation that could potentially change lives. Louise Brown was the first of many test tube babies, conceived in a lab and born from her mother's womb.

Above: Throughout the 80s, Sony refined the original Walkman design and added new features. The durable and partly waterproof Sports Walkman was one of the best-selling models.

Right: A familiar sight during the 1980s, a young man listens to music on a brightly colored personal stereo. From the launch of the first model, Sony actively marketed the Walkman toward the young, active and fashion conscious, and while other companies produced their own models, Walkman remained the most prestigious brand.

AT A GLANCE

Released on July 1, 1979, the Sony Walkman personal stereo became an iconic gadget during the 1980s and sparked a massive industry in personal entertainment devices that flourishes to this day.

FIRST SONY WALKMAN GOES ON SALE

JAPAN
JULY 1, 1979

The 'must have' gadget of the 1980s, the Sony Walkman personal stereo was the first truly portable cassette player, allowing its owners to listen to music of their own choice through headphones wherever they were. Although portable radios – and relatively small cassette players – had been previously available, the freedom of choice and ease of use that the Walkman represented made it a massive success across the globe, and a fashion accessory for hip youngsters everywhere. Instantly copied by many other electronics manufacturers, the Walkman inspired a huge industry in personal entertainment systems that continues today, though, as technological advances have been made, the Walkman-style personal stereo has evolved from cassette to compact disc to minidisc to MP4 and similar.

The first device was built in the Sony laboratory for the company's co-chairman Akio Morita, who was a frequent flyer with a taste for opera. After he complained that he was unable to listen to his favorite music while taking long-haul flights, an engineer from Sony's audio division, named Nobutoshi Kihara, constructed the a prototype device in 1978. Within a year, the first portable cassette player – the silver and blue Walkman TPS-L2 – was available in Japanese stores. Marketed in other countries as the Soundabout, the name was quickly standardized around the globe.

The gadget proved an instant hit and through the 1980s, Sony brought out a range of different models that remained at the forefront of the industry, despite fierce competition from rivals such as Aiwa and Panasonic who had quickly started producing their own versions. While others may have been cheaper, Sony's Walkman was seen as the most prestigious brand, and was the one that lasted. In 1984, the company adapted to new technology by producing a personal CD player called the Discman – but reverted to the iconic Walkman name for later devices such as their minidisc player and their latest range of MP3 and 4 players.

Since the Walkman's 80s heyday, other companies have pioneered new designs and options, resulting in devices such as the Apple iPod, which is a fraction of the size of the original Walkman but can store thousands of songs, and photographs, and even has an in-built video camera in the latest models. Nevertheless, the success of all of today's personal entertainment systems is owed to the trailblazing Sony Walkman.

Above: Lech Walesa, pictured in front of a Solidarity banner in 1989, the year before he became Poland's president.

Right: Walesa is carried on the shoulders of a crowd in front of Warsaw's Supreme Court as Solidarity is recognized, 1980.

AT A GLANCE

When the Polish government recognized Solidarity, acceding to demands for independent self-governing trade unions and the right to strike, it let loose powerful forces it could not control. It gave rise to hopes for freedom and a better future for workers. It also provided a stimulus for all who had believed, up to that point, that communist rule could not be challenged. Inevitably, the example of 'people power' in Poland inspired successful movements in other European countries, bringing many changes the political map of Eastern Europe.

RECOGNITION OF SOLIDARITY BY THE POLISH GOVERNMENT

GDANSK, POLAND
AUGUST 30, 1980

The Solidarity (Solidarnosc) movement struck a strong blow for workers' rights when their charismatic leader, the mustachioed Lech Walesa, obtained the right for Polish trade unions to strike and to be independent. The deal was signed, most reluctantly, on the part of the communist government by the first deputy prime minister, Mieczyslaw Jagielski. By this agreement Poland became the first Eastern Bloc country to take such a step.

The key moment had come when around 17,000 Polish strikers had assembled in the Baltic shipyard in Gdansk, threatening to shut it down altogether. The catalyst for this upsurge had been a recent hike in food prices, but in fact the grievances were deep-rooted and based on longstanding social injustices. It was as a result of this demonstration that the agreement with the government was negotiated.

Lech Walesa, an unemployed electrician, was an unlikely leader, but he proved to be a good mouthpiece for the organization, mobilizing 20 other areas to join the strike. He became the undisputed leader of Solidarity, a national confederation of independent trade unions brought together under a single name.

The workers were promised, amongst other concessions, better social services, increased pay and more reliable food supplies. In return the government asked that the leading role of the communist party in Poland be acknowledged. This was no hardship for many Polish workers, who at that time were under the illusion that the communist party could be reformed from within.

It is impossible to exaggerate the feelings of excitement and hope that were felt as the news of these events was broadcast throughout the world. Very soon there were 9 million members of Solidarity. From the start, the Pope and the Polish Catholic church backed it to the hilt, sustaining popular support for the organization.

It could not last. the USSR was not slow to realize the importance of these events and put pressure on the Polish prime minister, General Jaruzelski, to act forcefully against the movement. In December 1981 he declared martial law, making Solidarity an illegal organization, and had its leaders arrested, including Lech Walesa; he spent almost a year in jail and was put under surveillance for the next seven years. Walesa's moment in the sun came in 1990, when he became Poland's president. But his success was short-lived; he eventually left the confederation, which declined steadily from then on.

FIRST COMMERCIALLY AVAILABLE CELLPHONE

USA
OCTOBER, 1983

It is hard to remember life without them, but it was only in 1983 that the first, brick-like cellphone was available to buy. Now, nearly three decades later, there are thousands of models used by millions of people the world over.

Portable telephone technology had been under development since the early 20th century, and included two-way radios and phones in vehicles that could latch onto networks. But the world at large relied on landlines and letters to communicate with far-off places. That is, until American telecoms giant Motorola emerged out front, to provide ordinary people with a portable handset they could buy themselves. It was the result of a race with fellow innovators AT&T and their Bell Laboratory, which had focused on portable communication through cars up to that point. But at Motorola, Martin Cooper led a team to create a device that could be hand-held, and used independently from a building or a vehicle.

Cooper made the first call from a cellphone a decade before its release, in 1973, using what would be known as the Motorola DynaTAC 8000X. It remained in development for a decade while a network was found from which it could operate, and the phone was released in October 1983.

It was far from perfect, however; and at a cost of over $3,000, only the rich could afford it. The handset itself was by today's standards large and bulky, at over ten inches long, and weighing nearly a kilogram (2.2 lbs).

Six years later Motorola followed up its success with the MicroTAC series, which saw the handset scaled down. The revolution had begun; by the end of the 20th century, second generation phones were widespread through manufacturers such as Sony and Nokia.

Rapidly advancing technology has meant cellphone capabilities have been greatly enhanced over the years. SMS messaging became a revolution in the 1990s when users could type messages instead of communicating through the spoken word.

The next step was the introduction of the Internet onto phone handsets in the first decade of the 21st century; cell phones had become much more than a simple communication device.

The call made by Martin Cooper over 30 years ago had lit the touch paper on the fastest evolving technology of the turn of the century. With an estimated 60 per cent of the planet's population now owning a cellphone, it is undoubtedly seen as one of the world's most essential accessories.

Above: An early 21st-century mobile phone, showing some of the applications available for them.

Left: Martin Cooper compares the Motorola DynaTAC phone, the world's first commercial handheld cellphone, with his current model during a news conference in 2009.

AT A GLANCE

It took two decades for the cellphone to slim down from the boxy prototype to the slim, pocket-friendly device we know today. Martin Cooper's vision in 1983 has revolutionized the way we communicate, making our arrangements on the move and sending messages at the tap of a keypad.

251

Above: An image showing the ozone hole over the Antarctic in 2000, at the time the largest such hole on record.

Left: French scientists launch a research balloon that will circle 20 km above Antarctica to inspect the ozone hole in the atmosphere.

AT A GLANCE

The discovery by three British scientists in 1985 of a hole in the ozone layer over the Antarctic ensured environmental issues a place at the top of news agendas. Refrigerators and other users of the CFC gases that deplete ozone have been redesigned to reduce their environmental impact. The ozone hole is a different phenomenon from global warming, although there are links in their causes.

ALARM SOUNDS ON HOLE IN OZONE LAYER

ANTARCTICA
1985

For nearly a billion years the ozone layer has protected the Earth's surface from ultraviolet (UV) radiation. But a discovery in 1985 brought environmental issues into every political party's agenda for the coming decades – scientists discovered a hole in the ozone layer.

In the 1970s research into the effects of certain chemicals and gases on the ozone layer around the Earth was in its infancy, but as it grew so did the recognized extent of the potential damage.

In 1985, British scientists Joseph Farman, Brian Gardiner and Jonathan Shanklin discovered that there was a substantial-sized gap in the protective ozone layer over the Antarctic during its spring months of September to December. This was due to the cold air causing man-made CFC gases to react with polar stratospheric clouds; when the tilt of the Earth means that the sun shines more directly onto the Antarctic, this causes the layer to degrade, creating a hole that can reach 1.5 times the size of the USA.

The revelation of this hole, coupled with the awareness of a worldwide decrease in the ozone layer estimated at four per cent per decade, changed the way the world thought. Environmental issues started to dominate news bulletins, and the press speculated about apocalyptic possibilities. In 1987, an international treaty was devised to prevent further damage to the ozone layer by limiting the amount of harmful gases created. The Montreal Protocol was signed in September that year, and implemented two years later, and was by all accounts considered a success.

The realization that the Earth is not indestructible has not only had an effect on environmental science and policies, but has also been reflected in our culture. Hollywood has capitalized on the subject's relevance and fear-provoking qualities with the release of environmental disaster movies like *The Day After Tomorrow* in 2004. The threat to the environment has also been coupled with the threat to humans; an increase in UV radiation leaves people at risk to cancer and other ailments, and this further heightened international concern.

As the noughties drew to a close, it was stated that the ozone hole was slowly reducing in size and was the smallest it had been in a decade. Even so, the planet's vulnerability had been exposed.

GORBACHEV ELECTED GENERAL SECRETARY OF THE SOVIET UNION

MOSCOW, USSR
MARCH 13, 1985

Above: President Reagan and General Secretary Gorbachev together at the concluding summit ceremony at the International Press Center, Switzerland, 1985.

Left: General Secretary Mikhail Gorbachev stands at the podium with US President Ronald Reagan at a 1987 White House summit.

AT A GLANCE

Mikhail Gorbachev tried to reform the stagnating communist party and the similarly moribund Soviet state economy by giving the people new freedoms. This, combined with improved relations with the West, inevitably led to the collapse of the Soviet Union. However, his concepts of glasnost *and* perestroika *are still remembered today.*

As the Soviet Union buried its third leader in less than three years, the baton of power was passed to a new generation, in the shape of 54-year-old Mikhail Gorbachev. The son of an agricultural mechanic on a collective farm, he was at the time the only Soviet leader to have been born after the October Revolution of 1917, and his election as General Secretary of the Communist Party of the Soviet Union signaled a new era. He would preside over the Soviet Union's final years, as his reforms inevitably led to the collapse of the old system.

Gorbachev led the funeral procession as his predecessor, Konstantin Chernenko, was buried near the Kremlin alongside fellow former leaders Leonid Brezhnev and Yuri Andropov. Gorbachev, the youngest man to take charge in Moscow since Stalin, immediately proposed a series of economic, political and cultural reforms including *glasnost* (openness), *perestroika* (restructuring), *demokratizatsiya* (democratization) and *uskoreniye* (acceleration of economic development), all launched in 1986 with the intention of making the Soviet economy more efficient.

He aimed to establish a free market economy by encouraging the private ownership of Soviet industry and agriculture – but existing structures ensured that these reforms were ineffective.

Gorbachev sent conciliatory messages to the West, confirming his wish to reduce arms stockpiles all round. He established a rapport with US President Ronald Reagan, British Prime Minister Margaret Thatcher and Germany's Chancellor Helmut Kohl, seeing improved international relations with them as a key to reform in his own country.

January 1986 saw him propose the elimination of intermediate range nuclear weapons in Europe, and in February 1988 he announced the full withdrawal of Soviet forces from Afghanistan – both moves at odds with past Soviet thinking. Then his publicly stated non-interference with the internal affairs of other countries allowed demonstrations to be made against communist governments in Eastern Europe without fear of reprisal, hastening the collapse of the communist bloc.

He was elected President of the Soviet Union in 1990, the same year in which his efforts toward ending the Cold War earned him the Nobel Peace Prize. But his attempts to make the Soviet Union a more democratic country made him unpopular with conservatives still in positions of power. Although in August 1991 he survived a coup staged by Communist party hard-liners, with the Soviet Union disintegrating into separate states he resigned later that year, ceding power to Boris Yeltsin.

Above: *Thousands of fans pack Wembley Stadium for the 1985 Live Aid concert.*

Right: *Chrissie Hynde and Bob Geldof hold programs for the Live Aid concert.*

Overleaf: *A view from within the crowd of the stage during the Philadelphia Live Aid concert.*

AT A GLANCE

1985's Live Aid was the world's biggest ever charity rock concert, aimed to raise money for the relief of famine in the Sudan and Ethiopia. It was the idea of Irish rock star Bob Geldof. 50 acts appeared in London and Philadelphia, the music transmitted worldwide via satellite. An estimated £150 million was raised.

LIVE AID CONCERT

WEMBLEY ARENA, LONDON AND JFK STADIUM, PHILADELPHIA

JULY 13, 1985

The power of rock music and television came together in 1985 to create a showbiz spectacle designed to raise money for African famine relief. Fifty of the biggest names in music including Queen, Paul McCartney, Madonna and U2, plus a re-formed Led Zeppelin, performed for a global audience reached through satellite transmission. There had been one-off charity concerts before, like George Harrison's Concert for Bangladesh in 1971, but Live Aid eclipsed all-comers in reach and ambition, setting a template for future events.

The concert followed the 1984 charity single 'Do They Know It's Christmas?' recorded by Bob Geldof (Boomtown Rats) and Midge Ure (Ultravox) with a galaxy of UK pop stars under the name Band Aid. Geldof had been touched by a BBC news report of the famine in Ethiopia and wanted to make a gesture. When the record sold three million copies, it was clear the public had taken the cause to heart.

USA for Africa's single 'We Are The World' followed suit, but a visit to Africa convinced Geldof that a greater effort was needed. Live Aid was conceived in March 1985 and organised in just 20 weeks. As well as the concert itself, the means to dispense the proceeds had also to be created – a yet bigger challenge.

Geldof's relentless harrying of the era's biggest stars ensured few turned him down. From Adam Ant to Neil Young, the Beach Boys to the Who (who re-formed for the event), the A-Z of pop was represented. Springsteen, Prince and Michael Jackson were the most notable absentees. Throughout the concerts, TV viewers were urged to donate money to the Live Aid cause – often by Geldof himself, whose on-air use of the f-word when disappointed by the amount thus far raised increased giving to £300 per second.

Each act was given just 15 minutes to perform at Wembley Stadium in London and JFK Stadium, Philadelphia; New York's Shea Stadium, the first-choice American venue, was unavailable. Phil Collins flew by Concorde to play on both sides of the Atlantic. While 72,000 people attended in London and 99,000 in Philadelphia, the TV audience amounted to an estimated 400 million viewers across 60 countries thanks to an unprecedented global link-up.

One of the organisers later put the final figure raised as £150 million ($284 million), far more than the originally hoped-for £1 million. Irish-born Geldof received a knighthood from Queen Elizabeth II in 1986 in recognition of his work. In 2005, Sir Bob Geldof marked the 20th anniversary with Live 8, a series of global concerts intended to persuade leaders of the G8 countries to 'make poverty history'.

CHALLENGER DISASTER

CAPE CANAVERAL, USA
JANUARY 28, 1986

Above: Challenger explodes 73 seconds after liftoff, killing the entire crew of seven.

Inset: Challenger crew members (front to back) Christa McAuliffe, Ellison Onizuka, and Gregory Jarvis leave their quarters.

Left: Space shuttle Challenger leaves the launch pad en route to imminent disaster.

AT A GLANCE

The USA's space program received its biggest blow in early 1986 with the crash of the space shuttle Challenger. Its loss, witnessed by millions of TV viewers, was the worst accident in the history of US space exploration and brought the program to a standstill. An unforgettable pall of white smoke marked the deaths of the seven crew members.

Nearly 17 years after NASA's greatest moment came its worst. While years before the planet had watched in awe as man set off to land on the moon for the first time, millions tuned in their televisions on January 28, 1986, to witness disaster as the space shuttle Challenger exploded just 73 seconds after take-off. It had been a catalogue of errors from the start; the mission had originally been scheduled to launch on January 22, but a series of setbacks, five in all, forced the delay of nearly a week, despite several attempted launches.

The mission was notable for its inclusion of the first civilian ever to go into space. In 1984 President Ronald Reagan had announced NASA's Teacher in Space project, designed to stimulate interest in mathematics and science, and a year later, Christa McAuliffe had been selected from over 11,000 applicants to teach some lessons from space as part of the exercise; but Challenger's main mission was to deploy a tracking satellite to observe Halley's Comet.

The decision to go ahead with Challenger's tenth space mission was a contentious one, as the weather on the morning of the sixth attempted launch was, at -1°C, freezing – borderline for allowing a mission to proceed.

Concerns before take-off were about the spacecraft's solid rocket boosters; it was said the freezing temperatures overnight would compromise the performance of their O-ring sealants, putting the mission in danger, but at 11.40 a.m. the launch went ahead regardless. Just 73 seconds into its mission, broadcast via US television, Challenger exploded in mid-air, resulting in the death of all seven crew members on board. An investigation was immediately launched as to the cause of the tragedy, and it was discovered that O-ring malfunction had indeed been the root cause of the explosion.

The confirmation of the engineers' fears was a blow to NASA, as the report revealed the organization's decision to launch despite repeated warnings of danger had been a key factor in the catastrophe. The disaster set their manned space program back years, and they didn't launch another manned vessel until September 1988.

The bodies of the crew were found at the bottom of the Pacific Ocean six weeks later, still in their compartment. The manual activation of a number of their emergency oxygen packs indicated they had not died in the initial explosion, but instead a couple of minutes later when the shuttle was crushed on hitting the surface of the sea.

Challenger remains to this day the world's worst space disaster, and it reshaped the way the public viewed space travel as well as the way NASA pursued it.

FOUNDING OF PIXAR STUDIOS

CALIFORNIA, USA
FEBRUARY 3, 1986

Above: Ralph Guggenheim, one of the founding executives of Pixar, stops to talk to an animator. The company encourages toys and games in its offices in order to create an atmosphere of creativity and fun.

Right: John Lasseter, the creative genius behind Pixar's early successes, poses with Woody and Buzz Lightyear, characters from Pixar's first feature-length animation, Toy Story.

Steve Jobs, the co-founder of Apple, purchased the computer graphics division of Lucasfilm in 1986, and he dubbed the new company Pixar. It has become one of the best-known and most successful movie studios of all time, changing the landscape of movies and technology, and paving the way for a new generation of superb on-screen visual effects.

Jobs had originally set the company up to develop the Pixar Image Computer, a high-end imaging machine that was designed to be used primarily in medicine. Although the computer was years ahead of its time, and revolutionary in terms of computer visualization, less than 300 were sold. But one of them was bought by Disney, quick to spot the possibilities offered by the machine with the RenderMan software Pixar had produced to run on it.

The general lack of interest in the machine, in which Jobs had invested millions, was disastrous for the company, but one of Pixar's employees – John Lasseter, who had previously worked as an animator with Disney – had begun making short animated movies to demonstrate the system's capabilities. These were acclaimed at computer imaging conventions, and with Pixar still losing money, Lasseter began producing computer-generated commercials in 1990 as a Pixar sideline in order to raise funds. The same year, the Pixar Image Computer side of the business was sold.

In 1991 Pixar's fortunes began to turn when they signed a multi-million dollar deal with Disney to make three computer-animated movies. Even so, the company was still in serious financial difficulties and Jobs was close to selling it before deciding to wait and see how the first movie – *Toy Story* – performed at the box office. Released in 1995, it was a massive hit, earning $350 million worldwide and critical acclaim from all quarters, including four Academy Awards.

This began a run of massively successful movies such as *A Bug's Life* (1998), *Finding Nemo* (2003), *Cars* (2006), and *Up* (2009); meanwhile, RenderMan swiftly became the industry standard for visual effects, changing the way that movies are made, and allowing directors to create astonishing scenes that had been impossible to generate until then. Every special-effects blockbuster in the last ten years owes its computer-generated graphics to Pixar; RenderMan has been used in the making of movies from *Titanic* to *Avatar*.

Steve Jobs sold Pixar to Disney in 2006 for $7.4 billion, becoming Disney's single biggest stockholder in the process. To date, the company's movies have between them been awarded 24 Academy Awards, six Golden Globes, and three Grammys, while RenderMan has won numerous industry and science honors.

AT A GLANCE

Founded by Steve Jobs in 1986, Pixar has revolutionized visual effects in the movie industry. It has produced groundbreaking computer-animated movies, from Toy Story (1995) to Up (2009), and the RenderMan software the company developed has been used by many other movie-makers to create the incredible photo-realistic scenes that define many of today's blockbusters.

Above: The global response to AIDS attracted the support of numerous world leaders and celebrities, including Princess Diana, seen here carrying a young, HIV-infected girl at a care facility in Washington, D.C.

Left: First displayed on the National Mall, Washington, D.C., in 1987, the AIDS Memorial Quilt included at that time 1,920 panels, each recording the life of someone lost to the AIDS pandemic.

AT A GLANCE

In the face of mounting worldwide panic over the spread of AIDS during the 1980s, the World Health Organization released a cool-headed, compassionate and constructive strategy for dealing with the disease at every level, from local to global. Adopted around the world, it had an impact on the spread of the disease, and the treatment of those infected with HIV, which has been hugely positive and beneficial.

WORLD HEALTH ORGANIZATION APPROVES GLOBAL AIDS STRATEGY

GENEVA
MAY 4, 1987

In June 1981, the Center for Disease Control (CDC) in Atlanta, Georgia, USA, published a report that detailed the outbreak of the rare lung disease *Pneumocystis carinii pneumonia* (PCP) among young gay men in New York and California. The center was also becoming aware of other disturbing cases of unusual illnesses and opportunistic infections that seemed to have no identifiable cause. At first, scientists thought that whatever was causing them was confined to the gay community, but by December of that year it became clear that other groups, such as injecting drug users, were also affected. While these were not the first victims of the HIV/AIDS virus, 1981 was the year that the scientific community and the public became aware that a new killer disease was at large. By 1982, although it did not yet have a name, 452 cases from across the USA had been reported. Four years later, amid mounting public alarm, Dr H. Mahler, the Director of the World Health Organization (WHO), suggested at a conference in Paris, that up to 10 million people around the world might be infected.

By 1987, the disease, now a recognised panedemic, had a name–AIDS. By December, 71,751 cases had been reported to the WHO. Fear, made worse by ignorance of how it was transmitted, gripped entire nations. After intensive discussion throughout 1985 and 1986, the WHO approved a document that was to reshape the global response to AIDS. Setting out the principles on which the disease could be battled at local, national, and international levels at a time when many of those who suffered were being treated as modern-day lepers, the WHO policy also established that every country should create a 'supportive and non-discriminatory social environment'. The objectives were 'to prevent new HIV infection; to reduce the personal and social impact of HIV infection; and to mobilize and unify national and international efforts against AIDS.'

The strategy provided the catalyst for action. The next year, delegates from 148 countries met in London to discuss AIDS prevention strategies, concluding that that a massive program of public education was needed, and as a first step the WHO announced December 1, 1988, to be the first AIDS Day. Since then, the strategy has been renamed the UNAIDS Program and is operated in partnership with other UN agencies in 193 countries. It has been updated with new aims, including the acceleration of HIV treatment, but its underlying principles remain the same. The number of new cases prevented by adopting the strategy, and the difference it has made to those living with HIV and AIDS, is impossible to quantify, but it is beyond doubt that the WHO strategy has been a monumental force in the fight against the disease.

FALL OF THE BERLIN WALL

BERLIN

NOVEMBER 9, 1989

The Berlin Wall was a stark reminder of the division between communism and capitalism that had split Europe after the end of World War II. The defeat of Hitler led to Germany being partitioned into East and West, the former under communist rule. The city of Berlin, situated deep in the new East Germany, was also partitioned, with the US, Britain, France and the Soviet Union each controlling a zone; as with the country, this arrangement became East and West Berlin.

The 28-mile-long Wall, built in 1961 at the bidding of German Democratic Republic leader Walter Ulbricht, became a stark reminder of the division between communism and capitalism. The Wall succeeded in stemming the steady flow of refugees from East to West, estimated at 2.5 million in the years since 1949 – but there were still those desperate enough to try; between 1962 and 1989 some 5,000 succeeded, and an estimated 100 lost their lives in the attempt.

The year before the Wall's fall in 1989 had seen Soviet leader Mikhail Gorbachev announce a unilateral cut in weapons levels in Eastern Europe – a reduction of half a million troops and 10,000 tanks. This followed a passionate speech in 1987 given by US President Ronald Reagan at the Brandenburg gate urging his Russian counterpart to 'tear down this Wall'.

Mass demonstrations in East Germany had led to the resignation of Erich Honeker, and this groundswell of public opinion was the immediate prelude to the fall of the Berlin Wall. On November 9, new GDR leader Egon Krentz opened the crossing points, and the once seemingly impregnable barrier became a site of rejoicing as separated families poured through the gates for joyful reconciliations.

In the first two days, over a million East Berliners took advantage of the new freedom to visit the West. And when, the following July, former Pink Floyd musician Roger Waters staged a performance of 'The Wall' in the nearby Potsdamer Platz, his special guests, German rock band the Scorpions, were inspired to write 'Wind Of Change' in honour of the event.

Souvenir hunters ensured the hated Wall was soon dismantled, and by the first anniversary only three short sections remained as a reminder of Berlin's divided past. On 3 October 1990, Berlin became the German capital once more. The reintegration of East and West Germany, with their markedly differing levels of economic prosperity, as the Federal Republic of Germany would prove rather more difficult, and the process is still ongoing.

Above: *A traffic jam at Checkpoint Charlie after the opening of the Berlin Wall.*

Left: *Man attacks the Berlin Wall with a pickaxe on the night of November 9th.*

AT A GLANCE

The Berlin Wall divided Germany's former capital between 1961 and 1989, dividing families and causing over 100 fatalities as would-be escapees were shot by East German border guards. When a new spirit of liberalism provoked by mass demonstrations convinced East Germany's leaders that partition was now impractical, the crossing points were opened, and the following year both city and country were officially reunited in the Federal Republic of Germany.

NELSON MANDELA RELEASED FROM PRISON

PAARL, SOUTH AFRICA
FEBRUARY 11, 1990

Above: Mandela's freedom is demanded by South Africans in a demonstration the year before his release.

Right: Nelson Mandela and his then wife Winnie, moments after his release from Victor Verster prison in February 1990.

Below: Removing graffiti from a wall of King's College Chapel, in Cambridge, UK, in 1965.

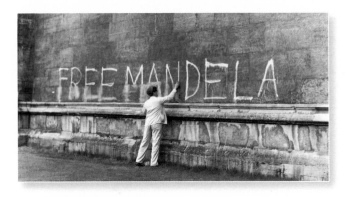

AT A GLANCE

Jailed African National Congress leader Nelson Mandela had become the figurehead of the opposition to South Africa's apartheid system. His release after 27 years signaled the overthrow of apartheid and the country's first free elections, after which he became South Africa's first black president. He stepped down in 1999.

South Africa was a country that had been divided by racial issues for over 100 years, and the introduction of apartheid (complete racial segregation) in 1948 by the country's government cast a deeper shadow over the country for nearly 50 years.

One victim was 46-year-old Nelson Mandela, jailed for life in 1964 for planning to sabotage the administration and the country's economy with his party, the African National Congress (ANC). His release 27 years later would signal the end of apartheid in that country.

Under the existing regime, racial segregation had been legal for many years, and Afrikaners – white Africans of European descent – enjoyed minority rule. Mandela and his party spent the 1940s and 1950s attempting to fight for equality and derail the system. But the government banned the ANC party. Mandela was a believer in non-violent resistance, inspired by Indian independence pioneer Mahatma Gandhi, but he changed his views after the Sharpeville massacre of 1960, in which nearly 70 peacefully protesting black Africans were shot dead by police. Having been acquitted of treason in 1956, Mandela was convicted eight years later and jailed for life.

He spent the majority of the time incarcerated in Robben Island prison. Whilst he was inside, apartheid continued to hold sway, but the resistance movement was gathering pace; Mandela's imprisonment meant he was seen as a figurehead in the struggle, and his reputation grew apace.

He was moved to Pollsmoor prison in 1982, home to some of South Africa's most dangerous criminals, before being transferred to the low-security Victor Verster prison. Pressure for his release was now mounting in both Africa and further afield, and this appeared a very real possibility when President Pieter Willem Botha suffered a stroke and was forced to resign from office. His replacement was National Party leader Frederik Willem de Klerk, who immediately began dismantling the apartheid regime, lifting the ban on the ANC. Six months after taking office, he released Nelson Mandela.

Mandela, 71, walked free on February 11, 1990, just days after de Klerk lifted the bans on the ANC and other anti-apartheid groups. Mandela emerged to address a crowd of thousands, and pledged to continue his people's fight for freedom.

Mandela and de Klerk contested the country's first multi-racial democratic election in 1994, with the ANC triumphing and Mandela being elected the country's first black president. It was a turnaround that few had thought possible just a few years earlier, the result of half a decade of struggle.

Above: Left to right, Internet pioneers Vinton Cerfy, Lawrence Roberts, Robert Kahn and Tim Berners-Lee, after jointly winning the 2002 Prince of Asturias Award for Scientific and Technological Research.

Left: Tim Berners-Lee, inventor of the World Wide Web, stands at a chalkboard on which he has written notes on Web development.

AT A GLANCE

The arrival of the World Wide Web in 1991 made the Internet a user-friendly phenomenon. Created by Briton Tim Berners-Lee, it turned the chaos of online communication into order, allowing users to click links and explore cyberspace in a logical manner. Thanks to the Web, the world shrank in a matter of years.

INVENTION OF THE WORLD WIDE WEB

SWITZERLAND
1991

While many people think the World Wide Web is the Internet, many do not realize that they are separate entities, though without the Web the Internet would never have evolved the way it has.

The Web was the brainchild of British physicist and computer scientist Tim Berners-Lee, who realized that the growing technology of the Internet needed a public interface in order to expand and become user-friendly. The idea of the Internet as a 'network of networks' had been around for decades, though it had not yet reached mainstream awareness.

Berners-Lee was working at the European Council for Nuclear Research (CERN) in Switzerland when he first proposed the idea of 'a large hypertext database with typed links' – that is, a way of connecting the many pages of information in a network through links that can be read both by humans and by computers. It was a simple idea that gave the world a way of presenting and sharing data through the Internet.

His ideas converged with those of a fellow worker, Belgian Robert Cailliau, and together they created the names and all the relevant protocols that we take for granted today, such as html to format a page, and http to travel between them. Their initial aim was to make it easier for their colleagues to access information on company computers, but it was rapidly becoming much more than that.

Student Nicola Pellow adapted the Web system to run on any computer, and soon software was developed through which to view the Internet. Early developmental browsers preceded market leaders like Mosaic and later Netscape, before Microsoft's Internet Explorer became the number one way to view the Internet. The Web was snowballing, and websites were popping up all over the Internet.

Fast forward just one decade, and the Web had created countless businesses and revolutionized the Internet in ways that in its infancy were unimaginable to most of us. We now have things we take for granted like searching for information at a touch of a button through Google, or buying practically anything we can think of through online shopping sites such as ebay and Amazon.com.

In December 2009 there were an estimated 233 million websites on the Web, and if a company or even an individual doesn't have an online presence they are considered to be behind the times. The Web has changed the way the planet works, and it has never seemed smaller.

Above: Bezos announces the Kindle 2 electronic reader, a device that now permits Amazon to sell electronic or e-books.

Right: Amazon.com founder Jeff Bezos poses in his Seattle headquarters three years after launching the Internet bookstore.

FOUNDING OF AMAZON.COM

NEW YORK, USA
1994

Only a few years after the invention of the World Wide Web, the Internet was growing fast, and many people were jumping onto the bandwagon during the dot-com boom. It was in 1995 that the retail site Amazon.com was founded. It's now the number one choice when buying online, but it wasn't always that way.

Jeff Bezos worked as an analyst for New York-based firm D. E. Shaw & Co after his graduation from Princeton University. While at work, he began looking for gaps in the rapidly expanding market of the Internet. He came up with the idea of Amazon, which he originally planned to be an online bookstore.

He chose books, as opposed to a mail order catalogue, due to the sheer volume of listings he could store online. He was realistic about the chances of failure in an unproven industry, but realized he couldn't let the chance pass. "It was like the wild, wild West, a new frontier. And I knew that if I didn't try this, I would regret it. And that would be inescapable."

The company's early days were characterized by rapid growth but an even faster-growing uncertainty, as the venture was making heavy losses – by the early noughties its share prices had plummeted and staff were being made redundant. This, despite Amazon adding much more than books to its repertoire; in its first five years it had expanded from books to CDs, electronics and similar consumer goodies, toys and home improvement goods.

In the face of extreme adversity and near-certain closure, Amazon made its first profit towards the end of 2001 – the faith in it had paid off. In the years that it had been hemorrhaging money, it had been expanding at such a rate online that other companies could not keep up; in retrospect it was only a matter of time until it turned a profit. Amazon had become the number one e-commerce business on the planet.

Amazon is not only the USA's largest online retailer but the biggest in the world, selling goods from books to electronics to jewelry. It is also a story of perseverance in the dot-com industry where although success may look inevitable it is far from guaranteed.

AT A GLANCE

From its inception in 1994 as an online bookstore, Amazon has become the best known one-stop solution for Internet shopping. Jeff Bezos' creation survived its loss-making early years to become a household name, one that will very likely continue to serve millions worldwide for years to come.

Above: The world's press is introduced to Dolly in 1997, the year after her successful cloning.

Right: Dolly, the world's first cloned sheep, at age two at the Roslin Institute in Edinburgh, Scotland

FIRST CLONED SHEEP

EDINBURGH, SCOTLAND
JULY 5, 1996

In July 1996, experimenters cloned the first animal. Rather than call the creation Frankenstein or something equally horrifying, they named her the rather placid Dolly after country and western singer Dolly Parton; the quick-witted stockmen who had attended the delivery made the link between the busty singer and the mammary gland that had been used to clone the sheep.

Dolly was the only lamb that survived to adulthood from 277 attempts at somatic cell nuclear transfer, a technique where the nucleus from an adult cell is transferred into an unfertilized developing egg cell from which the nucleus had been removed. Most embryos created this way and implanted in a surrogate proved to have defects, and were terminated. Dolly's birth was kept under wraps for nearly a year, because while it would be heralded a scientific miracle it would also spark controversy and heated debates over the ethics of the procedure. True to form, the world reacted with both awe and disgust when Dolly's existence became known in 1997.

It was not the first time scientists at the Roslin Institute in Midlothian, Scotland, had attempted a live animal clone, but the success of Dolly's case led to international debate. When the head of the team who created the sheep hinted that the technique might be viable for human cloning, the media went into overdrive.

During her lifetime, Dolly gave birth to six offspring after being regularly mated with a Welsh mountain ram. This brought yet more attention to the already infamous ewe.

Then, at five years old, Dolly was spotted walking stiffly; tests confirmed she was suffering from arthritis, unusual at such a young age. Debate once again raged over the ethics of cloning and the possibility of an advanced aging process; Dolly was rumored to have the body of a six-year-old at birth, the same age as the sheep she was cloned from. The arthritis was a blow, but was controlled – but when another cloned sheep died from a lung disease it was considered likely Dolly might suffer the same fate. Sure enough, tumors were discovered in 2003, and it was decided that she should not continue to suffer.

Dolly's creation was a scientific breakthrough, and captured the public's imagination. Soon wild theories starting flying around of Jurassic Park-style dinosaurs roaming the earth and deceased loved ones being cloned after their death. It was the merging of science fiction and reality, despite the ongoing feud about the ethics behind it. Dolly really was 'the world's most famous sheep'.

AT A GLANCE

The creation of Dolly, a sheep created from cloned embryonic cells, created a storm in the world's press when it was announced in 1997, a year after her birth. While horses and bulls have since been cloned, Dolly's arrival did not herald a 'brave new world' of mutant and/or previously extinct animals, and the sheep herself only survived to the age of six.

FIRST SOCIAL NETWORKING WEBSITE LAUNCHED

NEW YORK CITY, USA
1997

Above: Launched in 2006, the popular Twitter is a social networking service that allows users to send short messages to a limitless group of subscribers, known as 'followers', from a computer or mobile device.

Right: Facebook founder Mark Zuckerberg speaks at a conference in San Francisco. Over half of the website's members use the site on a daily basis.

Today, internet sites such as Facebook, Twitter, Bebo and MySpace are visited daily by millions of people around the world. Essentially comprising a user profile that can be linked to other individuals or groups using the same site, each site offers a range of other services, including the ability to create photo galleries, upload videos or play games across the entire community. While many members find such websites an effective way to keep in touch and share information with an immediate circle of friends and family, the sites also offer a chance for users to rediscover old friends, or to forge new relationships based on shared interests with strangers around the globe.

Internet-based communities appeared during the earliest days of the internet, and today's social networking sites include features – such as profiles and friends lists – familiar to the users of earlier networking tools, such as ICQ. The first to bear a recognizable resemblance to the social networking sites of today, however, was called SixDegrees.com. Launched in 1997 by Andrew Weinreich, founder of a company called MacroView, it brought together various features already in use across the internet to provide a site where people could link and send messages to each other. Although the pioneering site boasted roughly a million members at its peak, it was not a commercial success and was sold in 1998 at the peak of the dot-com bubble for a reported US$125 million worth of stock, only to be closed down in 2000. At that time, internet use was not so widespread as it is today, and many users found SixDegrees offered little more than the chance to exchange messages with strangers.

As more and more people around the globe came online, though, a second wave of social networking sites was launched, including Cyworld, Ryze and Friendster. Many were aimed at business communities, but in 2003 MySpace went online and by the following year had become a massive hit among young people – though it was soon eclipsed by the massively popular Facebook, launched in 2005. While the spread of social networking sites has not been without problems – privacy features continue to be an issue – they are now an everyday part of life for many around the world. Facebook alone has over 400 million active users in more than 180 countries. Operating across national borders and creating virtual neighbors of people living at opposite ends of the Earth, such sites represent a powerful tool for creating new social groups. It is arguable, in fact, that they have had as great an impact on the way that humans communicate and interact as the introduction of the telephone.

AT A GLANCE

The launch of SixDegrees.com in 1997 marked the beginning of an explosion in social networking websites. Although that site no longer exists, it provided a model for sites such as Facebook, which are now used daily by hundreds of millions of people.

DEATH OF PRINCESS DIANA

PARIS, FRANCE
AUGUST 31, 1997

Above: Diana, Princess of Wales, on a royal visit in 1983 as she would forever be remembered.

Left: Floral tributes left outside Kensington Palace after the death of Diana, Princess of Wales.

Inset: The tunnel in Paris where Princess Diana met her death in a 1997 auto accident.

AT A GLANCE

Diana, the People's Princess, lived a highly public life, but showed a common touch that endeared her to millions and deflected much criticism from the British royal family. Her death in Paris in 1997 has since been the subject of conspiracy theories. but was found to be a tragic accident due to negligent driving and the pursuing press pack.

Diana, Princess of Wales, had been a much-needed shot in the arm for the British royal family since her marriage to Charles, Prince of Wales, in July 1981. She was a young, vibrant and relevant member of the monarchy whose charity work drew admiration from many, as did the way she conducted herself in a family that some were saying was out of touch with the public. A nation mourned in August 1997, when news came through of her untimely death in Paris.

Diana, her partner Dodi Fayed, her bodyguard Trevor Rees-Jones, and driver Henri Paul, were involved in a car crash in Paris while fleeing paparazzi photographers. Everyone except Rees-Jones died as the car, having entered the Pont de l'Alma tunnel, struck a supporting pillar at an estimated 65 mph.

Diana had long been a target for the international media, her youth, looks and royal status making her a regular on newspaper front pages worldwide. The princess had graced those pages even more often than usual in the years leading up to her death, as after years of marital issues she and Prince Charles had separated in late 1992 and divorced four years later. Both had admitted adultery.

In the summer of 1997, Diana began dating Dodi, son of Harrods owner and Fulham Football Club chairman Mohamed Fayed. Diana and Dodi embarked on a romance which was highly publicized, as was inevitable with the Princess. After a holiday on the Fayed family yacht in the Italian and French Rivieras, they stopped off in Paris en route to London. They stayed at the Ritz Hotel, owned by Dodi's father, before heading out towards an apartment near the Champs Elysées.

As they set off in a blacked-out Mercedes, they were tailed by a number of paparazzi; as the car entered the tunnel the driver lost control and crashed into a pillar. Diana was taken to hospital but died a few hours later. It was later discovered the driver had consumed both drugs and alcohol before getting behind the wheel; he was blamed for the crash by a subsequent judicial investigation.

A nation poured out its grief as tens of thousands lined the streets of London, and over 30 million people watched the funeral on television, along with millions more across the world. At the service Elton John's rewritten version of 'Candle in the Wind' proclaimed, 'Goodbye England's Rose.' Though Diana had been a controversial figure in many ways, her impact on Britain, both in life and in death, has been undeniable.

Overleaf: Guardsmen of the Prince of Wales Company of the Welsh Guards attend the casket along the route of the funeral procession of Diana, Princess of Wales.

DOT-COM BUBBLE BURSTS

NEW YORK STOCK EXCHANGE, USA
MARCH 10, 2000

Inset: High-tech workers, unemployed and job-hunters, networking at a dot-com 'pink slip' party in February 2001; these parties, held to help people find new jobs, first came about following the huge job losses that happened when the dot-com bubble burst.

Left: Dismay at the New York Stock Exchange as the NASDAQ tumbles through April 2000.

At the approach of the 21st century, the Internet and the World Wide Web were thriving. The computer-based technology was coming into its own, with continually developing equipment creating many commercial opportunities to market products and services.

The emergence of online companies began apace, and their rapid arrival sparked a period of on-paper prosperity that would become known as the 'dot-com bubble'. Eventually that bubble would burst, with disastrous consequences.

The far-reaching ability of the Internet, along with its rapidly increasing audience, made it an attractive proposition for existing companies to expand and for new ones to form. The entrepreneurs who formed these companies did so by collaborating with venture capitalists – financial benefactors who had the resources to get the new ventures up and running.

There was no shortage of willing investors, as the general feeling was that the Internet was the future, and any foray into it would reap large financial rewards. These companies operated on the premise that to gain success they needed to 'get big quick', expanding their customer base very rapidly even if it meant trading at a loss for the time being. Though in retrospect this seems like a fundamentally flawed business plan, it ended up working well for a few enterprises, most notably Amazon.com.

Many of the dot-com companies entered the stock market to became publicly traded, even those with little to no history and who had turned no profit. Such was the optimism around these new companies then that their stocks rose dramatically and they became overvalued. The peak came on March 10, 2000; the US stock market, NASDAQ, closed at an astronomically high 5,048.62. The companies and their investors were very rich – on paper. But the only way out of this crazy situation was down; a four per cent drop the next day was the beginning of mass panic selling that signaled the end of the dot-com bubble.

Many businesses went bust in the years following, and many individuals were left with a lot less money than before. The incident proved yet again that in business caution is sometimes the best way to proceed. The Internet continued to flourish regardless, and is now the number one technological medium in the world – but a lot of its early companies did not stay afloat to see it.

AT A GLANCE

The modern equivalent of historical boom'n'busts such as the South Sea Bubble and the Gold Rush, the dot-com bubble was the result of investors being seduced by the advent of the Internet and overestimating its ability to turn everything it touched into gold. The inevitable result was a crash, sorting the well run ventures able to deliver on their promises from those launched on a wing and a prayer.

9/11 TERRORIST ATTACKS

NEW YORK, USA
SEPTEMBER 11, 2001

For years its twin towers had been an iconic point on the New York City skyline, a bold statement of strength and prosperity. But on September 11, 2001, the World Trade Center came crashing down, on a day that would stun not only the city but the entire planet.

The day began like any other, but reality was shattered at 8.46 a.m. when American Airlines Flight 11 from Boston to Los Angeles flew into the north tower, piloted by a hijacker. The Boeing 767 caused a huge explosion on impact, killing the 81 on board and sending New York into chaos. It was the beginning of the worst attack on the USA since Pearl Harbor six decades earlier.

As the world's news cameras focused on the burning tower, they captured a second plane flying into the south tower at 9.03 a.m. Another flight from Boston to LA, it carried 65 passengers. The footage was beamed around the planet as everyone struggled to believe what they were seeing. The scenes could have been from a Hollywood disaster movie – but they were all too real.

Shortly after the second plane hit, President George Bush was informed while reading to a classroom full of children in Florida. As firefighters attempted to battle the blaze a third plane, flying from Washington DC to LA, crashed into the US Department of Defense headquarters at the Pentagon shortly after take-off, killing nearly 200.

The disaster was compounded at 9.59 a.m. as the World Trade Center's south tower collapsed. It killed many aid workers and those still inside, engulfing downtown Manhattan in a blanket of smoke. The north tower fell half an hour later, at 10.28 a.m., pushing the death toll even higher. All the while, news cameras were catching the death and devastation, filming desperate office workers falling out of windows to their deaths.

Between the collapse of the two towers, at 10.03 a.m., a fourth flight – United Airlines 93 – crashed in Pennsylvania; passengers had foiled yet another hijack attempt, the target this time believed to have been for the US Capitol building in Washington.

In total, nearly 3,000 people died in the attacks, which had been orchestrated by Islamic terrorist group al-Qaeda. The USA launched a 'war on terror' which included extended conflicts in Afghanistan and Iraq that have continued through the first decade of the 21st century.

The event was one of the most shocking of modern times, one that shook the USA to its foundations. The images from its darkest day would forever be engrained in the minds of its citizens. Rebuilding at the site is scheduled to be completed in 2012, some 11 years after its destruction.

Above: This series of photographs shows hijacked United Airlines Flight 175 as it approaches and impacts the World Trade Center's south tower.

Right: Firefighters search the rubble after the collapse of the Twin Towers.

Overleaf: The South Tower of the World Trade Center begins to collapse following the terrorist attacks.

AT A GLANCE

The two airliners flown into the twin towers of New York's World Trade Center on September 11, 2001, struck at the very heart of the USA, destroying an iconic landmark and bringing the resentment harbored against US foreign policy by certain factions into shocking focus. President Bush's retaliation against Islamic terrorist group al-Qaeda was far-reaching, and a decade later the reverberations had still to settle.

ENRON INVESTIGATION BEGINS

HOUSTON, TEXAS, USA
OCTOBER 22, 2001

Above: Former Enron CEO Kenneth Lay, who cited his Fifth Amendment rights and refused to testify during a Congressional hearing into his company's demise.

Left: Enron Vice President of Corporate Development Sherron Watkins testifies at the Enron Senate hearing.

AT A GLANCE

The rise and fall of Enron exposed how accounting could be used to cover up corporate malpractice, deceiving regulators and shareholders and diverting money into the pockets of executives. Enron's bankruptcy in 2001 was the curtain-raiser to the most volatile decade in world business since the Great Depression.

When the energy company Enron collapsed in late 2001, it revealed a rotten, corrupt financial structure behind the illusory façade of all-American corporate success. In February that year it had been paying its executives million-dollar bonuses and advising the White House on energy policy, having been named Most Innovative Company in America for the sixth year running. But by Christmas it was bankrupt and under investigation by the US Securities and Exchange Commission.

What lay behind the glamorous veneer of multinational expansion and spectacular profit levels was a fraudulent accounting system which concealed losses in artificial subsidiaries. Enron deliberately misled shareholders into the belief that the company could deliver good returns on their investment, ensuring that money would continue to flow into the company – and into the pockets of its executives.

From its 1930s origins as a gas distribution company, Enron suddenly grew in the mid-1980s when Kenneth Lay became its CEO. He expanded the corporation's interests and overstretched its capacity with questionable dealings, covering up the resulting business failures with some fairly ruthless 'creative accounting'.

In 1990 he was joined at Enron by Jeff Skilling, from the failed First City Bank of Houston, and Andrew Fastow from the failed Commercial Bank of Illinois. The three men bought and created a multinational maze of interdependent companies amongst which they hid debts and exaggerated profits. They created a business culture at the company's Houston headquarters in which its directors and accountants went along with the trio's dubious practices, tolerating the sometimes illegal conflicts of interest instead of challenging them.

In August 2001, however, Sherron Watkins, vice president for corporate development at Enron, began to voice concerns about its accounting systems. She had formerly worked at Arthur Anderson, Enron's accountants, and knew what she was talking about. Her questions to Kenneth Lay triggered quiet panic in the offices of both Enron and its accountants, leading to executives ditching share holdings and Arthur Anderson shredding documents while insisting that Enron was in robust good health.

But the façade crumbled, and on December 2, Enron became the largest corporate bankruptcy in American history. Arthur Anderson, one of the five largest accounting firms in the world at the time, also collapsed. Skilling was sentenced to 24 years for felony. Fastow, convicted of fraud, money laundering and conspiracy, reduced his sentence by turning state evidence. Lay was convicted on ten counts but died of a heart attack before being sentenced. Watkins now speaks at conferences on the dangers of US corporate culture.

Above: An abandoned house three months after Hurricane Katrina hit the Lower Ninth Ward of the city of New Orleans.

Right: A US Army loadmaster surveys a flooded New Orleans from his Chinook helicopter.

Overleaf: A New Orleans fireman helps evacuate a man out of floodwaters as a home burns in the seventh ward of New Orleans during the aftermath of Hurricane Katrina.

Below: Evacuees take shelter from the elements in the giant Houston Astrodome sports arena.

AT A GLANCE

The natural disaster of Hurricane Katrina saw the residents of New Orleans pay the price for living below sea level. The levee system designed to hold back the surrounding sea could not cope with hurricane-force winds, and there was widespread damage. President Bush's response to the disaster was widely criticized as too little too late, and five years later the city had still not returned to its pre-Katrina state.

HURRICANE KATRINA

NEW ORLEANS, USA
AUGUST 2005

In August 2005 the US state of Louisiana was devastated by Hurricane Katrina. The week-long tropical cyclone became the biggest natural disaster in the history of the USA, causing damage estimated at over $80 billion.

The Atlantic hurricane season usually peaks in the northern hemisphere's late summer, September the most active month. The 2004 season had resulted in over 3,000 deaths and caused nearly $50 billion worth of damage, and many people in Louisiana and the surrounding states were bracing themselves for a repeat.

Katrina began on August 23 as a tropical depression just south of the Bahamas with winds of 35 mph, but it quickly escalated and clipped the coast of Florida by August 25, with winds peaking at 75 mph. In its brief journey through Florida, Katrina caused 14 deaths and left millions of people without electricity.

It was a sign of things to come. As Katrina crossed the Gulf of Mexico it became a Category 5 hurricane, intensifying with winds of 175 mph. By now the states of Louisiana and Mississippi were on the alert for the impending storm, with a mandatory evacuation ordered for the city of New Orleans.

Katrina reached land again as a Category 3 on August 29, hitting Buras-Triumph, Louisiana. The town was no stranger to hurricanes, having been heavily damaged four times already in the last century, the most recent experience having come 35 years previously with Hurricane Camille.

Sited below sea level, New Orleans was predicted to be in a catastrophic situation, as it was thought the strength of the storm would breach the city's system of levees, raised banks built to keep the water at bay. The levees and floodwalls did indeed prove grossly ineffective; Katrina left an estimated 80 per cent of the city submerged in its wake.

Destruction was severe, and while the evacuation of the city was considered a success by and large, many people – mainly the poor and the elderly – stayed behind. Buildings were destroyed, and nearly 1,500 died. The city descended into chaos, with no clean water, electricity or shelter. Shops and buildings were looted, and many residents congregated at the city's Superdome stadium, which quickly became overcrowded and filthy.

Reconstruction of New Orleans was painfully slow, and two years after Katrina, areas of it were still uninhabitable. In 2007 the city was estimated to have regained 60 per cent of its pre-hurricane population, and it was clear that the path of destruction left by Hurricane Katrina would take many years to be fully erased.

MR. MUDD

FEDERAL TAKEOVER OF FANNIE MAE AND FREDDIE MAC

WASHINGTON, DC, USA
SEPTEMBER 7, 2008

Fannie Mae and Freddie Mac were early casualties in a chain of crises amongst financial institutions that triggered a global economic recession. In their collapse they exposed all the risks of the property market boom of the early years of the 21st century.

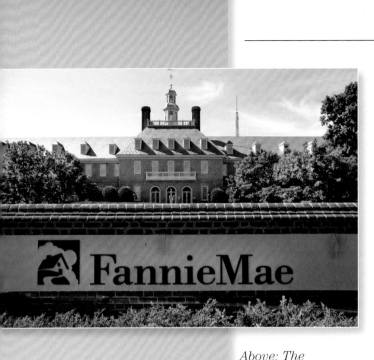

Above: The Washington headquarters of mortgage lender Fannie Mae, taken over by the US government in 2008 after bad debt problems had proved insurmountable.

Left: Former Freddie Mac and Fannie Mae CEOs are sworn in before the House Committee examining the extent to which their corporations' actions and policies may have contributed to the mortgage crisis.

Fannie Mae, more properly the Federal National Mortgage Association, and Freddie Mac, the Federal Home Loan Mortgage Corporation, acted as mortgage brokers to the subprime market – that is, clients with a less than prime, or good, credit rating. It is by definition a high-risk market, consisting of vulnerable people which the two organizations had originally been established to serve and protect.

Deregulation and political pressure around the turn of the century, under Presidents Clinton and Bush, undermined much of that protection. Unscrupulous lenders were able to offer deceptively low initial rates to the poorest members of society, inducing them to acquire debts which they could not afford to repay, especially when the housing bubble burst in 2006.

The proportion of subprime borrowers defaulting on their loans rose to one in four in early 2008. Thousands of homes were repossessed; house prices fell, and those who now owned these repossessed buildings found that their assets were worthless. Fannie Mae and Freddie Mac handled about half the mortgages in the USA, worth $5 trillion in mortgage-backed securities, and now faced combined debts of around $1.6 trillion.

The US government's move to take over the running of Mae and Mac in September was an unprecedented intervention in a country characterized by relatively unregulated, hands-off capitalism. The action sought to stabilize the housing market; but financial institutions all over the world had a finger in the property pie, and when confidence in that collapsed then so did they. In Britain, the Northern Rock bank had already been rescued by the government in February 2008, and other British banks were effectively nationalized a month after the US intervention. Banks everywhere restricted credit, and businesses large and small found themselves unable to operate. As many high-profile high street names were declared bankrupt, unemployment rose and spending fell. By the start of 2009, much of the world was deep in recession.

Although by the end of 2009 the world had emerged from the darkest phase, full recovery would, it became clear, take much longer. Those governments, institutions and businesses which had survived the recession must now count the cost, erase deficits and try to recoup their losses; belts must remain tightened for years to come.

AT A GLANCE

The failure of the US subprime mortgage market in which Fannie Mae and Freddie Mac were the major players had a knock-on effect that was felt worldwide. The American government moved to take them over, while similar nationalisation of overexposed banks took place in Britain as a worldwide recession loomed.

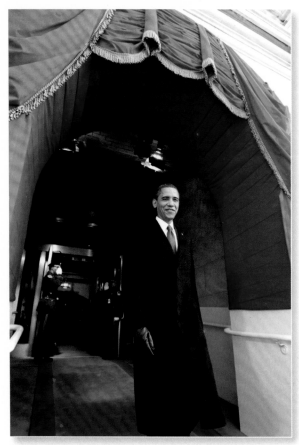

Above: Barack Obama on his way to be sworn in as the 44th President of the United States.

Right: Supporters of Barack Obama celebrate in Chicago as he wins the presidential election.

Overleaf: Thousands look on as Barack Obama takes the Oath of Office as the 44th President of the United States, sworn in by US Chief Justice John Roberts.

AT A GLANCE

With its history of institutionalized racism, the likelihood of the USA ever having a black president was considered a pipe dream by many. But Hawaiian-born Barack Obama proved in the 2008 presidential election that the American dream was indeed open to anyone at last, no matter what their color.

PRESIDENT BARACK OBAMA ELECTED

USA
NOVEMBER 4, 2008

When the United States of America elected Barack Obama as their 44th president, it was a historic moment for a country whose history had been peppered with racial prejudice, violence and the long fight for civil rights.

The early to mid 20th century in America had been a period fraught with tension between whites and their black counterparts, characterized by segregation and the campaign for racial equality led by iconic figures such as Martin Luther King Jr. At that time, the thought of a black man being elected leader of the country would have been unthinkable, but 44 years after the Civil Rights Act of 1964, it happened.

Barack Obama was born in 1961 in Honolulu, Hawaii, to a white mother and a black father. His parents divorced in 1964, and Obama spent part of his early childhood in Indonesia with his mother's new husband. He moved to Los Angeles as an 18-year-old, before studying in New York City, and later Harvard Law School.

After a brief spell as a civil rights attorney he entered the political realm in 1996. He began as Senator of Illinois, before becoming a US Senator in 2005. He was already making waves, and was spoken of as a potential Democratic presidential candidate.

Obama threw his hat into the ring for the presidential election in early 2007. With the desire for change prevalent throughout the country after eight years of President George Bush and his Republican party, Obama was seen as a favorite from the beginning; hopes were high for a new party and new figurehead at the helm.

It did not bode well for his opponent, Republican and former Vietnam prisoner of war John McCain. When the two Senators went head to head, calling on the country for their votes, the result was the highest voting election for four decades, with at least 130 million Americans having their say.

November 4, 2008, was results day, and it was Obama who triumphed, with a 52.3 per cent share of the popular vote. He finished with 365 Electoral College votes to McCain's 173, after taking eight previously Republican states, among them Florida and Indiana.

As he addressed his home state of Illinois after his historic victory, Obama proclaimed, "It's been a long time coming, but tonight change has come to America." Indeed it had – a new face and a new era for a country that was beginning to emerge from the shadow of its past.

DEEPWATER HORIZON OIL SPILL

GULF OF MEXICO
2010

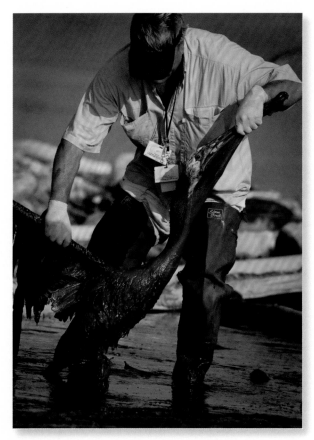

Above: On June 3, oil driven by strong winds came ashore at the Queen Bess Island Pelican Rookery. The oil-coated birds were quickly rescued and taken to Fort Jackson Rehabilitation Center for emergency treatment.

Left: Dispersant-clotted oil and fresh crude oil float on surface 9 miles (14 km) from the source of the **Deepwater Horizon** *oilwell spill.*

Overleaf: Fireboat response crews battle the blaze on the offshore oil rig **Deepwater Horizon,** *April 21, 2010. The rig sank the following morning.*

AT A GLANCE

Following an explosion on the drilling rig Deepwater Horizon, *millions of barrels of oil were released into the Gulf of Mexico from a leak 5,000 feet (1,500 meters) below the surface. Numerous attempts to stop the gushing oil failed, leading to the greatest ecological disaster in the USA's history.*

On April 20, 2010, the floating drilling rig *Deepwater Horizon* operated by the British energy giant BP, exploded 40 miles (64 km) off the coast of Louisiana in the Gulf of Mexico, killing 11 workers and injuring another 17. The rig, which had been drilling in the Macondo Prospect oil field, sank on the morning of April 22. The same day, a large oil slick could be seen spreading from the disaster site, and over the following days it became apparent that oil was emerging under pressure from a leak some 5,000 ft (1,500 meters) below the surface. Over the following weeks, estimates of the amount of oil being released fluctuated between 5,000 and 100,000 barrels of oil a day. Despite deployment of over 1,000 km of containment booms, tarballs have been found washed up on beaches as far away as Pensacola in Florida. It is feared that much of the oil remains below the surface of the water and that oil reaching the Loop Current will be circulated into the Gulf Stream and spread much further.

Efforts to stop the gushing oil have included trying to cap the leak with a 'coffer dam' intended to capture the oil as it escapes, and a 'top kill' method aimed to prevent the flow of oil by pumping heavy mud over the leak. Both failed. A more recent attempt has capped the leaking pipe and reduced the flow, though the oil continues to escape at about half the original rate. Meanwhile, BP is drilling relief wells that by August 2010 should allow engineers to block the original well with mud.

The long-term effects of the oil spill are impossible to predict, but it seems likely that the oil spill will become the greatest ecological disaster ever visited upon the USA, and possibly the world. Despite a massive response that has seen hundreds of containment workers and engineers working around the clock and BP's assertion on May 18 that the level of environmental damage will be 'very, very modest', the spill will certainly take terrible toll of marine life in the area. Fishing and tourist industries have already been hit hard, and oil has been washing ashore at wildlife sanctuaries.

It is also difficult to predict what ramifications the spill will have in a broader sense, but US President Barack Obama has established a commission to investigate the causes of the spill, which will also report on ways to prevent such a catastrophe ever happening again. At the very least, safety procedures for offshore drilling will be tightened, but it is very possible that the Gulf of Mexico disaster will have profound and far-reaching consequences for energy development around the globe.

PHOTO CREDITS

All photographs supplied courtesy of Corbis. Individual image credits as follows.

T = Top, B = Below, I = Insert

Front Cover: Main Image Najlah Feanny, Inset images (left to right) Hulton-Deutsch Collection, Bettman, Corbis, Joshua Roberts/Pool
Back Cover: Corbis, Front flap: Karl-Josef Hildenbrand/dpa, Back flap: Bettmann

Project Managed by BlueRed Press Ltd
Michael Heatley would like to thank the following people for their assistance: Mike Gent, Drew Heatley, Julian Heatley, Colin Salter.